The Name of the Game

GREG EMMERTH

Resolve Media, Inc.
Atlanta, Georgia

To Chad

CONTENTS

Tuesday

Wednesday

Thursday

Friday

Saturday

SUNDAY

1

"What do we have?" Detective Robert Carlyle asked.

It had already been a long day for the fifty-two-year-old California native, starting with a contentious meeting with community activists at eight the previous morning over the rash of assaults plaguing Hillcrest. As head of the task force hastily assembled to address the situation, it fell on him not only to arrest the culprits but also to play public relations with those accustomed to having their crimes solved within an hour-long procedural on CBS. It hardly helped that his partner was in L.A., leaving him to babysit the team of misfits under him.

He had just settled down onto his couch, Fox News Channel on in the background and an untouched glass of tequila in his hand, when his cell phone buzzed. It was, he knew as he answered the call, not the end of the evening. Now here he was at the UCSD emergency room just after one o'clock in the morning.

The junior detective sighed. "Our friends struck again."

"Where, exactly?" Carlyle asked, then winced as he took another sip of his latest cup of coffee. He regretted not finishing the drink he'd left on his kitchen counter. "Just so I know where I'm going."

"The alley off University and Third."

"I'm sorry," Carlyle said. "I'm having a hard time recalling your name."

"Patterson. Mark Patterson."

Patterson, with a mop of dirty-blond hair and dressed in what appeared to be his father's dark gray suit, looked about twelve. Carlyle thought back to his argument with the captain, who had handed him a short list of names with the order to make them his new team, and for some unknown reason, this kid had made the cut. "New detective, right?"

Patterson nodded. "Yes, sir. About two months."

"How old are you?"

"Twenty-eight."

"And how'd you get involved in this mess?"

Patterson shook his head. "Just lucky, I guess, sir."

Carlyle nodded toward the drawn curtains across the hall, the steady beeps of medical equipment filling the silence. "Gay?" he asked, though he already knew the answer. This was the sixth beating in as many weeks, and they were still no closer to determining who the three alleged perpetrators were.

"I suspect so."

"What's his condition?"

"Same as the others. Not pretty, but nothing serious."

"Any ID?"

"Here's the wallet," Patterson said as he handed over the plastic evidence bag, watching as Carlyle gave it a cursory examination. "Still got the cash, like all the others."

"And quite a wad of it, too. Anything else?"

"There are two driver's licenses."

"Which one's fake?" Carlyle reopened the wallet and took both out. The one on top was from California, the second from Illinois.

"I called it in. The California ID that puts him at twenty-one checks out. The one from Illinois—"

"Where he's… nineteen."

"Yeah. That's in the system as well."

Carlyle looked back down at both IDs, wondering how this kid had managed to get hold of a real California driver's license with an altered birthdate. Glancing between them, he noticed the same name on each: James Edward Byrne. "Anything pop up on either of them?"

"No. Nothing."

"Byrne," Carlyle muttered. "Chicago… nah, it can't be."

"Excuse me, sir?"

"Nothing."

Patterson pointed toward the wallet. "And there's also—"

"A UCSD ID, I see it." Carlyle said as he pulled it out.

"Talked to campus police. He's enrolled, and they're going to have someone from the school call us back."

Carlyle held up the California ID. "I'm taking this," he said, slipping it into his suit jacket. "You can return the wallet to the victim. Cell phone?"

"Not that we found."

"Sounds like you've got everything covered. Does this mean I get to go home?" he joked.

"Not hardly," a voice called out from behind him. "What, you're too good for a crime scene now?"

Carlyle turned, a smile appearing as he recognized his old friend. The fifty-nine-year-old had made detective only a few years before he had, although the subsequent decades had taken a more visible toll, his girth now beyond the tailoring of his rumpled suit. "I wanted to check in on the victim first," he answered, rolling his eyes. "You know—show my compassionate side."

"And here I thought you didn't have one."

"I don't." Carlyle nodded toward Patterson. "So… I take it I have you to thank for doing my job for me?"

"Something like that," Detective Boslin said as the two shook hands. "I was already here when the victim came in and thought I'd give some guidance to your new detective."

"You sure you don't want the case?"

"It's your task force. I just work here."

"As if I fucking want it," Carlyle said. "How'd you manage to dodge the bullet?"

"My hand jobs aren't what they used to be, I guess. I don't know—ask the captain."

Carlyle laughed. "So, what *does* put you in Hillcrest in the middle of the night?"

"Speaking of hand jobs, a couple of boys in a domestic. One's downtown and the other's getting some stitches." He looked over at Patterson. "No offense."

Patterson smirked. "None taken."

Carlyle looked between the two, the rookie detective's presence on the task force now clear. "Oh, that sounds like fun," he finally remarked.

"Absolutely," Boslin said dryly.

"Anything else I need to know about our latest?"

Boslin looked over at Patterson. "Can you excuse us, son?"

Patterson nodded. "Yes, sir," he said before stepping away.

Boslin feigned exasperation. "When did teenagers start making detective?" he asked.

"I thought he was twelve. He's gay?"

"Yeah, you didn't know? How the fuck else does a kid that green get on your task force?"

"I had no idea."

Boslin chuckled. "You need to get with the times."

"Yeah, sure," Carlyle said. "So… what did you want to tell me?"

"Just don't get mad."

"I'll get mad if I want to."

Boslin hesitated. "I took the liberty of calling Chicago PD."

Carlyle sighed. "Now why would you do something like that?"

"I couldn't help myself. Didn't you see the last name?"

"You don't think—"

"No thinking about it. That's Ciaran Byrne's youngest son in there."

"So?"

"I figured I'd let their snitches earn their money," Boslin said. Carlyle's face darkened. "The university was going to call them, anyway," he added.

"You've stirred up a real shit show, you know that?"

Boslin smiled. "Probably, but it was going to get that way regardless. And speaking of shit shows…"

Carlyle almost didn't want to ask. "What?"

"You'll see."

"*What?*"

"I don't know just yet," Boslin said. "A little present for you they found on young Mr. Byrne. It's at the lab."

"Care to give me a hint?"

"Oh, no. You'll have to see for yourself—especially with this family."

Carlyle sighed. "Just fucking great. Look, I appreciate you helping me out like this. Most of it."

"I owe you a few. And it seems your good-for-nothing partner isn't around."

"LA again."

"*Again*? What the fuck does he do up there?"

"I don't know," Carlyle admitted. "It's always a bullshit answer, so I quit asking."

"Must be one sweet piece of ass."

"I wouldn't know," Carlyle said.

Boslin laughed. "And on that note, you have a wonderful evening."

"I'll try. You talk to the doctor yet?"

"No, but I told the charge nurse to have him find you. I also took the liberty of requesting the crime scene photos and reports on your desk first thing in the morning."

"And here I am, already going over there. Thanks again, Ron. I owe you."

"Just let me catch up before you start doing me any more favors."

2

The three rarely spoke afterward, which Billy always found odd—as if the solemnity of the occasion somehow demanded silence.

He entered the apartment first, followed by Dan and Chris. The door slammed behind them, and Billy jumped. His hands were still trembling, his entire body sagging with the stress release that accompanied the completion of their work.

He went to the kitchen and opened the refrigerator, grabbing three tallboys from among the half-empty condiment bottles. He walked to the living room and passed them out, then slumped into the stained gray fabric chair that faced the front of the room. Dan and Chris were already sitting on the matching couch against the wall to his left. They opened their respective beers and silently hoisted them in the air before taking their first sips to honor another successful evening.

They were all in their mid-twenties. Dan was the oldest at twenty-seven, with Billy the youngest at four years his junior. Chris fell somewhere in the middle, though Billy could never remember the year—only that it fell on Halloween. Probably why he was so screwed up, he often thought, but Chris was the tallest and best-looking of the trio, so it was no surprise that he was the one that guy winked at on the street six weeks ago.

Billy finally noticed the blood on his knuckles and passed the beer to his left so he could inspect them. His hand hurt a little, although as he flexed it, he couldn't tell whether the blood was his, the guy's, or a combination of the two. That would be the worst. He'd heard fags could give you all kinds of disgusting diseases.

He took another healthy sip from his beer, hoping it would calm him. He wasn't sure why this one had been so different than the five before, but somehow it didn't feel right. Maybe because he didn't beg or plead for mercy. Sure, he tried to talk his way out of it at first, but it sounded more like a warning. "You'll regret this," he had said just before Chris's first blow landed across his left jaw.

Dan sat with his eyes closed and head against the threadbare couch as he relaxed in the moment. Chris was staring off into space, bobbing slightly to the music in his head, clearly still amped from their excursion. "You'll regret this," Billy heard again, and as he took another swig from his beer, he began to wonder if he should be worried after all.

■ ■ ■

"Fuck," he muttered as he stood back to examine his work, power tool still in his gloved hand.

He hated working in this space, the dim corner room of a basement in a nondescript commercial building off Clark. With no windows, it was hard not to feel claustrophobic. Besides, he reminded himself as he glanced at the water-stained cement on the far side of the room—another trick he used to distract himself—the room had perfect soundproofing and a concrete floor with a drain. Whining about the lack of windows was complaining just for the sake of doing so.

"What?" one of the kids standing behind him asked.

He held up the drill to examine the half-inch hammer bit. Small pieces of flesh still clung to it, a thin trickle of blood running from the partially exposed shank to the drill's chuck. "Nothing," he said. "This sure as hell doesn't work like it does in the movies."

"That shit is all fake," another of them said.

He dropped the drill to the floor and looked back over his shoulder. "You think I'm a fucking idiot?"

"No."

"Then shut the fuck up," he ordered before turning to the man in front of him.

His feet were duct-taped to the front legs of the metal chair, his hands bound behind him, his chin digging into his chest. He had been stripped to his white boxer briefs, now mostly a dark maroon due to the interrogation, which had lasted the better part of two hours. His torn body had begun to tremble slightly as the pool of blood grew to encompass all four chair legs within its circumference, and he had ceased movement only moments before.

"I bet he bled out."

"Yeah, no shit," he responded as he looked over the wounds he'd inflicted. "Those goddamn arteries are a real bitch."

He turned to face the group—the Three Stooges, as he thought of them. They would all need substantial work on his part if they were ever going to become part of his regular crew. He certainly didn't need any more groupies. There were plenty of them around without adding these dipshits to the mix.

He peeled off the purple gloves and dropped them by the drill. Next came the blood-spattered plastic medical apron. "You two," he said as he pointed to the one to his left and the one in the middle, "I want you to go to that address and clean it out. Flush the drugs, but I want that cash. All of it." He turned to the third as the others hurried out of the room. "Get me my fucking hacksaw and some trash bags," he said. "Then grab the hose and get to work."

3

Conrad Moretti lay in bed staring at the fan circling above, his intertwined fingers resting on his stomach as his mind searched for the source of the anxiety that had brought him here.

He wasn't a man who often lost sleep over the way he lived his life. A lesser man would have, but the years had ground Moretti's conscience into a fine dust. Something was off in the universe tonight, and he loathed the vague anxiety that accompanied it. It rarely happened to him, but when it did, bad things happened. Always.

He had been the Byrne family's personal attorney since earning his law degree from the University of Chicago decades earlier. The Byrnes had been good to him—very good. It wasn't so much the financial compensation, which was substantial, as it was the intimate connection to one of the most powerful families in the Midwest, a level of power most men could only dream of attaining simply by dropping the Byrne name.

His father, Salvatore, had worked for Liam Byrne Sr. since both men were in their early twenties, the bond between the Italian and newly transplanted Bostonian Irishman sealed when both had nothing but dreams and ambition. Now Conrad worked for Liam's second-eldest son, Ciaran. Both men now in their mid-sixties, they shared a relationship that, though not as close as their fathers', was nonetheless tight.

Then there was Ciaran's older brother, Liam Jr. Decades before, when his two sons came of age, the patriarch had, for reasons of expediency, decided to reverse their inheritances. Shortly thereafter Liam Jr.—who had grown up dreaming of little else but running the North Side—was sent west to take control of what was, at the time, a chaotic Las Vegas. Threats had been made, although nothing would ever come of them. Hollow words from a violent, impetuous young man who would, like all Byrne sons, heed his father's wishes.

Since that time, it had been Moretti's responsibility to coordinate the brothers' interests, keeping Chicago—and their New York partners— supplied with drugs, guns, and anything else that could be shipped east and sold for significant profit. Liam Jr. kept to his world as he consolidated and expanded his gaming interests, and Ciaran kept to his as he took the reins from their father. The two brothers built rival empires in parallel, driven by a competition never addressed as their wealth and power grew. As long as the proverbial trains ran on time, neither interfered with the other. Moretti liked to think that he was the sole cause for this being so.

His official title at the conglomerate known as Byrne Holdings, LLC, was chief counsel. From his corner office in a nondescript office tower on South Wacker, he helped oversee the three branches of their legal investments: Byrne Construction, Byrne Restaurant Holdings, and Byrne Wholesale Distribution. Each had been established during Ciaran's early years as a façade of legitimization, designed to mainstream their power into something less likely to catch the attention of entities that could bring them to heel. The Byrnes, everyone could now pretend, were upstanding members of the greater Chicagoland community.

Most of their concerns were handled at any number of their off-the-books establishments in Wrigleyville, places where needs could be met, favors given, and the levers that gave force to their interests manipulated. Ostensibly aboveboard or not, the Byrnes took whatever was required to maintain their perch. Power, even when legitimately earned, occasionally required force behind it. One necessitated the other. That was—and always would be—the name of the game.

Ciaran and his wife, Isabella, had been married just past forty years. What started as an arranged marriage to forge an alliance between the Byrnes of Chicago and Valcos of New York, to both cement their respective power bases while expanding opportunities, had quickly flourished into deep affection and an unwavering love between the two. Before the handshake between fathers to finalize the agreement, however, the willful twenty-year-old would have her say.

"I will not marry that fucking Irishman," Conrad had overheard her shout as he returned from the bathroom. He had just seen the attractive young woman in the dark blue skirt and fitted white blouse, a single strand of pearls loose around her neck, storm toward the back of the large Brooklyn townhouse as the heels of her shoes clicked loudly against the hardwood floor. "I will not do it."

The silence that followed felt eternal as Conrad remained frozen in the hallway, fearing the worst for their pilgrimage to New York, Liam Sr. and Ciaran still awaiting his return in the library where they would all soon meet. "Fine," her uncle Carmine, who had helped raise her in her father's absence, eventually answered. "Okay, fine. Will you at least meet him? For me?"

"No."

"Isabella… please. For me."

A pause. "I hear they're sending him to Las Vegas."

"It's something that benefits us all."

"I will not go there," she threatened. "Do you hear me? I will not go to that desert hellhole in the middle of nowhere."

"Then what would you have me do?" he seemed to plead.

He heard her sigh. "I don't know," she said. "Perhaps Chicago, but… I will not go to Las Vegas." And with that single utterance, Conrad's life—and that of his employer—was forever altered.

4

They had four children: Thomas (Tommy), thirty-seven; Enzo, thirty-two; Sarah, thirty; and James (Jimmy), nineteen. The elder two boys had worked for their father—the only two to do so—since entering their early teens, when they learned the family business and the subtle dance of moving between their various interests without attracting unnecessary attention. Tommy did so down the hall from Moretti's office; Enzo worked in the shadows on the streets—as two sides of the same coin.

Tommy, his father's right-hand man, would succeed Ciaran at his passing. He had officially been made CEO of Byrne Holdings four years ago and, in many ways, was already in full control of all their businesses—or at least to the point where no one save Ciaran ever questioned his decisions. He seemingly enjoyed his burgeoning responsibilities as their enterprises continued to transform and grow.

It started innocently enough. The young man with a new MBA from Northwestern's Kellogg School of Management sat across the table from his father, Moretti between them, as the three had lunch in one of the holes in the wall they owned near Wrigley Field.

"Pop," Tommy began, "I've been looking things over and I think we could really do something with some of these properties. They could make some real money for us."

Ciaran laughed. "They make plenty of money for us."

"No, I mean *real* money, Pop."

Ciaran shook his head. "Tommy, my boy. They're not supposed to make real money. That's the point."

"But what if they could?"

Moretti remembered Ciaran looking to him, his advisor lightly shrugging his shoulders before the father had given his blessing for the experiment. "Let us see what the boy can do," Ciaran said once the two were alone, although little did either know the extent to which their interests would change.

Moretti watched as Tommy dove with gusto into their legal investments, turning one shell company after another, theretofore merely vehicles to move product and wash their own and others' cash, into thriving, profitable businesses. A company that once owned a few rundown apartment buildings now controlled a half-dozen luxury condo towers with several more in development, including a high-rise near the lakefront. A few dive bars on the North Side had become an array of sports bars, clubs, and dubiously sourced "farm-to-table" restaurants, all supplied by their alcohol distributorship, the largest in the city. Gentrification had come to Chicago, and Tommy Byrne intended to mine it for every last dollar while other entities, buried in bureaucracy, continued to shelter their duplicity.

Moretti could not fault the boy his ambition. It certainly had been profitable for all of them, but as of late it was clear that their traditional concerns were now something only to be tolerated, and Moretti knew that Tommy would phase them into oblivion as soon as the opportunity presented itself.

He was a relatively weak young man compared to generations past, Moretti believed, and had been spared the rod far too often for his own good. Empires like this required a spine not yet possessed by its newfound leader. He chose not to live among his people, but in a luxury penthouse above the city skyline. There were times when Moretti could see traces of Ciaran within him, but he also knew that Tommy wanted no part of their old world, or only enough to please those who demanded its continuity. In time Moretti's generation would be gone, and Tommy could do as he pleased. In the interim, however, the battle would continue to preserve what those hard men had built.

Enzo, for lack of a better phrase, was the family's enforcer, and from what Moretti saw the young man enjoyed his position a bit too much. Named after another of Isabella's uncles, a notoriously sadistic individual in his own right, he was very much his mother's favorite, just as Tommy had become Ciaran's.

Sarah had followed in her eldest brother's footsteps and had also attended Northwestern, albeit briefly, where she met and eventually married a classmate from Highland Park who went into investment banking. Aloof from the family, she now lived in Water Tower Place on Michigan Avenue, content to raise two small boys as a stay-at-home mom with a large shopping district an elevator ride away from her multimillion-dollar apartment.

She smugly believed that she had gotten away from the family business, completely unaware that her husband had been surreptitiously recruited by her eldest brother into handling a substantial part of the Byrnes' legitimate financial affairs, and some of those less legitimate, and quite willingly at that. As a doctor's son born and raised in the northern suburbs of Chicago, Andrew Beaman had been intrigued by what he thought was the glamorous life of the Byrnes—and to Moretti seemed overly confident he could navigate it. He was useful to them— but otherwise harmless.

The baby was James, whom everyone called Jimmy. Like his eldest brother, he was part of the new generation of Byrnes intent on earning a college degree and putting it to good use, although he had no interest in doing so for the good of the family. He had also chosen to attend school as far away as possible within the contiguous forty-eight states and was now in the spring quarter of his sophomore year at the University of California, San Diego.

That was probably for the best, Moretti thought. Jimmy was a willful child, although having grown up with two inattentive parents already tired of raising a family after their first three, that was not wholly unexpected. Under the guise of toughening him up, the only consistent attention he received once he became a teenager was from Enzo. Moretti had never flinched at violence as a means to an end, but he thought the beatings sadistically cruel. Ciaran allowed them to continue, though, and so they did. Isabella seemed to never give the abuse a second thought.

By the time Jimmy left the middle of last summer—he had only been back a month before abruptly departing shortly after the family's annual Fourth of July party—a noticeable strain between Isabella and Tommy appeared. Moretti had asked her about whatever had transpired only once, and her response was a terse "Jimmy" before she immediately changed the subject. It was never broached again.

He took a deep breath as the fan above continued to circle, exhaling slowly as he tried to release the tension within.

He was angry, although only at moments like this, alone with his thoughts, did he allow the bitterness of his recent marginalization to surface. It was not quite a year since Ciaran, his friend and benefactor these many years, had been diagnosed with Alzheimer's. With that came an immediate transition of all their other interests from father to son. With that one decree, he had been all but cast aside.

Moretti rankled at taking orders from someone so many decades his junior, a boy whom he considered unworthy of the mantle he was assuming. He would spend his last days of productivity working Tommy's deals in their offices downtown, mentoring the new boss's own right-hand man, Sam Dorgan, on the finer points of controlling their interests in Wrigleyville— and cruelest of all, watching helplessly as the elder Byrne, a man he loved and respected above all others, increasingly lost his grasp on the world around him.

He would never regain his place in the inner circle, able to wield power without question, and he resented all but Ciaran and Isabella for this cruel turn of fate. They simply had no other choice, although he knew Isabella, a similarly proud Italian, was a kindred spirit in his resentment, the queen of the Byrne empire now reduced to nursemaid.

More than anything he wanted back in, if only to wipe away the smug looks of pity from those who understood that he was now little more than a dog with all the teeth pried from his jaws, and who now intentionally accorded him less deference than years past. When opportunity presented itself he would show them all that Conrad Moretti had plenty of bite left in him yet.

The phone on the nightstand beside him began to vibrate, proving his faith in his instinct correct once again.

"Moretti?"

"Yes?"

"This is Boone. We need to talk."

"I'm sure we do," Moretti remarked as he glanced at the alarm clock, which read 3:54.

"Got a call in a little while ago," the cop said. "San Diego police were asking questions about Jimmy."

"And?"

"Something happened to him."

Moretti sat up and threw his feet over the side of the bed, not caring if it disturbed his wife. "What?"

"Don't exactly know," Boone said. "He's in the hospital and they wanted some info. What do you want us to tell them?"

Moretti felt his heart pound as his mind wandered to a number of darker scenarios that could have befallen the youngest Byrne son. Never did he think he would get such a call. Family had always been untouchable. Even those animals on the South Side understood that, but San Diego had become Liam's territory over the last few years. Was Ciaran's brother now engaged in something that had brought this to their front door?

"Tell them that you'll notify the family and they'll be in touch," Moretti said. "If they want anything more than that, give them my number."

"Got it."

Fuck, Moretti thought to himself as he tossed the phone onto the nightstand. His knees popped as he stood. It was time to start the day.

5

Since joining the *San Diego Times* in the late nineties, Susan Hendricks had focused on local stories—especially those relevant to the LGBT community. Once an activist, always one, and at fifty-three, she had no plans to change anytime soon.

As she had for the past few Sunday mornings, she stared restlessly at the ceiling, waiting for the phone to ring.

The police were no closer now to catching them than they had been since the rampage started five weeks ago. Their first victim had been a twenty-two-year-old barback on his way home after a long night cleaning up after a club full of drunken queens, an unfortunate end to an evening at a thankless job whose only promise was eventually making bartender—if you were considered attractive enough to work the front lines.

The screen on her phone lit up a moment before it began to vibrate. Without bothering to look over, she unplugged the phone from the charging cable, only turning her head enough to guide her thumb to answer the call.

"What's up?" she asked, having recognized the name from the caller ID as one of her best sources in the San Diego Police Department.

"Sue, how's it going?"

It was too early in the morning for so much enthusiasm, she thought. Another overeager millennial, already torturing her with his chirpiness. "Doing just fine, honey," she quietly answered as she climbed out of bed. With what he was about to tell her, there was no point in lying there any longer.

"Didn't wake you, did I?"

"No, not at all," she said. "What do you have for me?"

"Another beating."

Her stomach knotted. Even when she knew what was coming, it still made her physically ill. "I assume no change in the target?" she asked as she walked out of the bedroom and closed the door behind her.

"Yeah. Another white male, this one in his late teens—UCSD Hillcrest, like the others."

The age struck her as odd but she said nothing. "Name?"

"Byrne. B-Y-R-N-E. James Edward Byrne."

"Byrne. What's the condition?" she asked, flipping on the light in her office. *James Edward Byrne*, she repeated to herself, struggling to imprint the name before it slipped away with the lack of sleep.

"About the same as all the others."

"I owe you one, dear."

"Yes, you do."

She set the phone down on her desk. "Fuck," she muttered, then opened her laptop.

■ ■ ■

Not wanting to miss an opportunity to talk with the attending physician, Carlyle kept his trip to the crime scene brief. There was little to see that he couldn't glean from the photos, but he had diligently examined the area from all angles with a pensive look on his face, playing to the crowd still assembled, phones in hand to capture the moment to share afterwards with the assorted masses trolling social media for entertainment. It was the least he could do to show the public, and their followers, that he took the matter seriously. How this happened yet again in a relatively open area beside a busy thoroughfare with no witnesses, he would never understand. These bastards continued to be lucky beyond belief.

"How is he?" he asked.

The doctor briefly closed his eyes. This was his fourth incident, and it wasn't getting any easier for him. He tried to reassure himself that their wounds were relatively superficial and would heal fairly quickly. The emotional scars, which would no doubt remain for quite some time, he would leave to others. "I take it you don't want the technical jargon."

"I'm too tired to understand it, anyway," Carlyle assured him, exhaustion pulling down on him despite the latest delivery of caffeine in his hand.

"Kid will be fine," Dr. Evans answered, feeling a sense of déjà vu. If this kept up, he thought, he and the detective were a week or so away from forming a regular friendship. "Just beat a bit to hell like all the others."

"Where is he now?" Carlyle asked, looking around.

"Oh, he's done down here. I sent him up to the ICU."

"Intensive care?"

"They tend to be a little more attentive up there. It's not that bad."

"Any particulars I need to be aware of?"

"A couple of fractured ribs are the worst we have, so it's more good news than not," Evans said. "No concussion, no damage to the major organs. Lot of bruising on the torso, some swelling, cuts and scrapes to his face, mostly superficial. It looks a lot worse than it actually is, though he may not feel like himself for a few weeks."

"Lovely. You got my number, right?"

Dr. Evans patted the breast pocket on his lab coat. "I got a stack of your cards right here."

Carlyle smiled. "Call me if anything develops. I'll be back in the morning."

6

"What is it?" Tommy asked, the phone cupped in his hand.

He hadn't moved since he got out of bed a few hours ago, slouching in his chair as he stared aimlessly over the city, worrying over what he couldn't yet name. Nothing productive came of this meditation, he acknowledged, but he did so nonetheless. Better here than lying in bed and doing the same—or overusing prescription sleeping pills. And now, at just after four in the morning, his waiting had come to an end.

"It's about Jimmy," Moretti said.

It took Tommy a few moments to digest the name. "*Jimmy*?" he asked, his mind still clouded. "What the hell is going on with him?"

Moretti looked across the round kitchen table. There were two place settings for breakfast: his cereal bowl, juice glass, and coffee mug in their spots, a cloth napkin beside the bowl. Her placemat mirrored his own, a small sugar container between the two. He loved her more than anything and prayed every day that nothing would befall her as it seemingly had Ciaran's youngest. "Something happened in San Diego."

Tommy sat up, once again picturing his youngest brother, bloodied and near death on the floor of his parent's downstairs den. "What?"

Moretti noticed Tommy's sudden change in tone. As of late he displayed a distinct indifference to Enzo, but with that came an almost overprotectiveness of his youngest sibling. "I don't have exact details," Moretti admitted, "but he's been assaulted. He's in the hospital, and the local cops are asking questions."

"What the fuck?" Tommy muttered.

"I know."

"That can't be my uncle Liam."

"No. Never."

Tommy paused. "Maybe one of his animals south of the border then."

"I think they learned their lesson," Moretti said as he thought back to several years ago, when thirty-three people had been massacred in Rosarito, south of Tijuana, the result of a realignment of business partnerships following an offhanded threat against Liam Jr.'s wife.

"Who else knows?"

"Just you. What would you like me to do?"

"I need to get out there—now."

"No… not you. Not until we know exactly what's going on."

Tommy paused. "I guess Sam then. He can—"

"I'll go," Moretti interrupted. "I can take care of this."

Tommy thought of one of their more recent arguments, when the man on the other end of the call lectured him on his priorities. "You? Are you sure about that?"

"Yes. Besides, your mother will need to be out there once we know what happened, and I'm best to handle that."

"I don't think she'll go."

"She has no choice," Moretti said. "There are optics involved, and neglecting her youngest son in the hospital invites unnecessary scrutiny into our affairs."

"I agree," Tommy said as two words reentered his mind: Las Vegas.

Like Ciaran had with Tommy, Liam Jr. had turned over day-to-day control of his family's affairs to his eldest son, David, freeing himself to tend to his latest passion project, a small winery in California. His other two sons, Michael and Arthur, also worked for the family, though the latter served more as their own Enzo with little to no interest in leadership. Michael, in due time, would present a similar dilemma to the one their grandfather had faced decades before.

Unlike their fathers, Tommy and David had a relationship, albeit a distant one. The cousins had met only once, at a meeting arranged by associates in Kansas City, but they continued to communicate occasionally, mostly through their respective seconds—Tommy through his lifelong friend and now right-hand man Sam Dorgan, and David through Michael.

"I'll call my cousin in a few hours and give him the heads up," Tommy said. "He can run interference with Sonoma County's newest vintner if there's an issue."

"What about…" Moretti said, allowing the name to remain unspoken.

Enzo, Tommy thought. He already knew the answer he would give, as his father would demand it regardless. "Okay. They have a man down there we can use, right?"

"Yes, but that request opens up its own problem."

Tommy pinched the bridge of his nose. He didn't want to take this step, but they would need someone local to assist. And he knew that his cousin would want Arthur to take part in the hunt. It was their territory, after all, and Tommy would have little choice if pressed on the matter. "Let's see if I can head that off."

"If not?"

"Then we live with it," Tommy said. "I'm sure they can all play nicely if it comes to that."

"I'll keep it under control regardless."

"Take Sam with you," Tommy added as he found himself pacing in front of the window. He glanced down, watching as a few stray cars made their way south across the DuSable Bridge. "He can help if needed."

"What about Wrigleyville?"

"I need to get up there anyway. Joe and the others can step in with everything else."

Moretti sighed, annoyed to have Tommy's spy tagging along. "Okay. Let me call Highland Park and tell your parents."

"Thank you."

"I'm not sure I fully understand what happened between you and her last year."

"You don't need to," Tommy said, then disconnected the call.

7

As a fist connected with his jaw, his eyes jerked open and the nightmare abruptly ended.

Repeated blinking did nothing to clear the blurriness in the room. A muffled beep pulsed rhythmically in the background, and unfamiliar voices spoke words he could not follow.

He tried to rub his eyes but couldn't move. The pain in his ribs quickly resurfaced, and he moaned as it enveloped him—unbearable as he lay trapped and helpless against its force.

The sedatives once more took hold, and he welcomed the heaviness of his eyelids before slipping back into sleep.

■ ■ ■

"Don't tell me you've been up all night."

Sue looked up from her laptop to see her partner of almost a decade leaning against the doorframe, dressed in flannel pajama bottoms and a long-sleeve T-shirt, a mug of coffee cradled in her hands.

"Almost. I napped a little after I got back around five."

"You can work during the day."

"Edie, I know. It was important though."

"So is your health," Edie said, tucking a lock of dark brown hair behind her ear. As a nurse, her partner's chronic stress levels and high blood pressure were a constant source of concern.

Sue raised her hands in surrender. "Yes, Mom."

Edie frowned. "Another beating?"

"Yeah."

"Any leads?"

"Not really. I talked with some people at the crime scene, then went over to the hospital to see what was going on, which wasn't much, so I left."

"Where are you off to now?"

"Back to the hospital, I think." Sue picked up her phone, checking the time. "I talked to the doctor before his shift ended—off the record—but I want to see if the family shows up. Or someone else."

Edie took a sip of her coffee. "When will you be back?"

Sue shrugged. "Depends on what I find. I'm also hoping to retrace this kid's steps from last night, and I don't know where that's going to lead me. I need to check the bars, but they'll be empty until sometime this afternoon."

"Are the police cooperating?"

"The ones I've spoken to. But the head of the mayor's new task force is hardly a fan. I'm not sure how much I'm going to get out of him, if he even lets me track him down."

"I've told you that playing nice with people will pay off better in the end."

Sue smiled. "Detective Carlyle loves me. He just doesn't know it yet."

8

"I'm looking for Jimmy Byrne," Moretti said to the duty station nurse. He and Sam stood at one end of the horseshoe-shaped nurses' station in the middle of the large open space, a succession of patient rooms flanking it on three sides. "He's a new patient."

The plane had landed in San Diego shortly after ten that morning. He and Sam had grabbed a rental car and immediately headed to the hospital. Meanwhile, Enzo and his man Eddie had driven down to Indianapolis and flown in through Dallas using two of the several fake identities reserved for such excursions. Arriving shortly after Moretti and Sam, the two men picked up another car and began their search.

"Byrne," the nurse repeated, looking over some paperwork. "And you are?"

"Richard Moretti. The family attorney."

"He suing already?" she joked.

Moretti glared at her. "Lady, I've been up all night, and I really don't need you to be a smart-ass. I'd like the fucking room number. *Now*."

She looked at Moretti, then glanced over at the man standing beside him, his hands casually in his pockets. He didn't look threatening, but she didn't want to take that risk. Between the emergency room rumor mill and a quick Google search, she knew everything she needed to know about the Byrnes. She pointed to the far side of the room behind her. "Room 412."

The two stopped at the door to Room 412. It was closed, with white curtains masking the glass wall, as Carlyle rounded the corner from the opposite side of the nurses' station.

"Can I help you?" he called out.

They looked harmless enough, Carlyle thought, though he wasn't sure what he should have expected. Certainly not a pair of tracksuit-clad extras from *The Sopranos*, but these two—the older one dressed in Brooks Brothers, the younger one in an oxford and khakis—could fit in at any WASP country club in Orange County. They had clearly been dispatched to present a genteel front while others, no doubt, lurked about in the shadows.

They returned the favor of looking him over. "And you are?" Moretti asked.

"Detective Robert Carlyle," he answered, extending his hand. "And with whom do I have the pleasure of speaking?"

The two shook hands. "Richard Moretti," he said, reaching inside his coat pocket to extract one of his business cards, mildly disappointed when the detective didn't flinch. "I've been sent out from Chicago on behalf of the family."

Carlyle didn't bother to look at the card as it was handed over. "Is any member of this kid's *actual* family coming out here?" he asked.

Moretti raised an eyebrow. "Shortly."

Carlyle pulled open the hospital room door and motioned him inside. "Well then, since we have some time, why don't you and I have a little chat?"

■ ■ ■

"Enzo, long time no see," Sean said as he climbed into the back seat.

Closing the door, he took a quick glance to make sure that the outfit he had picked up from Saks only days ago still looked good while he was sitting down. Insecure about whether he was projecting the image he wanted, he often overcorrected with clothes and jewelry best left as a faded cliché of days gone by. In this car, however, he was not alone in his tastes and so was none the wiser of how he appeared to others.

The two exchanged a quick, if awkward, handshake over the seat between them. "What's going on?" Enzo asked.

"Not much," Sean said. "Glad to be working with you again."

"It's a shame you moved out here."

"Someone had to be local to handle those shipments, and your uncle takes care of me."

Enzo sneered. "You fucked us over for them."

"You know it's not like that, man. Moretti sent me—"

"Fuck Moretti."

"It was his idea."

"My uncle's a dick, and my cousins are a bunch of douchebags," Enzo said. "I have no idea what the fuck you were thinking going to work for them."

Sean put up a hand. "To each his own. They've been good to me."

"Whatever." Enzo nodded at the driver. "You remember Eddie?"

"Yeah," Sean said as he offered his hand. "Good to see you again. How's it going?"

"Same old, same old," Eddie replied, extending his own hand.

Sean turned back to Enzo. "So, what's up?"

"My brother Jimmy's in the hospital."

"Holy shit. What happened?"

"Don't know yet, but Moretti and Tommy's little bitch Sam are there right now. We're supposed to track down whatever stupid fuck hurt him and take care of it."

"It wasn't us," Sean said. "Our friends down south are behaving."

"I don't give a fuck. I'm just here to hunt down the son of a bitch."

Sean settled back into his seat. Arthur could be a sadistic bastard, but from his time in Chicago Sean understood he was a rank amateur when it came to torturing people the way Enzo could. This would be a very bloody week indeed.

"We're not here, of course," Enzo added.

"Of course," Sean replied as he pulled out his phone. "I got someone who I think can help with this one."

Eddie glanced toward the back. "Even down here?"

Sean laughed. "We have those kinds of friends everywhere. Everyone wants in on this shit."

9

Moretti walked to the foot of the bed, where little Jimmy—he would always be known as that, no matter how old he was—lay sleeping. Even though he had seen worse, he recoiled slightly at the bruising and swelling reminiscent of Enzo's beatings.

"What happened?" he asked after saying a quick prayer.

"From what we can tell, he was cornered and beaten a couple blocks from here," Carlyle answered as he remained by the door.

Moretti looked at the detective. "Do you know who did it?"

"We don't have many leads, no," Carlyle admitted.

"What *do* you know?"

Carlyle briefly paused as he stared at the man he believed to be Ciaran Byrne's consigliere, or whatever the Irish equivalent of that was, not wanting to help him—or whoever else was nearby—track down the perpetrators before he had the chance to. "We believe there are three males, probably living in the neighborhood or relatively close by, all around five-ten to six feet tall, mid-twenties or thereabout, all white, with one possibly being Hispanic. Most of that we've gotten from the other victims. Unfortunately, what surveillance cameras we have in the neighborhood haven't given us much."

"Remarkably vague," Moretti mused. "There have been others, though?"

Carlyle cleared his throat. He already knew where this was headed. "This is the sixth assault of this type in the past six weeks."

"What type?"

Carlyle shrugged. "You know," he answered, his tone softening as he resigned himself to being the bearer of bad news. "Some punks come along and beat up a... a homosexual for fun."

"You better watch your fucking mouth," Moretti snapped. "He's not a fag."

"Okay, then. My apologies."

Moretti glanced back over to the bed, his unease deepening. As if the assault of a member of their family hadn't been enough, now this. "Why the hell would you even say something like that?"

"He was beaten up in a predominantly gay neighborhood."

"*So?*"

"We were also able to confirm his presence in at least two gay bars that evening," Carlyle added, having received that information only moments before.

"And that proves what, exactly?"

"Our suspects only target young gay men."

"I guess they fucked up this time."

"Perhaps," Carlyle remarked, wondering whether there was a greater meaning to the statement. Moretti continued to glare at him. "I'm just waiting to talk to the victim to clarify things."

"I'm his attorney," Moretti said. "I can already tell you exactly what he's going to say."

Carlyle raised an eyebrow. "Perhaps," he repeated. "But since you're the attorney, I just wanted to let you know that he was out drinking last night."

Moretti laughed. "So?"

Carlyle pulled out the California driver's license and handed it over. "Care to explain this?"

Moretti stared at the altered birthdate for a moment, then forced a sneer. Jimmy had clearly tapped into some network to get hold of this, most likely one of their own. The boy was more creative than he had given him credit for. How the hell did he get himself involved with Liam Byrne's local crew, and was that why he was in intensive care?

He handed the license back. "I think we can find a more appropriate time to discuss a driver's license. Right now, I want to speak to the doctor."

"Where will you be staying, in case I need to reach you?" Carlyle asked.

"That has yet to be determined. I came straight from the airport."

"How can I reach you then?"

"My number is on my card," Moretti answered. "You have his cell phone?"

"It wasn't on him."

"Stolen?"

"I doubt it."

"And why is that?"

Carlyle pointed at the table beside the bed, the wallet still in the evidence bag. "They leave a wallet full of untraceable cash and take the phone? Not very bright."

"They are definitely not very bright." Moretti nodded at the door. "Now if you'll excuse us."

■ ■ ■

Sue entered one side of the ICU, spotting a very unhappy-looking Detective Carlyle as he passed the final patient room and turned toward the exit opposite hers. She stepped up her pace, scurrying along the back of the room toward the double doors that were now closing behind him.

"Detective Carlyle?" she called out. "Detective Carlyle?"

Carlyle stopped between the two elevators and turned to face her, forcing a smile. "Sue. Good to see you."

"Can I talk with you a moment?" she asked. "We kept missing each other last night."

"I wasn't avoiding you."

"I didn't say you were."

"Make it quick. I'm hungry, and I need to get some sleep."

"Any new leads?"

Carlyle glared at her as he hit the down arrow on the elevator panel. "Sue, you're a better reporter than that."

"How's the victim?"

"He'll live."

"Can you be more specific?"

"Haven't you already annoyed the doctor with these questions?"

"You've seen the victim," she said. "I wanted your impression."

"What do you expect? The kid looks like hell."

"You've been assigned to oversee the investigations for these beatings. What do you hope to—"

"Sue." The elevator doors opened and he stepped inside, turning around to face her. "This has been a shit day for me, and it's only just started. Call me later and we'll talk about it, I promise."

■ ■ ■

Still with Jimmy, Moretti stared down at his phone.

It wasn't as if it hadn't occurred to him on more than one occasion, and he couldn't have been the only one to suspect. There had always been something different about the boy. Each had a unique path to follow, he understood, and he never expected all of Ciaran's children to follow into the family's concerns, so he'd given very little thought as to why the youngest of his sons had gone to California.

He looked over at the sleeping teenager, a slight grin appearing as he recalled happier times: the toddler bounding up to him with ice cream dripping down his arm, the preschooler who gave him bear hugs, the lanky teenager enthusiastically trying to teach his "Uncle Conrad" how to play video games. But as he approached adulthood, that wonderful child had ceased to exist, replaced by a withdrawn young man with dead eyes.

Ciaran Byrne had a gay son. He still didn't want to believe it, but he was a practical man. Times were changing and people were comfortable expressing all sorts of things better left private. Tommy's wife even had a brother who was, and whenever he and his partner were around there had never been issue. Gay or not, Sabrina Byrne's brother was family and was shown that respect. Only Isabella had commented on it—privately—saying they would burn in hell, but such talk started and ended there.

As Moretti looked back over the last year or so, Jimmy withdrawing as he had and fleeing to California, it began to make perfect sense. The one place he could never be himself would be Chicago. To be that way around his family, around their associates, would cause too many problems, even in this day and age. He had done the right thing in trying to keep that part of himself as far from them as he could. But no good deed ever went unpunished, he reminded himself as he returned his focus to his phone.

"What's the word?" Enzo asked from the burner he had grabbed before heading west. Somewhere in Chicago, someone was using his phone, creating a long record of activity in case someone at the Bureau forgot his place.

"It's not as we thought," Moretti said without bothering to elaborate.

There was a pause on the other end of the line. "It's not?"

"No."

"Then what the fuck is it?"

"I don't know yet," Moretti lied. "We're still trying to figure it out. The police suspect it's random."

"So, what does that mean?"

"Nothing as far as you're concerned," he answered. "The message still has to be delivered. You are to continue as discussed."

"Good."

"Oh, and his phone is missing. Start there."

10

Chris had slept in, as he did every Sunday, especially after a night such as the last. The drunken evening, like the five prior occasions after they'd beaten up some poor, unsuspecting fag, had been a long one.

He thought back to the first assault six weeks ago. He, Billy, and Dan were walking down University on their way to one of the mixed clubs in the area. The other two were certainly willing to let it go—it was Hillcrest, after all, and these things were to be expected—but Chris had found it obscene that another man had clearly checked out his crotch before winking at him with a smirk on his face.

It was something that he had to respond to, something he had been incapable of when he was entering his teens and living with his bachelor uncle while his mother—he'd never known his father—struggled with her various addictions. That year and a half had been absolute hell, wondering how and when his uncle would decide to take advantage of their time alone.

Though Chris had felt the insult much more personally than his friends, both of them willingly partook in luring their unsuspecting victim into an alleyway and pummeling him unconscious before walking away as if nothing had happened, save for the incredible high that they felt. It wasn't as if they had intended it to become a weekly ritual, but by the following Saturday they longed for that feeling of superiority, of release, of the ultimate control the moment had provided them. Their only choice, of course, was to venture back out to sate the thirst, to improve upon what they had done the week before, to get that sensation back.

Looking up at the ceiling as he reached down and adjusted himself, he wished he could sleep all day to rid himself of his hangover, but he had to be at work and rent was coming due. He hated that he'd had to stop selling Ecstasy to the stupid disco fags after his supplier got busted, or that he couldn't live with himself by letting older men go down on him for cash. Money was never a problem then.

He rolled out of bed and noticed the dried blood on his hand. He first thought he had cut himself somehow, but after finding no open wounds on his body, he realized that it was the fag's blood on him.

"Holy fucking shit!" he yelled as he ran to the bathroom, wearing only his white briefs.

"What's your fucking problem?" Billy yelled back from the living room.

"I got that fucker's blood on me."

Billy glanced down at his own hand, now cleaned of his own reminder of the night before. "So?"

"Ever hear of AIDS, you stupid prick?" Chris asked as he ran his hands under the water, rubbing them vigorously with a bar of soap. "I swear to God if that fucking fag gave me AIDS, I'm going to kill him."

"You should have done it last night, then," Billy remarked, his anxiety from the night before dissipated, as it always had by this point. He glanced over at Dan, who was still watching the Padres game.

"Dumb fuck," Dan muttered.

■ ■ ■

"What do the police know?" Tommy asked.

The place to himself now, he had holed up in his home office overlooking the Chicago River south toward the Loop. The large tumbler of coffee his wife had delivered had long been consumed, as had two subsequent refills. As he watched the ebb and flow of traffic down on Wacker, he wasn't sure whether the slight tremor in his hands was from caffeine or fear.

He had already made the call to his parent's estate in Highland Park, a follow-up to Moretti's, a decision he quickly regretted. His father, taking it as an assault on the family, was still wound into an indignant rage. The old man had convinced himself it was the result of his brother's affairs in Las Vegas, cursing Liam and his inept children for placing his own son's life, and their mutual interests, at risk. Particularly since the diagnosis, he was very much one to fixate without end.

His mother, conversely, said very little, which was not unexpected. She had only taken the phone to calm her husband, greeting her eldest son with a terse, "What did he do now?" It had not gone well from there, but he was thankful that the conversation was short and relatively more cordial than usual of late. When it came to family, wagons were circled regardless.

Moretti paused as he stood outside Jimmy's room, watching the nurses mill about at their stations, comfortably out of earshot, still undecided on how to relay Detective Carlyle's theory. "Not much," he finally admitted. "They'll release him in a few days. Did you speak to David?"

"Yes, and we're solo for now," Tommy said. "Is it related to us?"

"No, I don't believe so."

Tommy let out a long sigh. "Thank God. Anything else?"

Moretti paused as he thought about the license. "No," he lied. "I'm still waiting to speak to someone besides a nurse."

"Where the fuck is his doctor?"

"The one who treated him has already left, and no one else seems inclined to give me anything."

"What's Sam doing?"

"Watching Jimmy sleep, doing whatever it is people your age do on those phones."

"I guess we need to cancel the party then," Tommy said.

"I told them it was still on."

"Why?"

"We don't have a choice. Your uncle—"

"He and David don't have a say in this."

Moretti cleared his throat. "Tommy, with all due respect, we're here with his blessing, and I'm willing to bet that your uncle doesn't give a good goddamn what these scumbags were thinking. He'll want a message sent regardless. We step out with that not taken care of and he *will* fill the void."

Tommy scoffed. "He can have it."

"I strongly advise against that, if only for your father."

"What are you not telling me? Why do *we* need to take care of this?"

Moretti paused. "Tommy, the police are calling this a hate crime."

He laughed. "Get out of here."

"I'm serious."

"We're Irish, for fuck's sake."

"Tommy," Moretti snapped.

Tommy paused. "Never mind. Don't say it."

"I don't *have* to say it," Moretti said, his voice raised. "It's hanging out there like a goddamn dick swinging in the wind." He looked up to see a middle-aged male nurse glaring at him.

Tommy groaned, relenting to the obvious. "Okay," he said, his voice barely above a whisper. "Okay."

"Look… I don't give a shit what the kid does out here—"

"You think I do?" Tommy asked.

"We just have to contain things," Moretti said. "*We* do. Or your cousin will send people here, and this is not something they need to know. All we have to do is make Las Vegas think we took care of the problem and it goes away."

"Okay. Agreed."

"Let's just focus on the optics for now. Your mother has already agreed to visit, which should keep them from wanting to meddle."

"Good luck with that."

11

Within moments of Eddie working the lock, he and Enzo found themselves in the middle of James's living room. Sean remained outside, smoking a cigarette and keeping watch as he continued his efforts to reach out to his contacts, busily putting out the word that whoever had attacked Jimmy Byrne was living on borrowed time, and that anyone who located the culprits would be handsomely rewarded.

Leaving Enzo to search elsewhere, Eddie first went to the bedroom, where he quickly went through several piles of clothes before tossing a pair of jeans, a T-shirt, a pair of underwear, and flip-flops into a backpack he found on the floor of the closet. He then returned to the living room, where Enzo was standing by the dining room table, staring blankly at the iPhone in his hand.

Enzo looked over, glancing down at the backpack. "What the fuck is that?"

"Clothes."

"Why?"

"Because Moretti asked me to."

Enzo furrowed his brow. "You two butt-fucking or something?"

"Huh?"

He motioned toward the backpack. "That. You're like his little bitch—fetching stupid shit for my retard brother."

"Look, Enzo," Eddie said, "Moretti asked me to grab some clothes, and if we managed to find the phone, to put them together for Sam to pick up. I'm doing what I'm told." He pointed to the one in Enzo's hand. "Is that it?"

Enzo scoffed. "It isn't fucking mine," he said as he examined it once more. "How the fuck do you work this stupid thing?"

Eddie tossed the backpack by the door and walked over, his hand out as he motioned with his fingers. "You don't know how to use an iPhone?"

"Fuck no. These things are for chicks and fags. Give me a flip phone any day."

Eddie swiped across the bottom of the phone. "There isn't even a password. Fifteen texts, five emails, and three voicemails. Where do you want to start?"

"Fuck, I don't know," Enzo said. "Voicemail, I guess."

A few buttons later the first message played over the speakerphone. "James, it's Matt. Give me a call when you get up. We need to talk."

"I bet you do," Enzo remarked. "Sounds like a fag. Next."

A different man's voice. "Hey, girlfriend!" he shrieked. Eddie paused a moment before looking over at Enzo, whose face wore an all-too-familiar frown that always foretold trouble.

"You and Matt just need to chill out and quit fighting in public like that," the message continued. "Everyone's talking about it, and that isn't cool. Call me when you get this. Bye."

"What the fuck?!" Enzo shouted.

Eddie glanced at his boss, took a deep breath, and played the third voicemail. "James, it's Matt again. I'm sorry that I was being so jealous. Look, it's just… well, you know how I am. Call me. I love you. Bye."

Eddie looked up from the phone and met Enzo's eyes.

"If you say one fucking word—" Enzo warned, jabbing his finger at Eddie.

"Man, I didn't hear a fucking thing," Eddie assured him as Sean walked in, his own phone in hand.

"Enzo," he began as he closed the door behind him, "I got some news about what's been going down, but you are *not* going to like it, man."

■ ■ ■

"Have you heard from James today?" Tim asked his roommate as the two recovered from the night's outing as they usually did—watching television and eating junk food—today being Cartoon Network and a pizza that had been delivered an hour before. As usual he was slouched in the chair facing the television, Matt comfortably lying on the couch to his left, both hands resting on his stomach.

He hated even asking the question. As the eldest of the group, at twenty-six, he was quickly becoming drained by the never-ending crisis mentality that obsessed those only a few years younger. Matt, a friend since he'd met the then-freshman during his senior year at UCSD, was especially so, and James was just the latest to bear its brunt.

Tim wasn't even sure why the two were together, their only commonality the penchant for bar-hopping that only the young or immature seemed to crave. In the few months they'd been together, they spent most of their time either drunk or stoned, a means to an uneasy truce amid their raging fights. Last night was just the most recent example of the two states merging into one.

Tim genuinely liked James, who was generally quiet and rarely talked about his past, although he could sometimes become what Tim referred to as a three-cocktail conversationalist. There was certainly a wall there, one both high and thick, and Matt would never be the one to get through it.

He thought back to last night, when he and James had wound up alone while Matt was on a beer run before heading out. The young couple rarely ventured outside an invisible five-foot boundary when together, so Tim was somewhat surprised when James decided to stay behind while Matt went out for the beer. The latter seemed annoyed but didn't argue—there was already tension between them over James wanting to go back to La Jolla to retrieve his phone; slamming the door behind him was all he needed to express his displeasure.

Tim had sat as he did today, beer in hand, as he watched James on the far side of the couch. The two enjoyed the silence, a rare occurrence with the always gregarious Matt around.

"You'll survive," he assured the younger man, whose knee was nervously bobbing up and down.

"Huh?"

"One night without your phone will probably do you some good."

"I hope," James joked, although with an underlying tone of seriousness. "It's like… how fucking stupid was that?"

"Got you thinking about something, though, without the distraction."

"What do you mean?"

"Who is he?" Tim asked.

"Who?"

"The one you're thinking about."

James cracked a reminiscent smile as he glanced down. "He's no one. Just… someone from my past."

Tim laughed. "You're nineteen. How much of a past could you have?"

James looked away once more as his knee continued to twitch. "You'd be surprised."

Tim thought of his father, a Republican state senator, with whom relations were, at best, strained. None of his friends ever thought to put two and two together with his surname, something for which Tim was thankful. He certainly didn't need the aggravation, especially since he would wind up agreeing with them that the man really was an asshole.

"I'm not trying to break you two up, but what are you even doing with Matt?"

James shrugged. "I don't know. A fresh start?"

"I don't think it's working."

James laughed. "No, it isn't. I'm… I don't know. I'm thinking of breaking up with him tonight."

Tim let out a long, slow sigh. This evening would be more of a train wreck than usual. "Thanks for the heads up."

James faked a grin. "You're welcome."

Thoughts of last night ended, and Tim looked back at Matt. "Have you heard from James today?" he repeated.

"No."

"I wonder what his problem is."

"I told you, we got in a fight," Matt said.

"You shouldn't have gone crazy like that."

Matt turned his head and glared at him. "He shouldn't have been talking to that guy."

"Oh, it was harmless."

"It didn't look *harmless* to me."

"Did you at least call him?"

"Yeah," Matt said as he looked back at the television. "I've already left him two messages, the stupid shit."

12

Alex Mullens had grown up in Andersonville on the North Side of Chicago. Like his father, Big Joe, Alex worked for the Byrne family, though having just turned twenty-one, he didn't get to do much beyond running odd jobs for his father and the rest of the crew under him. It wasn't glorious work, but it had its perks, namely the respect that working for the Byrnes entailed, not to mention the money, which was far more than the degree he never earned from his ill-fated attempt at Notre Dame would have gotten him.

It wasn't as if he didn't aspire to more, which was what had driven him to higher education in the first place. This was his father's life, not his, and though he knew he was being groomed to take over for his old man, he also could see that times were beginning to change within the organization as the leadership passed to the next generation.

Big Joe was generally cryptic about his feelings, although over a few beers, when it was just the two of them, he often grew animated enough to give his son a glimpse behind the curtain.

"How was your route?" his father had asked just last Sunday afternoon. The two of them were watching the Cubs in the living room while his mother cooked dinner in the kitchen.

Their love for the Cubs was the only thing they shared other than their respective employer. Alex was thankful there was even that. "Uneventful," he answered after taking a sip of his beer.

"You kids have it so easy," Big Joe said. "In my day we'd be lucky to go three stops without something blowing up."

"We got them trained, I guess."

"*We* got them trained," his father corrected. "You kids just skip along the path we paved for you." He paused for a moment. "Look at Tommy. Ciaran was in the trenches each and every day. His son? Sits in that fancy office tower playing businessman. He doesn't appreciate the hard work on the ground—working the streets, taking opportunities as they came, and demanding the respect that his old man fought for, man by man, block by block, neighborhood by neighborhood… just so he doesn't have to."

"I thought you said you were happy with how things were going."

"Don't be a smartass," Joe snapped. "That's not what I'm talking about."

Alex knew when to relent. "Okay, Pop."

"None of you understand what it takes to keep all this going," Joe continued, not one to prematurely end a good rant when the urge took hold. "None of you. The only reason there's a goddamn Byrne sitting in a building downtown is because of us. You can't run this family if you won't get your goddamn hands dirty."

Alex closed his eyes as he reflected on his father's words, one of many such sermons. They often came back to him on days like today, another in a long line of uneventful Sundays that melded together after a time. As always, it had started with attending Mass with his parents, who still insisted on a suit and tie, as well as being seated in the front pew a half-hour early. To do otherwise, his mother said, was an affront to God. To suggest he not go with them would be an even greater sin, and Alex feared the wrath of Sheila Mullens much more than the man above.

That was followed by his current chore, running pickups for his father, which normally took a few hours and had become rote. Even in a bad economy, people always made sure that the Byrnes got theirs. In the rare cases he met resistance, he only had to mention the name Enzo, one that only the foolish failed to heed.

For the past six months, his partner had been Chase Valco, a twenty-two-year-old member of Isabella's extended family whose father had sent him out to work for Big Joe, while a situation involving the discharge of a firearm in a trendy Brooklyn hipster bar, in front of a hundred or so witnesses, was being resolved. Joe put him under Alex's wing, where he would remain until he could return to New York without having to face an extended stay at Rikers Island. Glorified babysitting, Alex thought, not particularly caring for the overeager Italian show-off with whom he now spent the bulk of his time. Much like Alex's mother, Chase found it difficult to stop talking whenever the threat of silence approached.

"Oh, shit," Chase said as the two were halfway through their rounds. "Guess what I heard."

"What?" Alex asked as he glanced at his phone. Dinner with his parents was at six, and as with Mass, he was expected to be there significantly before the appointed hour.

"Something happened to Jimmy Byrne."

"What?"

"Don't know yet, but he's in the hospital."

"When did that happen?"

"Last night."

Alex's hands began to sweat as he pictured his friend lying in a hospital bed two thousand miles away. "How'd you hear that?"

"Theresa."

"How the hell did your girl hear that?"

"She lives next to Sam's sister, and Sam's girl said he left for San Diego with Moretti."

"Well… is he all right?"

"Fuck if I know," Chase said. "What, are you in love with the guy or something?"

"It's the boss's brother."

"I know who the fuck he is, asshole, but he's not involved in the family. I'm here busting my ass to make my old man happy and he's off being some fucking California freak."

"Jimmy Byrne is as much a part of this family as anyone," Alex said, a rare flash of anger in his voice. "We grew up together, so don't talk shit about him."

"Chill out, man. I just—"

"Just leave it the fuck alone."

13

"What is it?" Moretti asked as he stepped outside Jimmy's hospital room.

He watched through the glass panes as Sam continued to stare mindlessly at the phone in his hand and thought, not for the first time, that Tommy and his man would find out soon enough how important the empire's foundation was to maintaining everything they had. But probably not before it had been taken from them by others who understood that on a much deeper level.

"We're at Jimmy's apartment," Eddie said.

Moretti rolled his eyes. "And?"

"I got the clothes."

Moretti sensed a nervousness to Eddie's voice that disquieted him. He was almost hesitant to ask a second time. "*And?*"

"We found the phone like you asked. There are a couple of messages on it and Enzo wants to follow up on one of them."

Moretti sighed loudly to signal his growing displeasure at the pace of the conversation. "What sort of message? From whom?"

"A friend."

"*A friend?*"

"Yeah… you know. A *friend* friend."

"I don't have all fucking day, Eddie. What's your goddamn point?"

"We got a problem," Eddie said. "Enzo's climbing the walls right now."

This was going better than expected. "Put him on."

"Okay, hold on a sec."

"Yeah?"

"Enzo, I don't know what you heard—"

"You know what I heard? I heard a couple goddamn fags, and one of them is Jimmy's goddamn boyfriend. His *boyfriend*," Enzo repeated. "He's a fucking fag, Moretti. Fuck, he always acted like one, but—fuck me, the little douchebag *is* one. We have a fucking fag in the family."

"Enzo—"

"I can't fucking believe this. Jesus fucking Christ. And guess who else knows?"

"Who?"

"Sean, fucking Sean," Enzo said. "You know he's going to run back and tell Uncle Liam, and then we're really fucked."

That was unfortunate, but Moretti knew it was bound to come out at some point. "Did you warn him not to?"

"I told him I would personally cut his nuts off if he opened his goddamn mouth. Like that carries any fucking water. He's protected by those fucking assholes."

"Eddie said you wanted to follow up with one of the calls."

"You're goddamn right I do."

Moretti thought of Isabella and their conversation a few hours ago. Glancing at his watch, he estimated that she should already be in the air by now, or would be shortly. "Don't even consider it," he warned.

"Why not?"

"Because I don't need the headache of you fucking things up."

"What the fuck did you just say?"

"I think you heard me."

"What the fuck ever," Enzo said. "You don't tell me what to do."

"Yes, actually I do. Or do I need to have a conversation with your father about this?" Regardless of how easily Enzo could be manipulated, Moretti was not above showing him how tight the leash around his neck actually was.

Enzo grunted in stifled rage. "So, you're just going to let this stand?"

"On the contrary," Moretti said, his point made. "You do what you need to do."

■ ■ ■

Only once seated in the first-class cabin was Isabella comfortable dropping the façade.

She didn't wish what had happened upon the boy, satisfied with his being half the country away, but she also didn't want to carry on with the pretense of concern. Ciaran had been visibly taken aback, assuming the violence toward his youngest was the result of his affairs or those of his brother, his shock rapidly collapsing under the fury that took its place. It was not the time, she knew, to speak her mind.

Moretti, though, had truly impressed with his vision for making the most of a bad situation. "Never let a good crisis go to waste," he told her before requesting her presence at her youngest son's bedside, which she had recoiled from—until he explained what he had devised earlier that morning. It could solve several of their problems, even if it meant bargaining with the devil to get there.

Isabella finished off her wine as the flight attendant passed with the bottle, feigning a smile as the glass was refilled. She then looked out the window, gazing over the expanse of the approaching Rocky Mountains below, a smattering of clouds hovering just above the snow-covered peaks, and steeled herself to play the part as best she could. The day would come when this problem would be fully resolved.

She thought back to when she discovered she was pregnant with him. Her first instinct was to get an abortion, a secret that she would take to her grave. She had almost done it, only changing her mind in the parking lot of the doctor who would have discreetly performed it. After all, Ciaran was a ruthless man when required, and killing one of his sons would no doubt force that part of him upon her had it been discovered. The doctor had an unfortunately fatal traffic accident with a runaway trash hauler soon thereafter, though, ridding Isabella of any worry that her missed appointment might ever be disclosed.

So, she had the child, but never warmed to him, content with the three who were already there and allowing them, with the help of a nanny the others never had, to primarily deal with raising him. There was always something odd about the boy, something that she couldn't put her finger on until he was in high school, when she had finally put it all together. Nothing pleased her more than the day he left for California. And Enzo had taught the boy a lesson that would keep him out there for good.

■ ■ ■

Sue had considered getting in the elevator and pressing Carlyle until he told her everything she needed to know, but she had other sources who were much more accommodating. Besides, she didn't want to wear out her welcome with him just yet. There would be more than enough time for that.

She spent the rest of the morning and early afternoon calling a few contacts who could put her in touch with those who owned or managed the bars in the area, and from there a list of employees who had worked the night before.

"I'm sorry, I'm just tired," said the young man on the other side of the sidewalk table. A bartender from the last club James Byrne was known to have visited, he had begrudgingly agreed to meet after she had mentioned that his boss was a dear friend. She had been lying, but he wouldn't find out until long after this conversation, if at all. He looked as if he had the attention span of a goldfish.

"That's all right," Sue assured him, fiddling with the pen in her hand.

"Like I told the cops, I did see him in there."

She sensed something off in his tone. "And?"

"Well… he was with some friends, and then the next thing I knew he was gone. You know, it's busy in there, I don't have time to keep tabs."

"Yet you did with him."

He grinned. "Yeah, I guess I did."

She didn't respond, allowing the silence to do the work.

"Look—" He picked up his phone and quickly typed something before setting it back down. "I didn't want to tell the cops…"

"Tell them what?" she asked, her pen now hovering above her notepad.

"I used to go out with James's boyfriend's roommate. We dated for like… six months or something."

She nodded, picturing the early twenty-something dating his way through Hillcrest and swapping out boyfriends with each passing season. No wonder most of the gay men she knew were emotional cripples.

"Do you have any names?"

"Yeah. James's boyfriend is Matt Foss."

"Foss," Sue repeated as she jotted it down.

"Matt's roommate is my ex, Tim… Clark. His dad's kind of important." She looked up from her notes. "You know… he's a state senator or something like that."

"Oh, *that* Clark." Republicans, she believed, were lower than child molesters.

"Yeah. That's why I didn't say anything. Tim's dad is a real hard ass. I didn't want to get him in trouble."

"That's all you saw, then?"

"More or less. I mean… I wound up talking to Tim a little bit later when things were starting to wind down."

"And what did he say?"

"Just some drama," he said, sounding exasperated. "Something about a phone, and how Matt was bitching about James flirting or something with some other guy. Matt, you know… he apparently threw a fit over it."

"And that's why James left?"

"Yeah, I guess. I didn't actually see him leave, so I couldn't tell you what time it was or anything. I just… Tim told me about it later." He waved his hand in the air as if shooing away a fly. "He was just glad they had taken it elsewhere. He didn't want to deal with it."

"And you didn't tell the police this?"

"No. Like I said, Tim's dad and all… it's none of their business. They just wanted to track where he'd been, and I gave them that."

14

They were still in the living room watching television, down to one cold slice of pizza left in the box on the coffee table, when someone banged loudly on the front door.

Tim, lost in his thoughts as he scrolled through Facebook on his iPad, jumped at the noise. "Expecting anyone?" he asked.

"Uh—uh," Matt answered, shaking his head as he continued to focus on the television. "You?"

"No, but I guess I'll see who it is," Tim said, putting his iPad down and getting out of the chair.

"You do that," Matt said. He stood up and walked toward the bathroom. "And you need to call Ben and Darren. We're supposed to meet up with them later."

"Then you better make up with your boyfriend. We don't need a chill in the air."

"Don't worry about that. Just call them."

Tim walked to the door and threw it open without bothering to look through the peephole. Standing there were three men leering at him in a way that made him instantly regret the decision. "Can I help you?"

"Are you Matt?" the one on the left asked.

"No."

"Who are you?"

"Who are *you*?" Tim snapped back.

Enzo, who had been standing between and slightly behind Sean and Eddie, barreled between them, grabbing Tim's neck as he shoved him backward, then left, slamming him against the wall beside the open front door. He brought up his gun, silencer attached, and jammed it into Tim's left cheek. "Answer the man's goddamn question," Enzo barked.

"Uh… uh… uh," Tim tried to stammer out.

"Oh, Christ," Eddie muttered. "The kid just pissed himself."

Enzo glanced down and backed away, seeing a wet spot on Tim's pants that had also dampened his own. "Oh, fucking Christ!" he exclaimed, then knocked Tim to the floor with a closed fist.

Tim looked up, defiance flashing in his eyes. "Do you know who my father is?"

Enzo punched him again, and Tim's nose broke with a loud crack. "I don't give a good goddamn," he said as Tim grabbed his nose, blood flowing onto the hardwood beneath him.

Enzo put his gun to Tim's head as the latter began to cry. "Take it like a man, faggot, or I will shut you up myself."

"Sean, do me a favor and keep a watch outside," Eddie said, then kicked the door closed with his foot.

■ ■ ■

"Get your ass back down here," Carlyle said when his partner picked up the phone.

His intention had been to go home, enjoy the untouched glass of tequila still awaiting him, and sleep the rest of the afternoon—but he settled for a quick nap on a couch in the captain's office and a few more cups of coffee to keep him going for one more day. This had suddenly become a race between his task force and the Byrnes. Sleep would be a luxury until it was over.

"I'm already back. I got in about an hour ago."

"Everything all right?"

"Yeah," Seegars lied, frustrated at having been summoned like a dog. "What's going on?"

"Our little trio struck again," Carlyle said. "And… you won't believe this… they beat up Ciaran Byrne's kid."

A pause. "The mob boss from Chicago?"

"That's the one."

"Fuck me."

"Yeah," Carlyle agreed.

"His kid's…"

"Apparently. And I'm willing to bet the Byrnes will want to track down whoever did it."

"I'd hate to be them," Seegars mused. "They're dead."

"Not if I can help it," Carlyle said. "Be at the office in an hour. I need you to help me find them first."

"I thought you had a task force to help you with that."

"And you're a part of it."

Seegars sighed loudly into the phone. "We could just let the Byrnes deal with it. It's not like we've had any luck so far."

"Humor me, will you?"

Seegars grunted. "Headed your way."

■ ■ ■

"What the—" Matt exclaimed as he rounded the corner and entered the room to find a bloodied Tim on his knees, one hand clutching his nose, two men standing over him.

Eddie pointed his gun at him. "One word out of you, kid," he warned.

Enzo grabbed the collar of Tim's shirt and dragged him to the center of the living room as Eddie directed Matt to the same spot.

"*You* must be Matt," Enzo said after depositing a shocked Tim onto the couch, who pulled his legs to his chest and wrapped his arms tightly around them. Blood poured from his nose onto the cushion beneath him.

Matt nodded as Eddie's gun guided him to stand beside Tim. "Yeah."

"You the one fucking my brother?"

Eddie looked over at his friend. "Enzo…"

Enzo ignored him. "Answer me," he snapped at Matt, who flinched at the command.

"Who's your brother?"

"Don't get fucking cute with me, douchebag."

Matt paused. "Yeah, I mean—"

Enzo's finger pulled the trigger only when it was pointed squarely between Matt's eyes. Matt's head jerked back, his body collapsing onto the couch as Tim— yanked out of his stupor—looked up at Enzo. He was greeted by the barrel of the gun before his eyes measured a flash that his brain could not.

"What the fuck?" Eddie said, his voice barely above a whisper, as he tried to process the carnage. "What the fuck was that?"

Enzo gestured at Matt with his gun. The tan cushion behind his head was becoming a darker red with each passing second. "Stupid faggot fucked my brother."

"I wanted to talk to him."

"I heard all I needed."

"Enzo—"

"Fuck him. He got what he deserved."

The door opened and Sean stepped into the room. "Everything all right?" he asked as he surveyed the two bodies on the couch.

Enzo chuckled. "It is now. Let's get this shit cleaned up."

■ ■ ■

"Mark, I need an address," Susan said as she stepped out of the restaurant.

She hated using the rookie detective as much as she had of late, but he was a friend of a friend, and any hurt feelings could be smoothed over easily enough. Besides, she reminded herself, he was the one who had eagerly volunteered to help, yet another vain twenty-something who wanted to see himself online, even if he went by the name "police sources."

"Not even a please?" he asked.

She remembered why she generally disliked gay men. "Okay, Mark. *Please*, can I have an address?"

"What's the name?"

"I'll give you two. Matt Foss and Tim Clark," she said. "They're roommates."

"Foss and Clark," he muttered. "I'll call you back in five."

15

"What happened?" Moretti asked as he stood before the ancient coffee vending machine just outside the ICU, watching his latest cup trickle from the dispenser.

"Our friend took care of that situation," Eddie confessed. He was standing in the parking lot of a convenience store. Enzo, still on a high from the killing, was inside with Sean getting coffee. Just what he needed, Eddie thought. More caffeine.

He looked over at the car. The two corpses were in the trunk, wrapped in bedsheets taken from a hallway closet. That they managed to get them into the car unseen was a minor miracle.

It was one of their sloppier jobs, but also one of the more spontaneous, even for Enzo. There were generally plans in place, contingencies, rules to follow. Even in Chicago, where any evidence the police collected vanished, there were precautions taken to make sure that such things rarely, if ever, needed to happen. He could still smell the cleaning products on his hands.

Moretti couldn't help but grin. "Well, that's unfortunate."

"*Unfortunate?*"

"You know how difficult it is to control Enzo. What sort of mess did he leave behind?"

"Not much," Eddie answered. "It's taken care of."

"*Fuck*," Moretti mouthed. "Okay, good. I just need you to put that behind you and get him refocused on the task at hand."

"We're doing that now."

"Then get back to work."

■ ■ ■

Sue arrived at the given address, but no one answered her repeated knocks on the door.

The complex seemed oddly quiet for a weekend, although she suspected it was full of hung-over millennials who didn't get out of bed until late afternoon. She sighed, frustrated. It was her own damn fault, getting herself worked up by the chance for such an exclusive, the better to bring James's story—and her article—to a visceral level through their interviews.

She thought of trying a neighbor or two, but she didn't want that getting back to Matt or Tim and spooking them before they had a chance to talk. Resigning herself to finishing her article without an interview, she left her business card tucked between the door and the frame, the message "Please call me. I'd like to talk about James Byrne!" scrawled on the back. It was time to return to the office.

16

James slowly opened his eyes, the pain already returning. Most of the room remained a blur.

His head was tilted slightly to the left, his upper body raised on the adjustable hospital bed as his eyes moved about in a futile attempt to get his bearings. None of it made any sense—the faint rhythmic beeping, the swirl of colors on a muted television hanging from the ceiling across the room, an off-white railing only inches from his face.

Sam stepped into view, his brow slightly furrowed as if he were inspecting a strange new object. A grin appeared moments later. "Little Jimmy, how you feeling?"

"Sam? What are you doing here?" James asked. He winced as a new wave washed through him.

"Your brother sent me to look after you," Sam answered. "Moretti and I—"

"The kid's up?" Moretti asked as he entered the room, dropping the now-empty coffee cup into a garbage can by the door.

"Speak of the devil," Sam commented. "Yeah, he just woke up."

Moretti walked over to where Sam stood and carefully sat down on the edge of the bed, placing his hand on top of Jimmy's. "How you doing?"

James blinked several more times, the room finally coming into focus. "It hurts like hell."

"And it probably will for a while."

"What happened?" James asked. "What am I doing here?"

"You don't remember?" Moretti asked.

James briefly closed his eyes and grimaced, although this time not from the pain. "You'll regret this," he remembered telling them before it all went blank.

"You all right?" Sam asked.

"Yeah," James answered as he opened his eyes. "It just came back to me."

"Doc says you're going to be fine," Moretti said. "Nothing broken, nothing too serious."

"It hurts to breathe."

"You've got a couple cracked ribs. Between that and everything else, you're going to be sore for a few weeks."

An uneasy silence came between them. Moretti glanced at his watch. "Sam, I think it's almost time for you to head off to the airport."

"Okay. Take care, kid. I'll be back in a bit."

"Thanks, Sam," James said, his neck too stiff to follow him as he left.

Now alone, Moretti rose and walked to the wall beside the window, turning back to James as he leaned against it, his arms crossed over his chest. "Are you gay?" he asked at last.

"No."

"Are you gay?" Moretti repeated, his tone darker.

James snorted. "Whatever I am is none of your business."

"It is when it affects the family."

"Well, it doesn't."

"What are we supposed to do—just sit on our asses in Chicago?"

"Like they always have?"

"Don't get smart with me. Your family loves you very much and you know it."

James looked toward the television. "I'm sure they do," he said, barely above a whisper.

"Who the fuck do you think pays for all this?"

"Tommy."

"Drop the attitude, young man."

James looked back at him. "I'm fine," he said. "You and your crew can go now."

"This has to be taken care of," Moretti warned. "No one does this to Ciaran Byrne's son and gets away with it."

"This isn't Chicago."

"I don't give a flying fuck if you're in China. You know as well as I do that this does not go unanswered."

"Whatever," James muttered, too tired to argue further. They deserved what was coming to them anyway.

"What you've been doing out here—"

"What I've been doing is none of your damn business."

"It is when your family deems it so," Moretti said.

"What do they know?"

"Everything I do."

"Jesus fucking Christ," James muttered.

"Your mother's on her way out."

James blanched. "Why?"

"Because she's concerned," Moretti said, not even trying to be persuasive.

"I bet she is."

"Young man, you're getting very close to a line."

The door slid open, ending the conversation. The middle-aged physician Moretti had spoken to earlier peeked his head into the room, folder in hand. "Is this a good time?" he asked.

"Yes," James immediately answered.

He entered, glancing briefly at Moretti before opening the folder. "I'm glad to see you're awake," he said to James as he flipped through the pages. "I'm Dr. Michael Evans, the attending physician." He turned to Moretti. "I meant to ask you earlier… any word on family coming out?"

"His mother is on her way out from Chicago."

"Very good," he said, returning to his patient. "And how are we feeling?"

■ ■ ■

"Great article," her editor said as Susan entered his office.

It *was* good, she thought, despite being a rush job after spending the better part of the afternoon running around Hillcrest. She'd thought about calling Detective Carlyle as he had asked her to—not that he'd meant it—but she had seen the exhaustion in his eyes and didn't want to push him when she didn't need to. She assumed that she had everything he did—if not more.

"But?" she asked, knowing that a compliment from Sheraton was always followed by a qualifier.

"Why do you insist on putting the names of the victims in these stories?"

"The public has a right to know," she replied.

"For the sixth time in as many weeks, it isn't this paper's policy to name the victims of these attacks."

"That isn't my problem."

"Yes, it is. And just as I've done the last five times you've pulled this stunt, I'm not printing this guy's name. I already yanked it out of the website version."

"Charles—"

He raised an eyebrow. "Yes?"

"The community papers are going to publish it at some point."

"So?"

"*So*," she repeated, enough disdain in her voice to show her displeasure without pissing him off, "there's no point in hiding it if it's already public information."

"It's not public information."

"It will be."

"Susan, look… we don't do it, and we're never going to. Besides, the family specifically asked us not to print it. This comes from the top, so no matter what you say, what I say, what anyone else says, James Byrne's name does not get printed in this newspaper."

"That is such bullshit and you know it."

"No, I don't know it," Sheraton said. "Now remember, when I gave you this story, we talked about—"

"Yes, Charles," she interrupted, scowling.

"So then, if we're clear on your ground rules, please do me a favor and wipe that look off your face."

"Don't I have a right to be pissed off?"

"You're always pissed off," he said. "Which normally makes you one hell of a reporter. In this case, however—"

"Fine. Whatever you say, *boss*," she muttered, then turned and walked out.

17

Isabella glanced down at her watch as they arrived at the hospital entrance. It was already close to six, the sun hovering above the horizon as it signaled the end to another spring day in San Diego.

From the back seat, she exchanged brief pleasantries with Sam, who had driven out to pick her up, but the ride was otherwise quiet. She generally liked her eldest son's right-hand man and thought it was good leadership on Tommy's part to have sent the two out together. Better he learn by watching a maestro in action than muddle through on his own. Sam might have even made a suitable replacement for Moretti—but he probably wouldn't live to see the day the elder counselor stepped down.

Her hands began to shake subtly, and she clenched one over the other to steady them. She was rarely one to suffer this level of anxiety, much less to have it manifest physically, but she was out of her element here.

Her displeasure with her youngest—she could never bring herself to use the word hatred, even if she knew that was what she felt—drove this. She only had to make it through the next day or so; her duty completed, she would be safely back in Chicago to forget this ever happened. Playing his concerned mother was something she'd grown used to. This visit to the hospital wouldn't—couldn't—be any different from before.

As Sam guided them under the carport, she saw Moretti standing by the entrance with one hand clasped over the other. In his sour expression, she saw a kindred spirit likewise out of place this far from Chicago and its familiar rules. She knew she would have to broach the topic with him, if only to stroke his ego and remind him of his irreplaceability in their everyday lives.

Moretti opened the car door and helped her out. "Welcome to San Diego," he said as he gave her a quick kiss on the cheek. "How was your flight?"

She forced a smirk. "Uneventful," she answered, although the litany she could have given about the overweight, sweaty businessman and his three newspapers sitting next to her could have filled an hour.

"Excellent," he said as the two began their walk into the building.

She adjusted the purse on her arm. "How are things here?"

"Fine," Moretti answered as they arrived at the elevator. "Jimmy is awake and is talking, although he's a bit surly at the moment."

"That boy has always been surly." The doors to the elevator parted and they stepped in.

Moretti waited until their brief ascent to the fourth floor was underway before speaking. "You're welcome," he offered quietly.

She smiled. "Are you sure about this?"

"I don't think we have much of a choice in the end."

Isabella shook her head. "No, I don't think we do. As long as it works."

"It will."

"And the other one?" she asked.

Moretti chuckled. "Reacted as expected. You can count on him making a mess of things with some slack on his leash."

"We can control him when this is all over."

He nodded, their remaining few moments in the elevator now silent. As they stepped into the hallway, Moretti cleared his throat. "Isabella, about Jimmy."

She sighed loudly. "I've already talked to Tommy, and he's told me everything."

"Does Ciaran know?"

"Oh God, no," Isabella said. "We'll keep that from him… for now."

"Are you okay?"

She gave him a look. "Do I look okay? This is what I get for all my efforts—a goddamn fag for a son."

■ ■ ■

They had been friends since they were ten, when Eddie found himself trapped in an alley near Wrigley Field with two menacing twelve-year-olds closing in, the result of his juvenile fondness for the word fucktard, one that his mother had warned him about on quite a number of occasions.

His rescuer had been a scrawny kid wandering the neighborhood alone while his father was conducting business. Ciaran Byrne had sent his second eldest into the streets with the order to "keep busy," which proved to be Eddie's only saving grace that day. Enzo's idea of occupying his time was already predicated on a certain level of violence, and in that alley, he found both that and the unwavering loyalty of a new partner.

Eddie had seen the wooden board with the row of rusting nails, but dodging his two assailants to get to it wasn't something he could hope to accomplish. His savior, quickly making his way toward the trio, had picked it up while closing the distance between them still unnoticed.

Enzo drove the nailed edge of the board into the calf of the larger of the two, felling him instantly before two quick tugs ripped the nails out as the other boy turned in surprise. Continuing his self-appointed mission, the board was quickly flipped and slammed into the side of the other boy's head, knocking him to the ground unconscious. Enzo grinned manically, then tossed his weapon aside before climbing atop the first boy and pounding his face repeatedly with his fist. Then Enzo stood up, running his bloodied hand through his thick black hair, returning it to its slicked-back position, the style he wore to this day.

He had looked over at Eddie, still beaming, and extended his blood-speckled hand. "I'm Enzo," he said. Eddie frowned, unsure whether he had heard the name correctly. Enzo's left eye twitched slightly. "You fucking laugh I'll break your goddamn nose too."

Eddie violently shook his head. "No… no, no," he protested. "Never."

"What's your name?"

"Eddie," he answered.

"Good," Enzo said. "Now follow me. I got some people I want you to meet."

Their friendship had been lasting and solid. Despite Enzo's persistent recklessness, Eddie was always by his side as they did their part for the family. More than two decades later the two were still inseparable, although with this latest outburst Eddie began to feel as if he were straining against the breaking point of a bond tested one too many times.

As he stared out the back passenger window of the rental car, as Enzo drove and Sean rode shotgun, he took a deep breath and sighed as quietly as he could. He had seen more than his fair share of violence in his time with the Byrnes, but he hadn't seen any reason to kill those two kids, even if they had seen their faces, even if they were gay. People like that were intimidated into silence easily enough. Had they merely knocked on their door and talked to them like reasonable people—rather than indulging Enzo's preference for abruptly killing any and all witnesses—Eddie wouldn't have two dead bodies in the trunk, nor a boat ride in his future. This, he suspected, would not end well at all.

■ ■ ■

Susan slouched at her desk, still stewing over her argument with Charles, frustrated in her efforts to write the story she believed needed to be told.

It wasn't as if she was into outing civilians—though celebrities and other public figures were fair game in her mind—but she knew that if names and pictures were published for everyone to see instead of the generic moniker "victim," the people of San Diego would finally become outraged and rise up to insist that something be done. And nothing would please Susan more than to light a fire under the mayor's indifferent ass. She hated betraying the sisterhood, but the woman running City Hall was worthless when it came to matters Susan cared about.

Susan was, however, very surprised that the Byrnes had contacted the newspaper about not publishing the kid's name. None of the other five victims or their families had made a similar request—perhaps they knew that it wasn't going to happen anyway—and this one had done so less than twenty-four hours after the assault.

She sat up, wriggled her mouse to clear her screensaver, and typed "James Byrne Chicago" into the search bar.

■ ■ ■

Isabella stood with her hand not quite touching the door handle. "I'll wait here for Sam," Moretti offered.

Isabella nodded. She closed her eyes as she prayed for patience and guidance in this, her time of need. She then slowly opened the door.

She looked up only after it fully closed behind her, then leaned against the frame for support. He was sitting up in bed, fork in hand, a tray of half-eaten food in front of him as he quietly watched her. The television was on, the sound almost nonexistent.

She could feel the anger boil up inside her as she studied his face, the prior night's damage evident, as was the pain when he winced as he shifted against his bed. Despite their differences, family was family in this moment, and whoever had done this to her son was going to pay—dearly.

"How are you?" she asked as she sat in the chair against the wall near the foot of the bed. Looking down, she gently lowered her handbag to the floor before crossing her legs and placing one hand over the other in her lap.

"I'm okay," he answered, reservation in his voice. She was tense, and he knew that the latest round in their never-ending conflict was fast approaching.

"Look what those animals did to you," she said as she looked him over once more. "How do you feel?"

"It's not so bad," he said. "I'm fine."

Isabella nodded slowly. "Okay," she said quietly, looking away.

■ ■ ■

Carlyle was walking into the hospital when his phone began to vibrate.

"You're a popular man today," Captain Scott said. "Just got a call from the mayor's office."

"I always knew she was my biggest fan."

"They're starting to twist the screws a little tighter with these Hillcrest beatings."

Carlyle rolled his eyes. "Of course she is." Like most politicians, she was at her best when vociferously squawking—for public consumption.

"Six in six weeks makes us look incompetent, which makes her look doubly so," Scott said. "You know how this game is played."

"I most certainly do, Captain, but she *is* incompetent."

"Look, I know you're new to this investigation—"

"I don't know why I got stuck with this mess. Davis and Reinhardt were already working it."

"Because I needed a task force to quiet everyone down, and you're the better detective to lead it than either of those two," Scott said.

Carlyle laughed. "You don't have to suck up. We'll get it done."

"Where is Seegars, by the way?"

"I left him at the office to sort through some paperwork. He looked a little too hung-over to be of much use in the field."

"Why am I not surprised?"

"It's a typical Sunday for him, I suspect," Carlyle agreed.

"Well just know that City Hall isn't happy about things, and they're concerned about the pace and progress of our investigation. I need to feed them something, and soon."

"Fair enough," Carlyle remarked, now anxious to get back upstairs. "I'll talk to you later."

"Good luck," Scott said.

18

Isabella looked toward her son.

There had been an awkward few moments of silence as he finished the tray before him. They hadn't spoken in almost ten months, not since that final break last summer when Tommy had taken him out of her house—and her life—seemingly forever.

She had protested at the time, but it had been a matter of control, not actual concern for his well-being. Tommy had overstepped his bounds, and if he could not respect her role as the boy's mother, or that Jimmy lived under her roof, then he would respect very little. Certainly not her position in the family, but that was all due to change once Moretti had his way.

Her fellow Italian's plans made her slightly uneasy, but his loyalty to her and Ciaran was unwavering, and he would do nothing to place them in harm's way. No, she would trust him implicitly on this, as she had all else.

"What are you doing here?" James finally asked.

She feigned indignation. "I'm not allowed to visit my own son in the hospital?"

"I'm fine. You don't have to stay."

"I know that."

He sighed. "I mean... what are we going to talk about? We both know where I was last night. Do you really want to go there?"

"I suppose not." She shifted in her seat. "I guess I just don't understand your *lifestyle*, that's all."

"And I don't care anymore," he said

"I'm well aware of that."

"Well, you got what you wanted. I'm out of your hair."

"Yet you still find a way to disgrace us with your behavior, even from here."

"Mom, I'm gay. Deal with it."

She stood up, purse in hand. He seemed surprised by her reaction but said nothing more. She took a deep breath and exhaled loudly. She had done her duty. "Goodbye, Jimmy," she said calmly before walking out.

■ ■ ■

Carlyle was thankful for the time alone as the elevator doors closed. He rested his head against the plastic paneling, closing his eyes as the metal box lurched upward toward the fourth floor.

This would be a waste of time. The five prior assaults had yielded only vague descriptions of the assailants, all but unusable. A lineup would be a joke; his only hope was catching them in the act or hoping the Byrnes would show more resourcefulness than his department had so far.

Carlyle admonished himself for allowing the thought to enter his mind. He couldn't allow those thugs from Chicago to run rampant in his city even for the sake of expediency. Whatever the crime, they all deserved their day in court, he told himself once more. He just prayed he could figure out a way to get ahead of them, to see them to that point before the Byrnes' search gained any traction.

■ ■ ■

He was flipping through channels on the television when the door opened.

"What did you say to your mother?" Moretti demanded.

"The truth," James answered. "Why? Where is she?"

"On her way downstairs," Moretti said as he walked to the foot of the bed.

"Good."

"What the fuck is wrong with you?"

James snorted. "Why is everyone playing dumb with this?"

"With what?"

"Her and me. She hates me."

Moretti swiped his hand through the air to cut him off. "Your mother doesn't hate you."

"Oh, for fuck's sake—"

"Don't you take that tone with me."

"Or what?" James demanded. "You want to smack the fag around too? Send Enzo in. I'm sure *he'd* love to."

"You're in a heap of shit, young man. I don't think you quite understand the problems—"

He swiped his hand again, this time angrily, watching James's eyes flick toward the door.

"—this fuckup of yours is going to cause this family. You're goddamn lucky—"

Someone clearing their throat interrupted the conversation. "Should I come back?" Detective Carlyle asked as he stood in the still open doorway.

Moretti wheeled around, his expression already shifting. "Oh, Detective." He glanced into the empty hallway for Sam, who should have been running interference, but he had gone scurrying after Isabella. "Well, we're—"

"Not at all," James interrupted. "Please, come in."

"Okay then," Carlyle said as he entered the room, closing the door behind him.

"What can we help you with?" Moretti asked, urgency in his voice as he thought of Isabella waiting impatiently for him to join her.

Carlyle turned to James. "I got the news that you were up, and I just had a couple of questions I'd like to ask about last night, about what you remember." He glanced at Moretti. "I take it neither of you mind."

"I don't mind at all," James said. "It's still a little fuzzy though."

Carlyle turned back to Moretti. "I assume you'll want to sit in on this?"

"Yes, I would."

"Okay then," Carlyle said as he pulled out his notepad. "Let's begin, shall we?"

19

Isabella waited in the car under the portico of the hospital's main entrance, Sam behind the wheel as the engine idled. When Moretti finished with Jimmy, the three would go to the hotel a short drive away. Tomorrow she would continue her trip, as Moretti had dictated earlier.

She bit her lower lip as she looked out the window, watching as a young couple exited the building. The woman, who looked to be in her mid-to-late twenties, had clearly been crying, the man putting on as brave a face possible as he consoled her. Perhaps they were mourning the loss of a parent, she thought as they walked past.

Isabella had grown up an only child, though surrounded by a large extended family. Her father was dead, her mother, Alberta, had told her, although she wouldn't say what had killed him and could never fully suppress a bitterness in her voice when Isabella broached the subject. She had raised it with several aunts, although her inquiries ended after recognizing that, to all concerned, the door was to remain closed.

They were provided for by her uncle Carmine, her father's older brother who had come to accept her as his second daughter after his own, Angelica. The Valcos being who they were, she never went without—even if her own mother protested vigorously. Her uncle, though, would always answer the complaint with a broad smile. "Bert," he would repeatedly tell her as he waved a hand in the air, "Allow me this one indulgence, okay?" to which she would begrudgingly acquiesce. And then, despite her hesitations about the business arrangement that destined them to meet, she willingly—and happily—married Ciaran before her life began anew in Chicago.

The two had only recently moved to Highland Park, the house barely unpacked, when her father appeared in her life. One of Ciaran's men had spotted the elderly gentleman parked at the edge of the property in his Bentley, and as the car was approached, he got out and began to cross the lawn toward the house.

"That's a good spot right there," the old man was warned as Isabella watched from the sitting room window. He had complied, scanning the house quickly before turning his attention to the muscled young guard in the Armani suit. Though Isabella knew he couldn't see her watching him, chills ran up her spine when his eyes crossed her window. She knew instinctively who it was and that he was very much alive.

She stepped out the front door and walked down the steps to the circular driveway, watching as the two men talked. The kids were away save Jimmy, who was upstairs taking his afternoon nap. "It's all right, Arnold," she said, gently touching the guard's shoulder, and he immediately stepped aside to reveal the gaunt, elderly man in a now-oversized gray suit with a crisp white shirt and red paisley tie.

"Isabella," he said. "Do you know who I am?"

She remembered sneering, her mother's pain becoming her own. "What are you doing here?"

"I came to find you."

"And you did, so get back in your car and go back to wherever it is you came from."

"Let me explain," he begged.

"Explain what?"

"Everything," he answered, and he did.

They had settled into the sunroom at the back of the house, and he confessed that he had always been gay. With his strict Catholic upbringing and even stricter parents, it was expected that he marry and produce children. Anything else was certain damnation, he had been raised to believe, and so like many of his kind in those days, he had entered a loveless relationship.

Unlike most, however, it was not a life that he could endure for very long. He had told his wife about his preferences soon after Isabella's birth, and despite many nights of tears, she eventually acquiesced to allow him to seek whatever it was he needed. He had done so tentatively at first, both afraid to hurt her and be discovered by the family, but as time passed he spent more and more evenings away. He would, however, always return home before dawn, sliding into the bed beside her as if nothing had come between them.

Two years later he met someone and fell in love. The man was older, and very wealthy, though Isabella's father cared about neither. It was the first time he had been truly happy in his life with another person, and he would have followed him to the ends of the planet if that was required.

Alberta understood what the empty bed meant when she awoke that morning. There had been a light in his eyes that had begun appearing just a few weeks before, and by his sudden absence she knew which side of the battle raging within him had prevailed. He was gone forever, the empty Cadillac submerged in the bay near Jones Beach State Park on Long Island serving as the final proof, leaving a family to grieve but giving her the closure she needed to move on.

He had remained away for most of that time. It had been the better part of a life spent looking over his shoulder, constantly at first, then more sporadically, as he and his partner leisurely roamed far away from the place their lives together had started. It had begun with two years in a village on the outskirts of Paris, then another three in Dublin, and as years, then decades, passed, the cities and towns of Europe became as much a blur as the languages he half-learned before once more moving on.

He had seen the announcement of her marriage to Ciaran Byrne, as well as the subsequent news of the births of her four children. It was not the life he would have wished for her given their own family's past, but she seemed content, at least from the distance he kept once his partner passed and he had returned to the United States. In that, he found solace. His time, though, was running out, and it was his wish that the two could somehow reconcile before his last few years came to an end.

Isabella remembered feeling indifferent to this stranger, who with time and aging had become so comfortable in his anonymity that he lived just blocks from her eldest son in another nameless tower, confessing his sins and seeking an absolution that would never come. The look on her face never wavered, her contempt for him always visible as he told his pathetic story.

She hated him for his lifestyle, for his Bentley, for his gall to think they could forge a relationship. To abandon her and her mother for the bed of another man was obscene, and he deserved the hell of dying alone with his money.

When he had finished, a silence filled the space as she finished processing what he had shared. "I want you to leave now," she told him with as emotionless a voice as was possible. "If you ever come within a mile of me or my family again, I will have you hunted down and killed in the most vicious way possible; my husband is a very creative man."

20

Moretti, now settled into his hotel room, finally allowed himself to relax for the first time all day. A glass of scotch from the minibar in hand, he sank deeply into the chair and kicked one shoe off, then the other, before propping his feet on the ottoman. It was still early, but jet lag had found its footing, and his body yearned for sleep.

He took a quick sip of his drink, then laid his head back and closed his eyes. He was anxious to get back to Chicago—Sam was already on his way, and now that he had done his part he could leave too. It had gone well enough. The brief duration of the meeting between mother and son was something he had expected—had hoped for, really. Any doubts she might have held about his plan had been erased by the short exchange in the hospital room, although his yelling at Jimmy afterward had been unnecessary—especially with the detective appearing as he had.

Eyes still shut, he smiled as he pictured his house—his wife standing in the doorway as he arrived home tomorrow afternoon. And as happy as he would be to see her, he needed to be back in Chicago for when their plans began to fall into place.

The vibrating phone on the armrest yanked him back to reality.

"I think we may have found one of our missing packages," Eddie said.

Moretti immediately sat up. "You're fucking kidding me."

"We're on our way over right now. We'll be there in a few minutes."

"That quick?" Moretti asked.

"What can I say? A source for our local friend came through for us."

Moretti sighed. "That's good news."

"Yeah. If we can get this one, then we can get the other two."

"There are three of them out there?" he asked. At least the detective hadn't tried to deceive him on that.

"Not for long," Eddie said.

■ ■ ■

James reached over and picked up his phone, which Sam had returned on his way to the airport, along with a backpack full of clothes. Of all the stupid things to forget, he admonished himself once more. His texts and voicemails had been deleted, as had all his social media apps, probably by Sam, to keep Moretti from prying. Too late now, he thought.

There were still no messages from Matt, and as tempted as he was to reach out to him, he wasn't the one James wanted to visit. No, that person wasn't easily summoned.

He put the phone back on the table beside him. No, Matt could wait another day.

21

Lindsey had only been dating Dan for a few weeks, so she didn't feel all that guilty when she got the call asking whether she'd heard anything about the beatings in Hillcrest. Of course she had. Once Dan finally opened up about what he and his friends had been doing, it was practically all he could talk about, constantly bragging, until she was bored enough to scream.

But she'd been keeping quiet since he'd told her. Dan was great in bed and had, through one of his roommates, always managed to get his hands on the best weed. If it hadn't been for what she now viewed as a stupid fight over him not reciprocating oral sex, she never would have drunkenly complained to a couple of girlfriends about him, and *that*, last Saturday night. When she got the call, she considered denying it, but spilling a secret the second time hardly counts, since it's not one any longer. And once the man on the other end of the phone had promised her some of the good stuff from LA, it was that much easier for him to pry out what she knew.

Besides, Dan had it coming. Lindsey's oldest brother was gay, and had been beaten up in New York about a year ago. Payback is hell, she thought, as they lay in bed together in her apartment—his arm wrapped around her. Maybe some jail time would humble him a bit. She liked Dan, but he needed to be taken down a notch or two.

They were startled by a knock at the door. Who the hell could that be?

■ ■ ■

"I've got good news, and I've got bad news," Moretti said as he sat back down, his phone in one hand and a fresh glass of scotch in the other. "Which do you want?"

Tommy looked over the Chicago skyline as he contemplated the choice before him, his index finger tapping the bourbon glass on the chair's armrest. Sabrina was getting ready for bed, and for a change, he would be joining her. She was yet another woman in his life who rarely hid her displeasure, and his sitting out here night after night only aggravated that tendency. "Give me the good news first," he said, lifting the glass to take a sip.

"That missing package has been located."

Tommy grinned. "That *is* good news." He wasn't even sure why Moretti was being so vague—the phones on either end of the conversation were new enough—but better safe than sorry, he supposed. "What's the issue?"

"Some collateral damage."

Tommy nodded to himself, watching his reflection in the glass. That was to be expected with Enzo, although it wouldn't be as easy to clean up after out in California. "Sorry to hear that."

"Did you know your brother had a boyfriend?"

"Jimmy has a boyfriend?" Tommy asked as he turned to see Sabrina enter the room. She paused for a moment, a wry smile appearing before she turned and exited the room.

"Did," Moretti corrected.

Shit. "Does Jimmy know?"

"Not yet, but give it time."

22

"Here?" Eddie asked as the Bayliner lurched to a halt off Pacific Beach.

They had left Lindsey's place with exactly the information they needed. What Enzo had done to elicit the location of Dan's cohorts wasn't the most violent thing Eddie had been part of. The three of them agreed it was Dan's problem for not surrendering the information quickly enough. He learned that lesson the hard way.

"This is as good a spot as any," Sean replied as he looked around the dark waters. At this hour, any boat traffic here was nonexistent.

"What the hell is that buoy for?" Enzo asked.

Sean shrugged. "Don't know. I think they're shipping markers or something. They got all those fucking Navy boats coming in and out of here. Who gives a shit?"

"You sure it's safe to dump them here?" Eddie asked, his earlier suggestion that they be buried already dismissed. "The last thing we fucking need is someone finding them."

"Safe as anywhere," Sean said as he glanced at the depth gauge above the helm. "We're in a hundred feet of water. Who the fuck would come all the way out here?"

"Let's just get these damn queers overboard," Enzo said as he hefted a wrapped, weighted body. "It's been a long day already."

MONDAY

23

"Hey, partner. How goes it?" Seegars asked, a coffee in each hand as he sat on the corner of Carlyle's desk.

Carlyle feigned incredulity as he took the offered cup. "Just fine, Detective." He took a sip and leaned back in his chair, glancing none too subtly at his phone as he did so. It was just before seven in the morning. "And how are you this morning? Better, I hope."

Seegars smirked. "Can't complain."

"That's good to hear," Carlyle said. "How was your trip to LA, by the way?"

"Short."

"And you came back on your own volition. Must have been one hell of a night to want to get out of there so quickly."

"Well, I figured my jackass partner would order me back."

"What a prick," Carlyle deadpanned, choosing, for now, to accept the lie.

The two had been partners for almost five years, ever since the captain, in a fit of pique, paired them in order to express his displeasure with both. Carlyle, rigid and intolerant, had never warmed to any of his coworkers, deeming them too lazy, too sloppy, or outright incompetent. Seegars, his antithesis, had regularly found himself at the wrong end of a transfer request, if only because he deliberately exasperated those around him.

As if his life could get no worse, Carlyle's mother had finally succumbed to the cancer she had been battling on and off for the better part of the last decade, on the same day that he'd been burdened with the man now before him. Her death was something of a relief in the end, though he would never admit that aloud. He didn't believe in the nobility of suffering, especially when it involved someone he loved.

After spending the week in Carlsbad to tend to the estate—his father had passed away several years before—Carlyle had returned to his condo in the shadow of Petco Park and his beloved Padres, resigned to what the new partnership would bring. Not, however, before he enjoyed a few drinks out.

The half-broken neon sign that hung above the door read Lucky's, a name that hardly seemed to fit its sorry batch of regulars. Located around the corner from his condo, it was a community of last resort for middle-aged and elderly alcoholics, long ostracized by decades of bad decisions. But they kept the swarms of tourists away, and Carlyle liked both quiet and consistency, two things that Lucky's offered in spades.

When Seegars strolled in, he did his best to hide the reflexive sneer as his eyes adjusted to the gloom.

A few years into his forties, he was another who believed a youthful exterior appearance could be willed into being. His black and graying hair was overly teased, shooting out from all angles as if he had freshly arisen, his clothes best left to men half his age. A few inches short of six feet, he had kept himself fairly fit, although lifestyle and age had taken their toll, his once firm physique now slightly softened. And he hated to see himself in the mirror, his vanity unable to cope with decline, even if minor.

He was here thanks to the recommendation of a patrol officer—and he'd get his revenge for that soon enough—but though he preferred the upscale establishments of La Jolla when he wasn't in Los Angeles, after a date in the Gaslamp Quarter had gone awry he didn't feel up to driving thirty minutes for the privilege of mingling with tragic hipster wannabes.

Fuck me fifty times, he thought to himself as he saw Carlyle sitting alone, overdressed as always in pressed khakis and a white oxford, a blue sports coat neatly draped across the stool to his right. The man was clearly incapable of relaxing, even in a dive bar. But needing a drink, Seegars resigned himself to making the best of what would be a very uncomfortable situation. It couldn't hurt to reach out, even if their partnership was doomed to quickly fail.

He walked over to the stool on Carlyle's left, waiting a few moments before his new partner turned toward him, clearly surprised at what he saw.

"Mind if I sit down?" Seegars asked as he motioned toward the empty seat.

Carlyle, who had been in his usual spot for about an hour and three glasses of tequila, shrugged. "Do I have a choice?" he asked as he finished off his latest and flagged the bartender, who was staring down at his phone. He knew he was being somewhat hostile but didn't care.

An awkward silence between the two followed. "You don't like me very much," Seegars said once his beer had been ordered and delivered.

"Not really, no," Carlyle answered.

"Since I guess we're going to be working together, you mind if I ask why?"

Carlyle picked up his glass. "I don't like your attitude, your flippant disregard for procedures, general work ethic, or overall smug disposition. And I think the way you dress is a joke."

Seegars glanced down at his clothes before returning to his beer. Perhaps the designer jeans were a bit much, but the shirt, while colorful, set him back about two hundred dollars. "And I think you were born with a stick firmly planted up your ass," he finally responded.

Looking down at the refreshed drink, Carlyle thought once more of his dying mother. Toward the end, he visited as often as his erratic schedule permitted, the two sharing what remaining moments together they had, oftentimes her patiently listening to his grievances while he sat beside her bed. When she had her fill, a feeble hand would reach out, and she would place it on the edge of the bed as she draped her fingers over the side. "Robert," she would always begin. "Son, you need to learn to pick your battles. Trust me… none of it matters in the end."

Carlyle picked up the glass and downed it in one shot. He placed it back down on the counter, running his finger along the rim as he saw himself in the mirror behind the bar. He looked and felt like hell. His eyes drooped from both exhaustion and alcohol. As he continued to stare through the bottles on the shelf, the gray in his hair seemed that much more prominent, the lines across his cheeks deeper. Inspecting every flaw, he felt as if he were looking at a version of himself that would play out at some point in the indeterminate future, not here, not now.

His mother's words once more replayed in his head, Carlyle shifted on the stool before turning back to Seegars. "I'm not quite sure it's that firmly planted," he offered.

Seegars furrowed his brows. "Wait a minute. Was that a joke? Did you actually make a joke?"

"I'd like to think so."

The two watched as the bartender refilled Carlyle's glass. "Well, you got to start somewhere," Seegars said when they were once more alone.

Carlyle let out a hearty laugh, surprising his new partner and momentarily distracting the other patrons from the muted game show playing on the small flat-screen television suspended from the ceiling.

"I think you're probably very right on that one, partner," he said, raising his drink into the air.

Seegars picked up his beer bottle and tapped Carlyle's glass. "What are we toasting to?"

"A beautiful new partnership. And fuck the captain," Carlyle answered.

"You've heard what the office pool is up to, yeah?"

"Yes, and fuck them too."

■ ■ ■

Susan was still at her desk, nursing her second cup of coffee and staring blankly at her laptop, the half-written article on her screen resisting her efforts to finish it. At the moment, she had nothing to further her investigation, her calls to Detective Carlyle last night and this morning going unanswered.

She was also waiting to hear back from Matt or Tim, neither of whom had bothered to contact her after she left her card at their apartment. Maybe they were too hung over, but their silence surprised her; like everyone else, they must have heard about the attack by now. Even if most of them didn't

THE NAME OF THE GAME   103

know who the latest victim was, it was all that anyone in this part of town was talking about.

She resigned herself to stopping by their apartment once more while she was out getting some lunch. She also wanted to talk to James Byrne, though she doubted he would remember much. She had wrangled interviews with four of the past five victims, none of them able to recall anything beyond the blur of the assault. Most had been jumped from behind, not fully realizing what was happening until they came to in a half-lit alley or a hospital bed.

She was, she admitted, desperate to crack this case herself. As much as she once enjoyed reporting on pride parades and other special events in her community, this was a fascinating, if frustrating, opportunity. She had been given the chance, however slim, to make a name for herself in investigative journalism, and it was not an opportunity she intended to squander. If only someone would call her back.

■ ■ ■

"Speaking of pricks," Seegars said, still seated on the edge of Carlyle's desk, "Anything from our city's latest tourists?"

"Not the ones I met, but I don't expect them to dirty their hands with it. You have anything?"

"I made some calls, but nothing just yet."

"Sex lines don't count. What else?"

"Sex lines? God, you're old. That shit's online now." Carlyle raised an eyebrow. "I'm hoping sometime this afternoon if we're lucky. You know how my CIs are."

Carlyle nodded. Most of his partner's sources should have been incarcerated years ago, but somehow they managed to be of use in practically all their cases. And Seegars was able to keep them mostly in line and their infractions charged as misdemeanors, so on the streets they remained.

Seegars tapped the padded mailer on Carlyle's desk. "What's this?"

Carlyle snatched it and stuffed it in a desk drawer, then slammed it shut. "Nothing."

"Doesn't seem like nothing to me," Seegars remarked.

Carlyle sighed. "It's just something from the lab."

"About?"

"It has to do with our latest down in the ICU."

Seegars's eyes grew wide. "What comes from the lab overnight in a padded envelope that relates to one of our victims?"

"Nothing, until I deem otherwise."

Seegars raised his hands and looked away in frustration.

"I'll loop you in when I know more," Carlyle assured him.

"Okay, *partner*."

"Do you trust me?"

"Yes," Seegars immediately answered. "Do you trust *me*?"

"Yes. I just… I need more time with this."

"Okay." Seegars patted his shoulder. He walked over to his own desk, not bothering to sit as he aimlessly flipped through some newly deposited paperwork. "You know me. I live to serve."

"Well, why don't you go break some of your CIs' worthless fucking heads for me then."

"I'm thinking about doing just that. What are you up to other than that which we cannot discuss?"

"This dyke reporter from the *Times* keeps bothering me," Carlyle said, trying to change the conversation. Something was off with his partner, and he would hold his cards as close as possible until he could figure out what. "Just to be nice, I probably should call her back at some point."

"Oh, fuck her."

"I don't think she'd go for that."

24

"This suits you," Isabella remarked, looking out over the vineyard.

It was only an hour past dawn, though the twin heat lamps flanking their table removed most of the chill. The glass top had been covered with a white tablecloth, and two settings of china had already been laid out when she was escorted outside—this hastily arranged breakfast meeting marking their first face-to-face contact in many years.

Liam was showing his age far more than Ciaran, she thought. His once-lean frame had become somewhat portly, his short black hair now a long, disheveled salt-and-pepper name that danced in the frequent bursts of wind. He moved slowly, a cane resting against the railing behind his chair. His face, always perfectly shaven, had at least a week's worth of uneven growth about it. Had he not been immaculately dressed, down to his bespoke sports coat, she might have mistaken him for homeless.

He smiled as he set a cup and saucer down in front of her. He took the seat opposite her, sipping from his own drink as he turned to look out at the rows of grapevines rolled out before them. "Yes," he agreed. "It is magnificent."

"I'm sorry to have heard about Patricia," Isabella offered. "She was a strong woman."

Liam nodded as he placed his cup back in the saucer. "Thank you. That she was. God took mercy on her, though. It was quick."

"Is that why you're out here now?"

Liam looked back over the vineyard. "It's been a healthy distraction, I will admit," he said. He paused as he took another sip. "I take it, however, that you did not come all this way to talk about grapes or my deceased wife."

Isabella forced a smile as their eyes met once more. He was as direct as ever. "No, I did not."

"How is your youngest son?"

"He'll live."

"That is a shame what happened to him," Liam said. "Your family… it has been through much as of late."

"I'm not sure what you mean," she said.

He chuckled. "You don't have to play dumb with me, Isabella. Even out here I know what happens in Chicago."

"And what would that be?" she asked, not bothering to hide her contempt for this turn in the conversation.

"So, we will play this game," Liam said. "I know your husband is sick and is not himself a good bit of the time. I know that your eldest son would rather play Donald Trump than Don Corleone, and has no interest in continuing the traditions that made the empire he sits atop. And I know that your youngest is a… how do you Italians say it? A *recchione. One* who prefers the company of other men, which is what put him in the hospital—and this family at great risk." He paused, then smirked. "I hear that sort of thing can be genetic, but it certainly does not run in this bloodline. I wonder where he got it from?"

Behind her rigid façade of geniality, she was incensed. Had her husband been at her side the two men would have come to blows. "It is as it is," she said, making a dismissive gesture. "We will get through it all."

"I'm sure you will," Liam agreed. His brother, for all his flaws, did one thing right by marrying this woman. Despite her seeming position of weakness, she was still formidable, and he knew firsthand her ability to turn this, or any situation, to her advantage.

"You, though," Isabella began, "what are *you* going to do? Two wonderful sons, both of whom, I hear, could easily run things for you. I don't envy you having to try to split things between them."

"Who says I will?"

"You above all should know how messy that can be if such things aren't considered."

"Michael will most likely go to San Diego," he said. "We're expanding down there."

Isabella raised an eyebrow. "Are we now? And your son has agreed to go slumming with a bunch of illegals? I would have thought that was beneath a Byrne, but times are changing, I suppose."

"He'll do what I tell him to do."

"I'm sure he will."

Liam shrugged. "It is as it is," he said in a slightly mocking tone. "We might have some other opportunities open up for us."

She dropped her smile. "I wouldn't look east for that if I were you," she warned.

"No?"

"No," she repeated. "Our friends in New York like things as they are, especially you out here."

"Have you been whispering in ears, my dear Isabella?"

"My husband may not be the man he once was, but his wishes are well known. And they will be honored."

"You mean *your* wishes," he corrected. "It is you that put me out here, is it not?" She remained silent. "And what will your dear relatives in New York do when he is gone and Tommy begins to dismantle everything?"

"That will not happen."

"And how are you planning to stop him?" Liam asked. "For all our disagreements, I don't quite see you inviting the Valcos in to handle your affairs. Not yet, anyway."

She looked past him once more. Several Hispanic men were making their way across the field toward a large warehouse, pausing intermittently to check the vines. She wondered what their jobs were—and whether they knew who they were working for. She suspected yes, as Liam rarely passed on an opportunity to aggrandize himself.

Even the house she passed through on her way out back reflected the man and his personality. It was a cavernous mansion, overfilled with gilded artwork and assorted treasures from his travels. She dismissed most of it, pausing only as she entered a two-story great room that ran almost the entire length of the back of the house. Mounted above the cobblestone fireplace, which filled the middle third of the wall from floor to ceiling, was a large portrait of the estate's new owner, captured in an almost Napoleonic pose as he stood by a white horse in a field.

She looked over at him as his words began to resonate. It seemed a lifetime ago since she had been Isabella Valco, having been a Byrne for more than twice that time. It was with her husband's people in Chicago she now felt closest, and had for many years after they embraced her as one of their own, Italian heritage notwithstanding. She also knew that there was now little left for her in New York. Those adults that molded her into the woman she had become were long gone, her cousins more business partners than relatives. She had not been back east in almost a decade as time and distance weakened familial bonds.

Liam guided his finger along the platinum band on the edge of the saucer. "I find it hard to believe you came all the way out here just to visit your son in the hospital. And for how long? Five minutes? Maybe even less?"

"You spend too much time listening to your snoops."

"Perhaps, but I have a feeling this trip wasn't about him at all now, was it?"

"Don't flatter yourself."

He laughed. "I don't. Not on this, anyway. But regardless of why you find yourself in California, here in beautiful Sonoma County overlooking my bountiful grapes, perhaps you and I can take this most fortunate opportunity to find an arrangement that makes everyone happy."

She allowed herself a small grin. "Perhaps we can."

25

"When do we make our move?" Enzo asked. "All these fags are giving me the creeps."

The three were seated in an otherwise empty coffeehouse on Fifth Avenue in Hillcrest. Eddie watched the two baristas—a guy and a girl in their early twenties—banter between themselves. He took another sip of his coffee, still lethargic despite having spent most of the morning in bed.

Eddie glanced at his phone. "I think it's best if we wait until dark," he said, relieved his partner was cooperating to this extent and hadn't barreled in and started shooting up the neighborhood in broad daylight. They had gotten away with that in Chicago once, but wouldn't be so lucky out here.

"We should have done it last night."

"Then you shouldn't have pushed for us to go out and get drunk after that boat ride," Eddie said as he watched a middle-aged man in tattered jeans and a T-shirt enter and walk over to the counter, his flip-flops slapping against the wooden floor. Their conversation interrupted, the barista stepped to the register while her coworker grabbed a rag and began wiping down tables.

"We could have done both," Enzo insisted.

"Hey, Billy," the girl behind the counter yelled out. "What time you out of here tonight?"

"Six or seven," Billy shouted back. "I think seven."

Eddie looked at Enzo. "Patience, boss. They're not going anywhere."

■ ■ ■

"Wanting to get out of here, are we, Mr. Byrne?" Dr. Evans scowled as he entered the room. The day when patients actually listened had long since come and gone, and the surly teenager before him was no different. At least he was alone this time. Familiar enough with the name, the boy's entourage gave him pause—few others ever had.

"Yes, I would," James said.

Evans made the effort of picking up the chart and giving it a once-over, knowing his next words would be wasted. "I think it would be best—"

"Yes, I heard that before. Repeatedly. I just want to go home."

"I'd feel more comfortable if you stayed another day. We can look at it again first thing in the morning."

"I'm fine," James said. "I can breathe. I can walk. I can do pretty much anything. I'm just a little sore. Nothing to keep me in the hospital."

"Well—"

"Unless you're planning to physically restrain me, I'm leaving this hospital today."

Evans glanced back down at the chart, focusing once more on the name "Byrne" across the top. Perhaps getting this kid out of here would be for the best. "Go home then," he said before abruptly walking out of the room.

■ ■ ■

Sue was back at her desk in the *Times* building, fork in hand, chewing on the half-consumed salad before her while turning over the mysterious disappearance of Matt Foss and Tim Clark. She had returned to their apartment and found her card exactly where she'd left it.

Were they out of town, were they hiding, or had something unanticipated—and perhaps sordid—happened to them since James

Byrne's assault? So many theories were roiling her mind, all of them equally plausible.

She had left her card undisturbed, deciding it best not to seem like she was pestering them, then headed off to grab her meal and drive back to the office, where a side article awaited her attention. An art festival in Balboa Park didn't seem all that interesting these days. Perhaps a call to Senator Clark's office was in order.

26

Chris had been in the apartment all day, mindlessly playing Xbox. Billy had left around noon to get something to eat before his shift, and Dan had spent the night elsewhere. At least one of them was getting laid.

Chris felt slightly on edge, which he attributed to their latest outing. It certainly wasn't a delayed sense of guilt. It was a generalized unease, one that even video games and a few shots of vodka couldn't shake. The words *you'll regret this* still lingered in his thoughts.

Not that he worried that they would ever get caught. They had been careful enough, avoiding crowded areas and the assorted surveillance cameras, and they were all so nondescript that it would be difficult for their victims to pick them out of a lineup. Waifish, twenty-something white and Latino guys of average height were a dime a dozen in San Diego.

This evening, though, he would suggest they lie low for a while. It wouldn't be hard to convince the other two. Coverage of the beatings was becoming relentless, and Hillcrest was sure to be crawling with cops. No, six was a good enough run for now.

■ ■ ■

"You text like a teenage girl," Carlyle finally commented, having watched his partner type away on his phone for the better part of half an hour. "She'd better be fantastic in bed to make all that worth it."

"First," Seegars said without looking up, "unlike my Luddite partner, I don't mind texting."

"Clearly."

"And second, I thought you would be more sensitive to gender stereotypes and ageism after that PC training class we enjoyed last month."

"I'm very sensitive to it," Carlyle said. "I just don't give a shit."

Seegars chuckled. "I *am* working, you know."

"On getting laid."

"Patience, grasshopper. Some of my sources prefer to text."

"It better be one hell of a lead."

Seegars continued on for a few more moments before pulling his feet off the desk and sitting up. "How's this for worth the wait? My source knows this girl."

Carlyle looked up from his screen, where he'd been reviewing surveillance footage, hoping to spy something useful one of his team had missed. It wasn't what he considered a constructive use of his time, but there was nothing else to do until something moved the case forward. The look on his partner's face told him that was about to happen. "Don't we all?"

"Yeah, but this is a special girl."

"Really?"

"Yeah, her name is... Lindsey," Seegars said, looking down at his phone.

"And?"

"Lindsey's been banging this guy named Daniel Field. And it seems that Mr. Field has a bit of a big mouth and has been bragging about some extracurricular physical activity in Hillcrest."

"And how did your source come to hear about this?"

Seegars paused. "Some of my sources prefer a strict don't-ask-don't-tell kind of policy."

Carlyle stood. "At least tell me you have an address."

"It's hers, but he's been staying there a few nights a week."

"It's a start. Let's go," Carlyle said as he grabbed his jacket off the back of the chair.

27

"So, how was your day?" Sabrina asked as Tommy entered the kitchen, slipped off his suit jacket, and tossed it onto one of the bar stools by the island.

She knew that look well, the pensive façade masking an inner anger that he would never release to the world. At least not to her. She often thought his outward calm was a rebuff to his upbringing; of the few topics he would never discuss, his childhood as the heir to Ciaran Byrne's empire was at the top of that list.

Without saying a word, he came over and kissed her, and she could both smell and taste the alcohol on him as he slipped his arms around her and pulled her tightly against him. Whiskey this time, which meant he had been up in Wrigleyville to do family business in Sam's absence. He went there less and less, but she understood the need to continue doing so, at least for now. He would hear no complaints from her.

As he rested his chin on her shoulder, his arms still firmly around her, the faint smell of his cologne brought her back to when they first crossed paths seven years ago. She could sense in him now the same discord she had witnessed back then, the result of a birthday party abruptly ended by a bar fight brought about by too many beers and too much bravado. By the time she entered Room 13 at the end of the emergency unit, having been ordered to do so since no one else would go near the patient, he had seemed to have mellowed considerably from his raucous entrance into the ER.

He was seated at the edge of the examination table, wearing a gray suit and white shirt, both spattered with blood. The hospital gown he had been given was discarded on the floor beneath him. He was holding a bandage above his right eye, the white gauze spotted with crimson.

There had been two others loitering outside the room as she approached, but only one inside with him, all of them similarly dressed —including the blood—although he was the worst off of the group.

She eyed the one standing beside him as he eyed her back, a slightly younger, shorter, and scruffier version of her new patient with a head of wavy maroon hair and a week's worth of stubble on his face. "You need to leave," she ordered.

He looked to her patient for guidance. "You don't need his permission," she admonished. "I need you to leave. Now."

Tommy smiled. "It's okay, Sam. I'll be fine."

"He pouts too much," she said once they were alone.

"Yes," he agreed as he looked over her light blue scrubs. "He's the strong, silent type. Now who exactly are you?"

"Sabrina—"

"You a doctor?"

"Nurse."

"I want a doctor to look at this," he said, briefly removing the gauze from above his right eye to show her the wound.

"Well, you got me," she said as she retrieved some gloves from the dispenser and began to put them on.

After glancing at the other superficial wounds, she gently took hold of his wrist and attempted to pull the bandage away, but he resisted her effort. She gave him a look and tried more forcefully, but again he held firm. She slapped his wrist. "Stop it."

"I want to see a real doctor."

"Tough. You scared them all off. Now move your hand so I can see what you did to yourself."

He laughed as his hand finally dropped away. "I didn't do this to myself."

"You stumble and fall?"

"Not exactly. I ran into something."

"Something or someone?"

He seemed to think it over. "The latter."

Sabrina shook her head in feigned disbelief. "So, you *did* do this to yourself."

"You saying it's my fault?"

"I'm saying you probably did something to earn this. I don't see many who haven't."

Tommy slouched in resignation as he allowed her to examine the wound more thoroughly. "You're not afraid of me," he finally said after she took her hands away, the tips of her gloves now lightly blotched with his blood.

Her eyes met his. "No. Should I be?"

"I don't know. You know who I am?"

"Really? Did you seriously just ask me that?"

He chuckled. "Yes."

"I know who you are, Mr. Byrne, but to be perfectly honest, you don't seem that scary to me." She walked over to a rolling cart and pulled it toward him.

"When are you free for dinner?" he asked.

She leaned back to look him in the eyes. "You're asking me out? Here? Now?"

"I'm going to ask you to marry me one of these days."

She scoffed. "I doubt that."

"Just you wait."

She smiled at the memory, as her husband finally released her. He walked over to the refrigerator and opened it, hand still on the door as he studied its contents.

"How was your day?" she repeated.

"Fine, honey." He pulled out a beer and closed the door. He gave her another quick kiss. "What do you want for dinner? I'll cook."

"Hungry already?"

"Yeah."

"You don't have to cook," she said. "Let's just go out."

"I don't want to go out. I've been out all afternoon, and I feel like sitting home. How's take-out?"

She raised her eyebrows. "No pizza."

"Deal," he said as he walked to the other side of the island and sat down, watching as she flipped through the day's mail and sorted it into piles.

"How's Jimmy doing?" she finally asked without looking up.

Tommy exhaled loudly, then took a long drink of his beer. He still felt guilty for dissuading her from going out to visit, especially with his mother already on her way. "He's..."

"What?"

"Gay."

Sabrina nodded. "I know."

"How?"

"When he was here with us, he and I... you know... we spent a lot of time together."

Tommy looked away. "I guess I didn't really notice."

"Tommy—"

"Sabrina, I *really* didn't notice."

"Well... is it a problem?"

"You married into this family. What do you think?"

"I don't care about the rest of your family. I didn't marry *them*. I married you."

"You married us all."

She rolled her eyes. "Okay then, is it or isn't it a problem *for you*?"

"It's not a problem for me. I like your brother and his... friend. I just... I feel kind of shitty about it, because my mother is—"

"You don't have to say it. I know your mother well enough by now."

"And my dad. Jesus, he's going to hit the fucking roof with this."

She walked over and gave him a kiss. "You Byrnes and your machismo."

He pulled her closer, gently kissing her neck as they hugged. With her in his arms, everything was right in the world. "I just feel bad for him." He pulled back, looking into her eyes. "We're creating a fucking mess out there for him, and he doesn't deserve that."

She frowned. "What do you mean, '*we*' are creating a mess?"

"You don't want to know."

"Probably not," she said, knowing not to press him when he used that line. "What are you going to do about it?"

He shook his head. "I haven't figured that out yet."

28

Chris had just finished showering and slipped on a pair of gym shorts and a T-shirt pulled from his pile of dirty laundry. He now stood in the kitchen opening a new can of beer—it was his fourth of the hour—when he was startled by a loud knocking on the door.

"Fucking morons," he muttered to himself. One of his roommates had locked himself out of the apartment again. Probably Billy, since he was always too fucking dumb to remember to grab his keys. At least there would be someone to talk into splitting a pizza with.

He flipped the lock open and walked over to the chair facing the television. "It's open, bonehead," he yelled as he sat down.

The door opened. Instead of his roommates, two men, each shorter but far more gym-hardened, marched into the living room.

"I think you've got the wrong apartment, dudes."

One turned back and slammed the door. "Are you Chris?" the other asked.

"Yeah," he answered. The fucking cops. Fucking Dan and his big mouth.

The man snapped his finger. "Get over here," he ordered, his thick Midwestern accent now evident.

"Huh?"

"I said get the fuck over here."

Chris's free hand began to shake as he felt his face go flush. These weren't cops, he instinctively realized. He dropped his beer on the coffee table and walked over as ordered. Whoever they were, they didn't seem the type to enjoy repeating themselves.

"Who are you?" he asked.

"Your worst fucking nightmare," the man answered, then delivered the first punch to Chris's cheek, knocking him back a few steps.

"What the fuck?" Chris was able to blurt out before the second blow knocked him to the carpet. He sat there dazed and rubbing his jaw. As he glanced up, he saw something that looked like a baseball bat come flying through the air.

■ ■ ■

She had been home for some time when Ciaran entered the sunroom, two glasses of burgundy in hand.

He looked tired as he crossed the room, as he now always did after an active day in Wrigleyville. His once robust gait had slowed to a near shuffle over the last six months, even more pronounced as he carefully balanced the two glasses while navigating the furniture between them. He could only do so much, she knew, before fatigue overwhelmed him into near total confusion.

Isabella took the offered glass, and he sat down beside her on the love seat. It was their first opportunity to see or even speak to each other since she had left for California the day before. Neither had any use for computers or cell phones, which were poor tools for their business at any rate. No, talking was done in person, or on rare occasion, over the phone. News was delivered by paper in the morning or on television in the evening.

"How was your trip, my dear?"

"It was fine."

"And Jimmy? How is he?"

Isabella paused. "He'll live. He'll be fine."

Ciaran nodded. "Good. Good. Do they know anything?"

"It was a random attack, that's all. And how was your day?"

He sighed. "Very good. We got a lot accomplished."

"Is he finally rising to the occasion?"

Ciaran glanced over, seemingly taken aback by both comment and tone. "Yes. They have all taken to him, and the respect is there."

"Probably because you were there beside him."

"No. No, I would have heard something by now," Ciaran assured her. "It's been over a year. They're fine. He's the boss and they know it."

Isabella sighed. "I'm just concerned—that's all."

"About?"

"That his heart isn't fully in it."

"He likes what he does with the buildings," Ciaran said, "but he will step up."

"I hope so."

Ciaran gently patted her leg, squeezing her knee before returning his hand to his own lap. "He will. You'll see."

Isabella took a sip from her glass as she allowed the lull in the conversation to continue a bit further. It was their way—to speak, pause to reflect, then move on to the next topic. After decades, with their precious time together nearing an end, this pattern would not change.

"Your brother reached out to me," she finally said, a reversal of reality that Ciaran would never be the wiser to.

He looked back over at her, his brow furrowed in annoyance. "How did he know you were there?"

"Tommy spoke to David about us going in to take care of the situation," Isabella said. "He probably said something about it."

"What did he want?"

She took another sip from her glass. "Peace."

Ciaran scoffed. "I hope you hung up on him."

She paused once more. "No," she said, deciding not to tell him of their face-to-face meeting. He had been provoked enough. "We did speak."

He looked away. "Why the hell would you do something like that?"

"I don't know," she lied. "I suppose I wanted to hear what he had to say."

"Whatever came out of his mouth, it was bullshit," Ciaran said, waving a dismissive hand in the air. "He is a goddamn snake who cannot be trusted."

"I suspect you're right."

Isabella took another sip of burgundy as the silence between them resumed. She enjoyed her role as a confident, one she shared only with Moretti, and to a lesser extent Tommy. Unlike the other wives, she was heavily involved in the business, and had been since before Ciaran assumed control from Liam Sr. She had never been content to play housewife, as most of them were, or to go out and have their own career like her daughter-in-law. This is where her heart lay, and she would not sit quietly when so much was at stake.

She looked down at his glass, watching as his untouched wine rippled slightly in his trembling hand, signaling a continued agitation within him. She knew him well enough to recognize that their conversation on the matter was not over.

"Michael will be here on Wednesday to meet with Tommy." She listened as he took a deep breath, his way of checking the rage inside.

"Michael should go to San Diego," Ciaran said. "He has no business here."

"Liam is sending him to San Diego to handle their concerns there full time," she said. "But we also have concerns there, and it's best if a dialogue is kept open."

"It is. And what we have in place has worked well enough all these years. I see no point in changing things."

"It is a different generation. If Tommy and David can work well together, then it is in all our interests."

"I don't know."

"It helps New York too if they can build something more, and we owe them. They have been very good to us."

Ciaran sighed. "Let me think on it."

Isabella put a hand on his knee. "Will you trust me on this? Please?"

He placed his own hand on top of hers, squeezing gently. "Okay," he finally said. "Okay."

29

"I thought you would have gone home by now," Sheraton said without bothering to look up.

He didn't need to, of course. He knew on instinct who had parked herself in his doorway, her presence something of a force of nature. If he had more reporters like her and the financial wherewithal to fund each of their passions, he would have one of the best investigative papers on the West Coast—if not in the country. That was assuming they didn't tear each other, or him, apart first. Ego clashes between journalists were second to none, though he had a few professor friends who would vehemently disagree.

"The police just found the bodies of one suspect and a woman believed to have been with him about a half hour ago," Sue announced. "I'm heading off to the crime scene now."

"Sounds good," he remarked.

"Had a chance to look at my email yet?"

Charles looked up with his best expression of concern. "You sure you want to pursue this one? It might be kind of—"

"I'm not worried about the Byrnes. They don't frighten me."

"I don't know what you hope to prove. They don't seem like the kind of people you want to be fucking with."

"You don't think that's a story?"

"Of course I do, Susan. I just don't want you to cut off your nose to spite—"

"Spare me the clichés. James Byrne's boyfriend, Matt Foss, and his roommate, Tim Clark, son of State Senator Edward Clark, are missing."

"You *think* they're missing."

"Yes, I do."

"And what facts do you have to back this up?" Charles asked. "Hunches are good. Hunches have launched many spectacular careers. But investigative reporting is still pretty new to you. It takes time to hone those skills."

She resisted the urge to roll her eyes. "Yes, I know that."

"So, why do you think they're missing?"

"I went to their apartment yesterday and they weren't home." She raised her hand to cut him off. "Let me finish. I stopped by again today. My card was still where I left it, twenty-four hours later."

"So?"

"You don't find that a little odd? That they hadn't been back to their apartment in a day?"

"Maybe they're in Vegas. Who knows?"

"Charles, James Byrne and Matt Foss got into an argument Saturday night at a club on University. James left, stumbled into whomever, and wound up in the hospital. Matt and his roommate haven't been heard from since."

"Are you saying our little mafia boy had them whacked from the hospital?"

"I don't know," Sue said, frustrated. "Maybe on a Sunday, they're out and whatever, sure, but it's Monday night already and they're both still missing. Something's happened to them. I just know it."

Charles tapped his pencil against his desk.

"Look, James's father Ciaran runs north Chicago," Sue said. "Ciaran's brother Liam controls Las Vegas, and the family, both sides of it, has a presence here that makes keeping this quite important to them."

Charles frowned. "What does San Diego have to do with any of that?"

"They work with the cartels to import guns and drugs, mainly cocaine and heroin. Liam takes the drugs, but Ciaran despises them. He'll let them pass through on their way to the South Side or onto New York, but the quickest way to a death sentence is to deal drugs in one of his establishments."

"And how do you know all this?"

Sue grinned. "I have friends."

"Of course you do."

She paused. "So… I take it you don't mind me snooping around a bit?"

"I think you might be biting off enough to choke on."

"I appreciate the concern, Charles. I really do. But don't worry. Nothing's going to happen to me."

■ ■ ■

James checked his phone, the fifth such glance in as many minutes, before dropping it back onto the blanket.

He had broken down after the doctor left and sent texts to both Matt and Tim, but neither of them had responded. Matt was not a surprise—he did tend to pout in forty-eight-hour cycles—but Tim was usually quick to reply. If anything, it was hard enough to end a thread once it started. But even turning the phone on and off in the hopes of triggering a wayward incoming message had produced nothing.

His mind wandered to dark places, that they had fallen victim to whoever his family would have dispatched to seek retribution. Of course, he knew that was absurd—none of them, save Tommy and Sabrina, cared one iota about him. Sam and Moretti had been sent at Tommy's request, he was sure, but with the exception of his last visitor, whom he would rather forget, that would be the last of them.

He was still hoping to be freed by day's end, but as he looked over at the window, the sky turning an amber-red as the sun began its retreat beyond the ocean a mile or so from where he lay, he felt that chance fading with the daylight. There had been a small parade of specialists soon after the doctor tersely agreed to discharge him, but nothing but silence since then. The final signature, he suspected, would be the doctor's last act of a very long day.

His phone vibrated and he lunged for it, hoping it was Matt or Tim but eager for any human contact at this point. It was Ben. He typed out a quick response, asking his friend to come pick him up.

■ ■ ■

Billy clocked out a few minutes before seven, then started the ten-minute walk back to the apartment, and another night of only God knew what.

Like his roommates, he wasn't one to allow the end of a weekend to put a stop to the ongoing festivities. In that sense it was a typical early Monday evening, the remnants of another perfect sunny day still visible as the last of the setting sun found its way between the buildings along his path back home. Hopefully, he thought as he climbed the stairs to his apartment, Chris had come through and bought the beer like he was supposed to. He usually did, with a little weed thrown in for good measure, which meant that everything would be just fine by ten.

He stopped in front of the door. "Fuck," he muttered as he patted down his front pockets as he realized that he had forgotten his keys in the usual last-minute rush to work. He cursed his stupid eagerness to please—none of his bosses really cared so long as he was within fifteen minutes or so, and most of the time he could hit that mark with even the worst of hangovers.

On a whim he tried the front door, which thankfully was unlocked. He stepped into the dark apartment, the only discernible light coming from the hallway toward the bedrooms and the single bathroom they shared.

"Chris, you stupid bitch, where the fuck are you?" he called out after slamming shut the door behind him and walking toward the kitchen. He glanced down the hallway and saw that the bathroom light was on, but Chris's door was closed, so who knew what he was up to.

As he flipped on the kitchen light, it occurred to him that he hadn't seen Dan today. When that guy found someone to fuck, it was all any of them could do to pry him off the poor girl. That would end soon enough as it always had. Dan, like they all did, eventually tired of too much of the same thing.

He walked to the refrigerator, tossing his dirty apron onto the counter by the sink. "Yeah, boy," he shouted as he clapped his hands together. The fridge, thankfully, contained a full case of beer. He popped one open, and as he turned around, saw two large men standing in the doorway, one with a wooden baseball bat in his hand, the barrel speckled dark red.

"Hello, Billy. Have we got some fucking fun for you."

30

"Un-fucking-believable," Carlyle muttered as he and Seegars stood by the front door of the apartment, the medical examiner and forensics team doing their work inside.

First on the scene, they had already been through the place, finding their intended targets still in the bedroom where they'd been taken. Dan and Lindsey had been dead less than a day, both bound, and Lindsey still gagged with duct tape—Dan's having been removed at some point. Their hands were tied behind their backs, their legs taped together. Though Lindsey had suffered only a single gunshot wound to the head, it was evident that Dan had been tortured for some time before presumably giving them what they wanted. His throat gashed open in what looked like a botched beheading to end the ordeal.

"We're probably just one or two steps behind these fuckers," Seegars said, typing on his phone with both thumbs.

"Oh, I'm sure of that," Carlyle agreed as he pulled out his keys. "You have the kid's address?"

"Just got it," Seegars answered as he held up his phone.

"Let's go. Patterson," Carlyle called out to the junior detective, who had been hovering nearby while awaiting his orders. "Stay here and let me know if they find anything they can use."

"Yes, sir."

Seegars watched the younger man enter the apartment, then followed as Carlyle headed toward the car. "We have a teenager on the task force?"

"See what you get for missing meetings?"

■ ■ ■

"You look like shit," Ben joked as James closed the door of the SUV.

"Thanks."

"I still can't believe it was you."

James shook his head. "I don't want to talk about it, and I don't want you to either. If anybody asks, I fell down drunk or something."

As the car turned onto Washington, James looked out the window, happy to see freedom again after the last few days, although at the moment he only looked forward to trading his hospital bed for the one in his apartment. It was the same city that he had been abruptly sidelined from—but forever different. The brutality of the assault, its randomness—he had been robbed of the comfort his new home had provided, the refuge he'd needed after Chicago and the history he'd dragged here.

He glanced at Ben, thankful the two had crossed paths online a few months after James had arrived in California, meeting up for a coffee in Hillcrest that had gone nowhere romantic. James's heart had still been elsewhere while Ben, at only twenty-four, wasn't interested in anything more than a passing fling to liven up an otherwise mundane life as a retail assistant manager.

But the two had managed to forge a meaningful friendship and deep affection for each other. The younger man found someone who never tried to manipulate him. Ben was a friend he could be himself around without judgment, unlike other acquaintances who mocked him for his numerous liaisons.

"Any word from Matt or Tim?"

"No," Ben said. "I can't get Tim to call me back."

"And Matt?"

Ben fought the urge to roll his eyes. He understood James's desire to get past whoever it was in Chicago, but Matt, as much as Ben liked him, was a poor substitute.

"*Please* don't tell them about this," James asked. He knew Ben wouldn't, but needed to break the silence as he continued to ruminate on his two missing friends. Where the hell were they?

31

The door to Apartment J stood partially open. Two uniformed officers were dutifully standing by, more on the way, while the two detectives assessed their options.

"Uglier than the last scene?" Seegars asked as they stood on opposite sides of the door, Carlyle staring intently at the handle.

He looked up. "What?"

"Inside. More blood?"

Carlyle shook his head. Even for Seegars this was bordering on the obscene. He seemed almost to be enjoying himself. "You're really doing this right now?"

"Ten bucks."

"No."

"Come on," Seegars pressed. "You know you want to."

"This is why I hate you."

"You love me."

"There could be two victims in here and you want to bet—"

"First off, they're scum."

"Drop it," Carlyle ordered as he pulled out his sidearm. "Let's go."

■ ■ ■

They rode in silence to one of several warehouses Liam Byrne owned under various shell companies, where imports were briefly housed before moving on to Los Angeles, Vegas, Chicago, and New York. As the warehouses were spread evenly throughout the city, Sean was easily able to direct them toward one without having to travel with their captives for very long.

Eddie, alone in the back seat, looked out the window, the blur of buildings becoming more industrial as Sean steered the car onto a street near the airport. He looked up at his two companions, watching as Enzo slightly nodded to the beat of whatever he was hearing inside his head.

Getting to Billy and Chris had been easy enough once they found Dan, thanks to his big-mouthed girlfriend. They had to eliminate her, of course—she was a loose end and had already talked once, and the Byrnes, in addition to not liking snitches, never left anything to chance. As a courtesy, though, she was immediately put out of her misery with a single gunshot to the head.

Dan suffered a much different outcome. He had tried to be a tough guy, as much as one could with his hands tied behind his back and his mouth gagged, but Enzo broke everyone in the end—partially in the false hope that giving up his friends would save himself, mostly to be free of the agony.

In Chicago, Enzo preferred power tools to get someone's attention, but today a simple four-inch blade had sufficed. "Time to return to basics," he announced before first cutting deeply into Dan's leg. Eddie was used to his friend's sadism, but he saw a deeper drive within him today. Family honor was being restored. Even if Jimmy was gay, no one screwed with the Byrnes.

Having practiced on dozens, Enzo knew how to keep a victim alive— how to maximize pain while doing minimal damage, a lesson he'd learned after accidentally severing a femoral artery a few years back. He still didn't always get it right, but more often than not those at his mercy lived for far longer than they wanted to.

They were still well ahead of the police, so Enzo hadn't started the inquiry for the first thirty minutes. "This is just to loosen you up a little," he told Dan in an eerily calm voice, "so, when I ask you a question you're going to tell me exactly what I want to know, okay?" Dan, tears rolling down his cheeks, barely had time to nod in acknowledgement before Enzo drove the knife into his arm.

The removal of his left pinky finger with some clippers Enzo had picked up in a local hardware store marked the beginning of Dan's end. Eddie was still surprised that he had lasted that long.

"Dan, my friend," Enzo said, a blue-gloved hand firmly holding Dan by the chin as he looked him in the eyes, his victim's face flush red and wet with tears and snot. "I'm going to take off another finger, and then I'm going to ask you about your two buddies. You better goddamn answer me," he warned as the clippers closed down on the bound man's ring finger.

With his answer in hand, Enzo took off the middle finger as well, and watched the kid squirm in agony for a few minutes before sawing into his throat. It wasn't something Eddie particularly cared to see, but the kid had it coming to him—and it was nothing compared to what the two in the trunk were going to get.

■ ■ ■

"What do you think?" Carlyle asked after they had finished canvassing the empty apartment.

Seegars briefly closed his eyes and shook his head. "Thank God you didn't take that bet."

There was an opened beer lying next to the refrigerator, its contents pooled around it. A floor lamp next to the couch was broken. There were two small areas of spattered blood, one in the kitchen and the other by the front door. The blood on the kitchen floor was streaked with thin lines, as if someone's scalp had been repeatedly slammed into the linoleum. The one by the entrance had a spray pattern, like the flick of a red paintbrush across the beige carpet.

"This is not going to be pretty," Carlyle said.

"What do you mean?" Seegars asked.

"If it was a simple matter of payback, their bodies would be here. They left the other two, but these they took their time with."

■ ■ ■

Moretti sipped his scotch, having arrived only moments after Ciaran had retired upstairs, the two alone in the expansive room.

What had once been a shared responsibility—which he had finally learned to accept after decades of quiet resentment—had been totally usurped by the woman seated in the middle of the couch ten feet away. What had once been a duet of their two voices in Ciaran's ear was now hers alone, and Moretti knew that his new role would be to speak as one with Isabella, to parrot her thoughts and words, for he had been part of this game far too long to delude himself otherwise.

"How was wine country?" he asked.

"We have our agreement," she answered. "Michael arrives Wednesday."

"Ciaran agreed to that?"

"Yes," she snapped. "Of course he did."

He nodded. "And Jimmy?"

Her lips pursed, as if an uncontrollable reflex. "That… is something Ciaran does not need to hear."

He finished off his drink. "How should we address the attack?"

"I already have. That it was random, which isn't a lie."

Moretti stood up and walked toward the bar. "As you wish," he said as he poured himself a double.

"You're more agitated than normal," Isabella observed. "What don't I know?"

"Enzo killed two of Jimmy's friends in a fit of rage."

She didn't flinch. "Did he take care of it?"

"Unfortunately, more than he should have."

"They'll be missed in time."

"Which was my first sentiment, but… I should have never sent Enzo down that road. Missing or not, this doesn't put us in a strong position once they link them to Jimmy."

"I thought that was the point," she said. "Or have I missed something? You said you wanted such a mess that there would be no choice but for Tommy to bend to our will to fix it or step aside, and now you're fretting like a neurotic child."

"You saw how defiant he was yesterday. If he starts to talk—"

"The boy knows nothing."

"He knows enough to do some damage above what I planned for."

"Then you should have thought of that sooner," Isabella said. "If it comes to that, then he is just as expendable as the others were. They are *all* expendable. I thought this was already settled, or did I waste my time in California?"

He paused. "It's settled."

Isabella stood up and followed him to the bar. "Let me tell you something. Nothing else matters except that the honor of this family is protected—that all we have created is protected." She paused, allowing the words to linger. "Enzo understands what is important and what needs to be done. I thought you did too. 'Never waste a perfectly good crisis,' you told me—what? Yesterday? Now you want to quibble about nonsense?"

"No."

Isabella placed the glass of wine down between them. "If Jimmy starts to create a *problem*, as you put it, he won't for very long. His cousin Arthur is at our disposal if necessary." She paused. "Now… are we still in agreement?"

"Absolutely," Moretti answered.

"Then grow some goddamn balls," she said, and strode out of the room.

32

"Good evening, boys!" Enzo said as he removed the pillowcases they had taken from the apartment. "I'm glad you could join us."

Billy and Chris found themselves hanging about six inches off the ground, their bound hands attached to a chain wrapped around a wooden beam ten feet above them. Their mouths had been stuffed with socks and duct-taped; their legs secured at their knees and ankles. The pain in their muscles was unbearable after hours bound like this.

Chris knew his jaw was broken, the throbbing pain worsening—if that was even possible—the one time he tried to move it. In the back of his mind, arrest had always been a realistic possibility. Having spent a long weekend in jail on a DUI a few years back, he could picture prison and figured he could handle a few years if it ever came to that. But as he hung from the rafters in the empty warehouse, he knew he would never see the inside of a jail cell. This was the end.

"Let me first introduce us," Enzo continued. "My name is Mr. Smith, and this… this is Mr. Jones," he said as he motioned toward Eddie. "Mr. Jones is here to help me make what's left of your lives *very* uncomfortable. Mr.… Mr. Miller is out getting us some food so that we'll have the energy to make this a night to remember. For most of us."

A single tear rolled down Billy's cheek as he came to terms with the end of his life. He never thought he would be this calm, this accepting of what was coming—even now. His body screamed from the abuse of the past several hours, pain he knew would pale in comparison to what was coming, but it was too much to fight. He simply wanted it all to stop.

"I take it the two of you know why you're here?" Enzo asked.

Eddie pulled out his Ruger and pointed it at Billy's head. "It's rude not to answer Mr. Smith's question, girls."

"Thank you, Mr. Jones," Enzo said. "Now do you know why you're here?"

Billy and Chris glanced at each other and shook their heads.

"It seems they're a bit slow, Mr. Smith."

"I would have to agree, Mr. Jones," Enzo said. "Perhaps we have something here to help their memories?"

"That we do, Mr. Smith," Eddie assured him. "That we fucking do."

33

The missing persons report for the son of a state senator and his roommate hadn't been out long before James Byrne's name was linked to the pair, a connection that pulled Carlyle from his In-N-Out burger and sent him to their apartment in North Park.

William Harvey and Christopher Estrada were still out there somewhere. He suspected the two would not survive the evening unless he caught a very lucky break. Given what had been done to their associate, Carlyle knew the next scene would be significantly more gruesome. Should that be the case, he simply hoped the Byrnes would deem their business concluded and return home.

Carlyle scowled as the thought crossed his mind, hating when the realist within him revealed itself. He hadn't dedicated himself to this grueling job because he was the type to be content with mob hit men dispensing justice in his backyard. His self-worth was built on an arrest record and conviction rate no one else in the department could touch. But that record had brought him to this, haplessly tagging along as one set of scumbags hunted down another.

"Detective Carlyle, good to see you," Gary Stevens, the officer first on the scene, said as Carlyle walked through the open door and entered the living room. He watched as Carlyle reacted to the powerful smell of cleaning products, pressing the back of his hand against his nostrils.

"Where's your partner?" Stevens asked.

"I left him at another crime scene while I went out to grab a bit to eat. He'll be here shortly."

"Unless he stops off at Cheetahs first."

"I think he likes the strippers at Pamela's better," Carlyle said as he extracted a pair of gloves from his suit jacket. "Where's *your* partner?"

"Thought she'd jump ahead and canvass the neighborhood before interviewing the neighbors."

"The smell?"

"Yeah, that too."

"Well, I appreciate her initiative. So… who are the missing again?"

Stevens glanced at his notes. "Matthew Foss and Timothy Clark."

"Who put the call in?" Carlyle asked.

"State Senator Jeffrey Clark, Timothy's father, had a member of his staff call headquarters and ask for someone to come by and check up on them. Says he hadn't heard from his son in a few days."

"And we jumped to attention, of course," Carlyle said dryly. "And Foss? Anyone report *him* missing?"

"No, not yet."

"What about the lab?"

"On the way."

Carlyle looked around. He saw nothing out of place, but the eye-watering sting of ammonia, which he'd mostly adapted to, foretold something else. "And how did James Byrne's name come up in all this?"

Stevens pointed to the cell phone on the kitchen counter. "I took the liberty of listening. There were quite a few texts and voicemails in the last day or so."

"Playing detective, are we? Who else is on there?"

Stevens glanced at his notes. "Texts are mundane. Several voicemails from the senator's office, two from a contact named Ben… no last name… and one from James Byrne. They were all about the same, though—just checking in to see where these two were. If you ask me—"

"They're gone."

Stevens nodded. "Millennials won't take a shit without their phones."

Carlyle nodded as he continued to take everything in. He hated jumping to conclusions, but he was going off instinct at this point, and it told him that once the Byrne crew left town, this would go into the unsolved-case pile.

"How exactly did we gain entrance? Is the landlord around?"

"The door was unlocked," Stevens answered. Carlyle gave him a look. "I had reasonable suspicion."

Carlyle said nothing. No time to argue the trivial.

Seegars walked into the apartmnt and made a face. "Jesus fucking Christ, it stinks in here."

"It gets better," Carlyle offered.

"I fucking hope so."

"How are things going over there?"

"I left Bieber to handle it," Seegars said. "I've got to tell you, the kid comes in handy when you have other shit to deal with."

"When do we get results from the blood samples?"

"I hope tomorrow morning."

"Fingerprints?"

"That apartment is such a goddamn mess it's going to take time for the lab to sort through what they found. They're still there, as a matter of fact. Tanaka cursed up a fucking storm when I asked her about it, but she said that she'd try to get what she could to us before noon." Seegars looked around the room. "What's going on here besides some weird obsession with ammonia?"

"Missing persons' case," Carlyle answered.

"Then what the fuck are we doing here?"

Carlyle shook his head. "You'll never guess whose apartment this is."

"Lisa Ann's."

"Friends of James Byrne."

"Fuck me."

"Oh, it gets better," Carlyle warned. "One of them is the son of State Senator Jeffrey Clark."

"Fuck me in the dickhole," Seegars muttered. "That guy's a douchebag."

"Sorry," Stevens interrupted as he held up a business card in an evidence bag, "this was tucked in between the door and the frame."

Carlyle took it, then chuckled to himself.

"What?" Seegars asked.

"It's Sue Hendricks's business card."

"That nosey dyke from the *Times*?"

"Yes, that nosey dyke from the *Times*." Carlyle waved the card in the air. "I'd like to know how she got here."

"She's a reporter."

"Yeah, but I don't think she's that bright," Carlyle said. "How did we miss these two?"

"The Byrne kid obviously didn't supply the information," Seegars observed.

"With that goon squad around his hospital room, I wouldn't expect him to. But why couldn't anyone on our team figure that out? We have a number of witnesses who put him at two different bars. These guys were involved somehow, but no one bothered to say shit."

"Maybe they were afraid to?"

"Yeah, I don't think the mafia family was something James Byrne would want to advertise. I'm willing to bet he came to California to get away from that."

"Well, he did a bang-up job in that department," Seegars said.

"Maybe the senator, then," Stevens mused.

Carlyle looked over at him. "Huh?"

"Maybe no one said anything because the guy's father is a wingnut and they didn't want it getting back to him."

"Maybe, but in any case," Carlyle said as he began to pace, "she got information we didn't, and that pisses me off. I'll have to give her a call after we're done here."

Carlyle stopped in front of the linen-blend couch, looking intently at it for a few moments as he looked between the cushions and arms before motioning Seegars and Stevens over. "What do you two see?"

Seegars looked at it for a moment. "A couch only a gay man could love?"

Carlyle slipped on the gloves he'd been holding. "Something is off with these cushions. They're too new compared to the arms." He flipped the center back cushion around, a new wave of ammonia hitting them.

"Shit," Seegars said as he saw the dark red stain.

"I think it's time we spoke to James Byrne," Carlyle said.

■ ■ ■

James lay on his bed with the lights off, flip flops now on the floor but otherwise dressed as he had been when he got home, his hands on his stomach as he stared at the ceiling fan slowly rotating above him.

He hadn't felt this alone since he first moved out here, despite the friendships he'd formed since then. But as he watched the fan cast shadows on the ceiling from the light bleeding through the partially opened horizontal blinds, the solitude didn't bother like it once had. No, all he wanted was for sleep to come once more so he could escape from this, if only for a few hours.

34

"Ms. Hendricks, how are you doing this evening?" Carlyle asked without bothering to hide the reluctance in his voice.

Their search of the Foss and Clark apartment had yielded nothing beyond what had already been discovered at the couch. Carlyle couldn't understand why the two bodies had been removed. Given the amount of blood and the lack of a corresponding trail there was no way they had departed that apartment breathing. Taking the remaining two suspects alive had made some sense—they clearly wanted time to torment the two undisturbed—but with Lindsey and Daniel left behind, why would they suddenly start removing corpses? He needed answers, and hoped the nuisance on the other end of this call could start to give him some.

"Detective Carlyle!" she said. "I'm doing wonderfully. How are you?"

"I've been better. Tell me what you know about James Byrne."

"I probably know what you do. Did you want to know that he's Ciaran Byrne's son, or what happened Saturday night?"

"I really hope you're not sniffing around on that first part."

"And why is that?" she asked, a new testiness in her voice.

"I get the sense they're not the type to appreciate any unwarranted attention."

"Oh, I think the attention is very warranted."

"What about Matthew Foss and Timothy Clark?"

"I suspect I know what you do at this point."

He chuckled. "Somehow I think we're just a little behind on the background on those two."

"Well, if you'd bother to return one of my calls."

"Duly noted."

"Would you like me to recite it all, or is there something specific you're looking for?"

Carlyle made a face. "How did you discover their relation to James Byrne?"

"Good reporting."

"I found your business card on their door."

"What brought *you* over there?"

"Senator Jeffrey Clark suddenly became interested in knowing the whereabouts of his son and kindly asked us to pay a visit."

"I called his office," she admitted.

"I suspected someone lit a fire under his ass."

"Did you find him? Is he all right?"

"No, they weren't around," Carlyle said. "But off the record, since I know how cooperative you're going to be with me in the future, I'll tell you what we did find."

■ ■ ■

Tommy remained in the darkened living room, absentmindedly stroking the stem of his glass of Barolo beside an all-but-empty bottle.

Sabrina had gone to bed an hour ago, leaving him to his reflections on last night's conversation with Moretti and the collateral damage that Enzo had unleashed. What had happened with the boyfriend and the other one troubled Tommy, although he knew that was the result of how overprotective he had become of his youngest sibling after what had happened last year. Since that time, he had been able to shelter Jimmy from the family, even if it meant the jettisoning of Tommy's once-close relationship with their mother.

But there was no getting around what had happened. It was only a matter of time before Jimmy found out.

Enzo was what had happened, his life of reckless disregard and the consequences that were never faced. Enzo made the messes, and big brother Tommy cleaned them up. That was simply the way it was, the way his father wanted it—that his middle son could do no wrong was a notion that had hardened to an axiom as Ciaran's condition accelerated. What Enzo did, they had all rationalized, was in service to the family, so the family was obligated to return the favor no matter what.

But now their dark bargain was affecting Jimmy, and at this moment Tommy felt helpless to prevent that.

■ ■ ■

Five minutes after getting out of the shower, his hair still wet, James heard a loud knock on the door. Somewhat ambivalent about answering it—assuming it was finally Matt coming to apologize in person—he quickly slipped on a T-shirt and a pair of shorts before making his way to the front door. As he approached the knock repeated itself, only louder, and he jumped slightly. That was not Matt. He stared through the peephole and saw the familiar middle-aged man.

"Yes?" he asked after opening the door.

"James Byrne?"

"Yes."

He held up a badge. "Hello. I'm Detective Robert Carlyle—"

"The man from the hospital."

"Yes."

"And this is my partner, Craig Seegars," Carlyle added, nodding toward a younger man as he stepped in front of the open door.

"What do you want?" James asked, not bothering to take Seegars's outstretched hand.

"May we come in, please?"

"Is this about the license?" James asked, recalling their conversation in the hospital. It had come up only briefly, and Moretti had quickly batted it away, but now apparently had returned.

"What license?" Seegars asked Carlyle.

"I'll tell you later," he answered before looking back at James. "No, son. We're here because we'd like to ask you some questions about Matthew Foss and Timothy Clark."

35

"There's a problem," Moretti announced after Tommy answered the call.

Tommy had just dropped his wine glass into the dishwasher—he was a well-trained husband—and was almost to the bedroom when the phone began to vibrate in his pocket. Staring at the screen, he had initially hesitated to answer, but knowing both the source and the hour, it was wiser to do so.

"With what?" Tommy asked as he reentered the living room, where he walked over to the window and stared into the blackness of Lake Michigan.

"Our friend, Detective Carlyle."

Tommy sighed loudly into the phone to express his displeasure. "What about him?"

"Jimmy called Sam. It seems the detective paid him a visit, but Sam didn't know what the fuck he was talking about, so Sam called me. I told him I would deal with it."

"Is this about—"

"Yeah. Apparently no one was at the 'party,' but they left something behind."

Tommy groaned. "Anything to worry about?"

"Not on that end, but Jimmy told Sam he knows Enzo is involved."

"He knows shit about Enzo."

"He didn't come up with the idea from me," Moretti said, "but we need to start being concerned about him not sticking to the script."

Tommy nodded. "I'll handle it."

"This is starting to spiral out of control."

"I said I'll handle it," Tommy snapped before ending the call.

■ ■ ■

As if on cue, Carlyle's phone started to vibrate just as he sank into his recliner, Fox News back on the television.

His visit to see James Byrne had gone as expected. He didn't feel great about heaping more shit onto an already troubled mind, but needed to provoke a reaction out of the family. The three queer stompers getting their comeuppance at the hands of the Byrnes he probably could have lived with, but Lindsey, Matthew and Timothy deserved better.

He'd been somewhat surprised by the kid's facial expressions as he tried to maintain his composure throughout the questioning. Carlyle could see James's mind churning as he tried to digest how his world had so suddenly crashed down on top of him, all because he happened to be at the wrong place on a random Saturday night. A name had definitely popped into his head, but even if James didn't seem the brightest bulb to Carlyle, the kid knew better than to talk to the likes of him.

"Yeah?" he asked after tapping the screen.

"You better get downtown," Seegars said.

"Not again."

"I just got a call. They found something that we might want to see."

"What?" Carlyle asked.

"Two crispy bodies dumped in an alley near the airport. Texting you the location in a sec. Something tells me it's our two Hillcrest hooligans."

Carlyle stood up. "I'm on my way."

■ ■ ■

"Hello?"

He almost didn't answer, but he didn't recognize the number and hoped it was someone, anyone, with news to counter what the detective had told him. Matt and Tim were gone, Carlyle had said in a matter-of-fact tone, and there was little to no expectation that they were alive given what had been discovered at their apartment.

He knew who, and he knew why—but how they put it together so quickly he could not fathom. From what the detective told him, they had gone missing sometime Sunday, less than twenty-four hours after he'd been put in the hospital. Why did they always have to recklessly barrel in and destroy everything? Couldn't they leave him alone just once?

"James Byrne?" a woman's voice asked.

"Yes?"

"Hello, I'm Susan Hendricks with the *San Diego Times*."

"I'm not interested in a subscription," he said, his thoughts continuing elsewhere. He gingerly pressed his fingers into his right side, confirming that it would hurt.

"I'm a reporter," she clarified.

"Oh."

"I wanted to talk with you about what happened in Hillcrest the other night and the disappearances of Matthew Foss and Timothy Clark."

"How did you get this number?"

"Mr. Byrne—or can I call you James?"

"Don't call me either. In fact, don't ever call me again," he said, then ended the call.

■ ■ ■

Enzo said nothing as the car continued north.

They were approaching Temecula on their way to Las Vegas, arrangements having already been made to return them to Chicago without having to bother with another commercial airport. He was in a bit of a mood, even if he should have been elated after the last few hours. Few things were as satisfying to him as torturing street vermin, especially a couple of punks who had attacked his brother, even if the stupid little shit was a faggot.

He glanced at Eddie, who was sitting quietly behind the wheel. It was perhaps their most gruesome outing yet, but there was no need to discuss it, and they would do it again if they had to. These scum could never forget what would happen to them if they crossed the Byrnes.

Those two lasted a little longer than he had expected, but that made it even better. With two at once, you could work on one while the other rested before another round. Enzo had learned that a person could only take so much before shock or death ended his amusement. No, it was better to pace himself and keep it going. It could have gone on even longer, but they were expected in Nevada within a certain window, so they had to cut the evening's festivities somewhat short and soak the two of them with gasoline, then set one of them on fire—so the other could watch what was about to happen to him.

36

Carlyle arrived on the scene a little before ten, having decided at his front door to take a quick shower and a change of clothes. He also had a drink to finish.

When he pulled up, the cast of characters had already assembled. Seegars was studying the two corpses from different angles. Patterson stood by the yellow tape demarking the boundaries of the crime scene, his face ashen. Carlyle could smell the vomit as he approached.

The two blackened bodies were stuck to the blue tarps they'd been disposed on, the stench of flesh and melted plastic becoming more pungent as Carlyle stood over them. He looked over the two, one face up, the other half-lying atop him face down, his left cheek resting on the other's chest.

"Tell me you have something," Carlyle said.

"Oh, like fibers or a nice bloody Bruno Magli shoeprint?" asked the lab guy, whose name Carlyle could never remember. "Don't I wish."

"No teeth, either," Seegars pointed out. "Looks like those fuckers took a hammer to their mouths."

"I hope for their sakes *after* they died," the lab guy said.

Carlyle snorted. "What a fucking mess."

Seegars jerked his head, and Carlyle turned around to face the captain. The two looked at each other.

"Can you and I speak privately?" Scott asked.

Carlyle nodded. "Of course," he answered, then followed his boss to about fifteen feet away.

"Why the fuck are you always two steps behind these pricks?" Scott asked without bothering with any small talk, not that Carlyle expected any. The captain was all business, all the time, which Carlyle respected even if he was on the short end of it now. "How the fuck can they roll into town and find these little bastards inside of a day when you two, and every other goddamn worthless person under you, can't seem to find your own dicks? Huh?"

"If I could have had the luxury of breaking someone like they did, perhaps I'd have found them first."

"Well, how the fuck did they find the first one?"

"I don't know."

"'I don't know' is not a fucking answer," Scott said. "It's the kind of shit my kids give me when I ask why they got a D on their goddamn report card. I didn't put you in charge of this for bullshit answers."

Carlyle nodded. "Okay."

"You got a goddamn leak or something?"

"What?"

"A leak," Scott repeated. "Is someone on your fucking team blabbing his fucking mouth?"

"Captain, with all due respect—"

"Oh, for fuck's sake," Scott interrupted. "That's the bullshit line I use with my boss. What the fuck is going on?"

"Captain, I'm working this thing directly. Right now, it's me, Seegars, and—" Carlyle motioned toward Patterson. "—the rookie over there who's been following me around like a lost puppy since you dumped him on me."

"He's a good detective."

"He's a fucking kid. He doesn't know anything. You put him on the team because of optics, not experience."

Scott's jaw tightened. "Careful."

Carlyle ran his hand through his hair. "Fuck. I have *no* idea how they tracked down the first one, but once they had him… we were never going to catch up."

"How about the other two kids?" Scott asked. "I've got a state senator's son missing and presumed dead with this."

"Captain… they sent professional hit men to track them down, torture, and kill them. I don't even know how long it's going to take to identify those bodies over there. We're chasing our tails here."

Scott glared at him. "I can't even begin to tell you how disappointed I am to hear that coming from you. Seegars—yeah, all day, every day. You? Never in a million years did I ever think you'd give me a line like that."

"Well, I'm sorry."

"Well, I don't accept it. Find those fucks. I don't care what it fucking takes. I want you to find them before I have to make this political. That won't end well for anyone."

TUESDAY

37

Sabrina set a mug of black coffee in front of Tommy as he mindlessly scrolled through the newsfeed on his iPad.

She had already dressed for the day in her blue scrubs, her new tennis shoes squeaking as she walked across the hardwood floor. He sat on one of the bar stools at the island, wearing black gym shorts and a bright red long-sleeved nylon T-shirt—his preferred uniform within the confines of their house, something he pulled on as soon as her alarm went off. It was all she could do to rescue them from the back of the chair where he tossed them before changing into a suit and tie and running them through the washer and dryer. Her one attempt at introducing additional colors was not well received. Her husband liked what he liked and that was that.

"Thanks, hon," Tommy said without looking up.

"Anything good?" she asked.

He pushed the iPad aside and looked up at her. "Same old shit. I don't even know why I bother."

"I saw something about city contracts under review, or something like that."

Tommy smiled. "Hmm. Interesting," he said, deflecting.

"Any more news on Jimmy?" she asked, knowing she was dancing close to the line between what she did and did not need to know.

"You haven't spoken to him?" he asked, surprised.

Sabrina shook her head. "A few texts to see how he was doing, but he… I thought I'd give him some space." She paused. "Why? Have *you* heard from him?"

"I know he's not particularly happy at the moment. He called Sam last night after the police paid him a visit."

She raised an eyebrow. "Why was that?"

He paused, regretting the slip in the unspoken protocol of silence that had defined a part of their relationship she had willingly, but begrudgingly, accepted. "Some of his friends are missing. He thinks we're involved somehow."

"Why would he think that?"

Tommy looked away. "I don't know," he said, though he knew she saw through the lie. "He's been through a lot. He's just not thinking straight."

"Do you want me to call him?"

"No." Tommy glanced at his watch to calculate the time difference. "This is one I need to make. You don't need to get caught in the middle."

Sabrina walked to the kitchen cabinets as Tommy turned his attention to the coffee before him. She grabbed a mug and poured her own cup. "Alex Mullens," she said quietly.

He looked up at her. "Huh?"

"Alex Mullens," she repeated a little more confidently.

Tommy frowned. "Joe's kid? What about him?"

"Send him to San Diego."

"Why?"

"To see Jimmy," Sabrina said. "To check in on him."

"*Why?*"

"You have your secrets, I have mine," she said, watching his initial bewilderment harden into something sharper. "And whatever is going through your mind right now, you will not act on it. Okay?"

He nodded. "Okay."

■ ■ ■

The nightmare had returned. He jerked upright, the physical pain of his attack fusing with the emotional—his heart seeming to seize as he gasped for breath.

James ran a hand through his damp hair to push it out of his face, wiping his hands on the sheets and begrudgingly climbing out of bed. His body ached as if he'd just been beaten all over again, and it was all he could do to hobble into the living room, where he immediately fell onto the couch, the cool leather a relief against his burning skin.

He reached up and yanked at the blanket draped across the back of the couch, clumsily pulling it over him as he closed his eyes once more. He felt several tears roll down his face, but he quickly wiped them away. No, he would not cry over any of this.

■ ■ ■

Alex traced the crack in the ceiling, as he did at times like these—a welcome distraction from the memories of last night.

This had been going on for six months—drinking at bars and sleeping with strangers, the mornings after an equal mix of shame and physical pain. What had once been a weekly effort to forget the past and escape the present had morphed into a pattern of self-destruction that he wasn't sure he could escape. Not that he was inclined to. Regularly numbing oneself to reality could make almost anything bearable.

Alex had never learned why—only that he was gone. Their late-night conversations about taking what they had out to California had been cut short by an abrupt departure, a changed phone number, and complete silence, and Alex realized that asking too many questions would only raise the suspicions he was paranoid enough to think were already brimming just below the surface. He had to leave it alone and move on, even if he found that all but impossible to do so.

Jimmy had now been away almost half as long as they had been together. Though they had known each other all their lives, what they had together only began the summer before Jimmy's senior year of high school, Alex having just returned from his one and only year at Notre Dame. The two had been celebrating Alex's 0.5 GPA from spring semester with a bottle of vodka as they watched TV and listened to music in the Byrne's pool house when that first touch, that first kiss between them occurred. He had been so nervous he couldn't remember who even initiated it.

It continued through that final year, and even though Jimmy had decided to head west for college, the two remained in constant contact through text and FaceTime. Alex had also taken more than a couple trips to visit, once cheering him on when he made his collegiate debut on the soccer field, and during the holidays the two were practically inseparable.

When last summer began they had picked up where they had left off as if those long months mostly apart had never been. Then came the Fourth of July party, when something transpired that tore Alex's world asunder. With no closure he was unwilling to let go, not now. He had convinced himself that they should be together, and short of a definitive sign that that would never happen, he would allow the dream to continue—even if he had to endure this version of hell to do so.

His phone buzzed on the nightstand. "Where the fuck are you?" his father demanded.

"Huh?" Alex asked.

"You got a hearing problem now?"

"Pop?"

"What the fuck are you doing?"

"Sleeping."

"Goddamn idiot," Joe muttered. "I'm sitting around with my thumb jammed up my ass while you play sleeping beauty? We got things to do."

Alex pulled the phone away from his ear long enough to see the time. "Oh, fuck!" he said, remembering that they'd made plans to grab breakfast before they went to work. "Sorry... on my way."

38

"What?" he grunted after a long pause.

"Jimmy?" Tommy asked reluctantly.

Tommy had arrived at his downtown office off South Wacker just under an hour earlier, though a few cups of coffee and some procrastination had staved off this task until now. He could count the number of times they had spoken in the past year on one hand with a finger or two to spare, and Sabrina rarely shared anything more than a superficial update on what Jimmy had been up to. That he was okay was what mattered, and Tommy knew she would have let him know if something had been amiss. But this was his call to make.

He leaned back in the leather chair behind the wood-paneled desk as he waited for his brother to pick up. This had been his father's office before he took over, and aside from changing out a few family photographs it remained as it had always been, the shelves behind him full of books his father had never touched. The expansive corner room advertised the persona of a powerful man in control of his empire. Since Ciaran had conducted most of his business in a few restaurants and back offices in Wrigleyville, this was a theatrical space his father used only for their more powerful friends downtown. For him, though, it had become something else entirely.

"Yeah, Tommy?"

"How you doing?"

James sighed. "I'm okay."

Tommy found himself at a loss, suddenly regretting not letting Sabrina talk him into making the call. "What's going on out there?"

Silence. "I think you know."

Tommy nodded. "Yeah, I just wanted to check in on you, see how you were doing."

"You said they would never hurt me again."

"I know I did," he said, his regret sincere. He would never forget that promise, not after all Jimmy had been through. "I didn't know. I just—I didn't."

"Two of my friends are missing."

"I heard."

"You know what happened to them, don't you?"

"No, I don't," Tommy said. "None of us do."

"Enzo knows."

"Jimmy, they probably just... they'll turn up. Okay?"

"No, they won't." James paused, needing his brother to say something, but knowing he wouldn't. It would have been hard enough to discuss face to face. Even if Tommy wanted to say something, he could never, would never, do so over the phone. "Look... I got to go."

"Jimmy—"

But the line was already dead.

■ ■ ■

"Hello?" Alex asked, dropping back a few steps as he and his father made their way down Halstead.

The irony of conducting some of their business in Boystown was not lost on him as they wandered between bars, none of which he could ever enter as a patron. The family had interests in a number of them, Ciaran and then Tommy having leveraged their alcohol distribution network into the retail side, both of which served an even more lucrative laundering operation the family offered to those with dirty money to legitimize. "The gays," as Ciaran called them, knew how to drink, and business was business no matter who was handing over the money.

THE NAME OF THE GAME   167

His father, who had never heard an ethnic or racial joke he didn't repeat incessantly, surprisingly had never said a disparaging word in all the times they had made their rounds here. On the contrary, he seemed to get along with the men they did business with, and they in turn appeared to like him as best they could under the circumstances. Not that Alex was tempted to test the limits of his father's tolerance.

"This is Sam," said the voice on the phone. "I need you to come by the downtown office in about two hours. We need to talk."

"Sure, sure," Alex answered, immediately wondering what it was about. He and Sam had spoken in passing on a few occasions, but only because he had been with his father at the time. "I'm out with my pop right now, but we should be done here soon."

"Just tell him I told you to be here."

"Okay."

"See you then," Sam said, then ended the call.

■ ■ ■

"So, how's our investigation going?" Seegars asked, carrying two coffees as he walked into the room.

Carlyle took the one offered to him as he scowled at the question. At least his partner had come in on time, and two days in a row at that. The captain's loud rebuke of their investigation must have motivated this most recent, albeit rare, gesture toward professionalism.

"Well, I managed to solve the Hillcrest beatings case," Carlyle said, running his hand through his hair.

"Great job. Congratulations."

"Fuck you too."

"You solved your big case. What's the problem?"

"You and I now have the—"

"No… no, no, no, no, no," Seegars said as he shook his head. "We don't do missing people."

"We do now."

"Give it to the kid."

Carlyle took a file folder off the desk and tossed it at Seegars. "Scott told me this morning that everything remotely connected to these beatings is ours."

"Well, fuck Scott."

"I'll let him know the offer's on the table."

"You spoken to your girlfriend lately?" Seegars asked. "Is she still being a busy little lesbian? Maybe that eager beaver could solve it for us."

Carlyle shook his head. "I wish. She left me a voicemail asking for an update, which means she doesn't have one of her own, but I'm not inclined to entertain her at the moment." He pointed at the folder between them. "Now back to our case."

39

Despite his asking her not to, Sue had made several more attempts to contact James Byrne. He hadn't answered, but she wouldn't give up just yet. A good reporter, she kept telling herself, never would.

Since the beatings began six weeks ago, she had talked to most of the victims' families and had amassed volumes of background information. Still, she had very little on James Byrne other than what she knew about the family, and her first self-imposed deadline for an article about the victims and the aftermath of the violence was approaching fast. Even with the outstanding issue of Matthew Foss and Timothy Clark's disappearance, the case was now all but solved, and the public would no doubt be ready to move on to the next big thing.

Sue still needed to speak with Carlyle, though she suspected he had nothing to barter with, and probably assumed she was as starved for info as he was. And she suspected he was still a little pissed that she beat him to Matthew Foss and Timothy Clark's apartment by a day, although that certainly wasn't her fault. She heard through her sources that he had ordered a second round of interviews even though the criminals had been identified and, in a manner of speaking, punished already. Probably, she surmised, it was simple petulance toward the witnesses for not disclosing more the first time around.

She was pleasantly surprised that he had been so forthcoming about what he had discovered at the Foss/Clark apartment. It was certainly the biggest scoop of her short career in investigative journalism, one that gave her far more credibility with those in the office who thought she'd been assigned the story more for her sexual orientation than for her skills as a reporter. Now that she'd shown those assholes she *was* competent, the next step was to prove that she was better at this job than anyone.

She also had something to prove to the Byrnes. She had yet to figure out how to do so, but they needed to pay for their crimes. The vigilantism she could almost excuse, save for the barbarity of how they extracted their revenge, but Foss and Clark were unforgivable. She knew they had been killed for their sexual orientation and friendship with James Byrne, and she would never let that rest until she exposed them for the evil homophobes they were.

She hadn't forgotten Charles's warning not to push too far. They were extremely dangerous—their recent body count alone proved that—but she couldn't help but feel secure in her position as a member of the press. Coming after her would certainly create a whirlwind of public attention, something that the Byrnes had to be desperate to avoid after all the murders they'd committed in the past few days. This was a vulnerable time for them, and a time for her to push ahead, and push hard.

■ ■ ■

"Nice office," Alex commented as he entered the room, Sam directly behind him.

The two had just met in the reception area one floor below, then silently walked up the curved staircase to the executive offices and then down the hall to their ultimate destination. This was, Alex had been told, where everything "on the books" was managed—just a front in Ciaran Byrne's time, but with Tommy's ascendency, it crackled with real energy now as people bustled about their work. Going legit, as his father termed it, seemed to be good for business.

Tommy was at his desk on the far side of the room staring intently at the large flat-screen monitor to his right. He grinned slightly as his eyes met Alex's, probably just an automatic gesture to put an underling at ease. He stood and extended his hand across the desk as Alex approached. "Thanks for coming. Can I get you anything?"

Alex could have used a drink to calm his nerves, but he shook his head. "I'm good, thanks."

Tommy motioned to one of twin leather chairs facing him. "Have a seat," he ordered as he sat back down. Alex glanced behind him to find Sam, who was sitting in a chair in the corner between a window and the now-closed door. Sam, as he always did on those occasions when Alex crossed his path, watched what was transpiring before him without expression.

Tommy briefly adjusted his tie. "How's it going?" he asked.

Alex was leaning forward, elbows on the armrests, fingers interlocked. "Good, good."

"I didn't pull you out of anything, did I?"

"Not really, sir. My father and I were down on Halstead."

"I thought you were babysitting one of my wayward New York cousins."

"I am… I mean, he's usually with me, but not today."

"Good that you and your father get to spend some time together then. How's your mom? I hadn't seen her in a month or two."

"She's all right," Alex said. "Same old, same old."

"Well good," Tommy said. "Glad to hear everything is fine."

Alex nodded, his fingers still clasped together, his right foot thrumming ever so slightly under his seat. "So, what's going on? How can I help you?"

"If my memory serves me correctly," Tommy began, "you and my brother Jimmy were somewhat… close over the last couple of years." His brief wince was noticeable.

"We were friends, yeah," Alex said as casually as he could.

"Good friends?" Tommy pressed.

Alex paused. "Yeah, I guess."

"You guess?"

Alex shifted in his chair. "No disrespect, but you got something to say?"

Tommy grinned. He had probably pushed their conversation a bit too far, but when he glanced at Sam to gauge a reaction, there was no recognition in the man's eyes. The passing innuendo had remained between himself and the kid. "Alex, I need you to do me a favor."

"Okay."

"You know Jimmy's out in California right now, don't you?"

"Yes, sir."

"I want you to go out there for a week or two and keep an eye on him for me. For my family."

"Yeah?"

"Yeah," Tommy said.

"What for, if you don't mind me asking?"

"You heard about what happened," Tommy said, and Alex nodded. "That issue has been resolved, but he could probably use a good friend right about now."

"Sure, absolutely," Alex said. "When do you want me to leave?"

Tommy stood, and Alex did the same. "Sam has those details," Tommy said, extending his hand once more. "Thanks for this. I appreciate it."

40

"How was lunch?" Isabella asked.

Moretti lingered in the doorway to Ciaran's home office for a moment before closing the door behind him. Even if his future was inexorably linked to hers, he couldn't help but feel unsettled by seeing her behind that desk.

It hadn't always been like this. Tommy's moves toward transforming the businesses had once seemingly been blessed by both parents, though Moretti had always been wary of releasing their grasp on the reins of power even slightly, fearing it to be a display of weakness that others would attempt to exploit. Only when it became clear how thoroughly Tommy intended to remake the empire once Ciaran relinquished full control did Isabella adopt those concerns. She said very little to Ciaran about her newfound misgivings, but when she was alone with Moretti, she rarely held back.

"It was fine," he answered as he seated himself across the desk. "I just walked him upstairs to his sitting room. He said he wanted to nap." He nodded toward the paperwork spread before her. "What's all that?"

She raised an eyebrow. "I'm seeing what my son is up to with his latest projects. Did he even bother to show up today?"

Moretti shook his head. "No. He and Sam were in a meeting downtown. He was coming in later."

"Couldn't bother to meet his own father for lunch, could he?"

"I guess not."

"What is the word down there?"

"I believe they'll fall into line."

"You hope so."

"I know so," Moretti said, a little too quickly.

She looked at him warily. "They're Irish. They have an innate issue with authority. Don't count on that." He remained silent. "When does Michael arrive tomorrow?"

"Early afternoon. He's bringing the other two with him."

"Anything else out of San Diego?"

"No," he answered, unwilling to tell her about Jimmy—or the detective.

"How do you think Tommy will react to his cousin's arrival?"

"I think it might unnerve him a bit. He might start to get a little suspicious, so we'll need to make sure Ciaran can speak convincingly to the upside if and when Tommy goes running to him."

"You leave that to me," Isabella said before returning to her papers.

■ ■ ■

Joe Mullens slid into the wooden booth, the boards creaking under his weight as he positioned himself in the center to directly face Tommy.

Giancarlo's Pizza had been a family meeting spot for years, the décor unchanged from when it had opened in the middle of the prior century, the menu begrudgingly updated only a few times to reflect society's changing palate. Pineapple and tofu would never be welcome, but low-carb beer could be tolerated.

The two sat in the back booth along the wall of the L-shaped dining area. Tommy, who had shed his tie before leaving downtown, was facing the front of the restaurant. Sam had seated himself at a table between them and the front door. He was already nursing a beer, and, without asking, the waitress brought one for Joe right after he sat down. Mr. Mullens, everyone knew, expected his Old Style within a minute. He was never disappointed.

"Thanks for coming," Tommy said as Joe gulped down half his beer.

"Good to see you," Joe bellowed, piercing the quiet of the afternoon lull between lunch and dinner. "I was getting tired of looking at Sam's ugly mug anyway."

Big Joe was a tree of a man who had been well on his way to seven feet had puberty not ended when it did. Practically as wide as he was tall, he lumbered somewhat gingerly, slightly hunched over, as if his knees would buckle from all the weight they supported. He was always impeccably dressed in a somewhat dated style, in a custom suit with a tie and matching handkerchief.

He had joined the family in his late teens as a runner. His father had been a shop steward in an electricians' union controlled by Liam Sr., where in high school Joe had sporadically worked at an apprenticeship he never fully appreciated. As Ciaran took over Joe had caught the eye of one of the family's associates, and much to his father's consternation the young man soon began working directly for the Byrnes.

Joe's rise to his current position had been swift, Ciaran being a man who appreciated talent and rewarded it handsomely. What had started with a few dive bars and a minor poker night with three men under him had morphed into controlling or collecting from dozens of establishments and by far the largest of the family's crews, and once they controlled all of the alcohol distribution on the North Side, Joe had cemented his place as both top earner and close confidant to Ciaran and Moretti. The family rarely ventured down a path without Joe's nod of approval.

And it had been Joe's embrace that had sealed Tommy's seamless ascent to power last year. There had been grumbling among the captains about what would happen once Tommy had free rein to remake the family. It wasn't so much a question of whether the change would be supported—they, or their replacements, would fall in line eventually—but there was real concern over whose status might be downgraded by the new regime. Joe throwing his considerable weight behind the next generation of Byrne leadership quickly dissipated any nascent discord within the organization.

Tommy let out an audible sigh. "Something I've got to tell you. I'm borrowing Alex for a few days."

"Sure… sure," Joe said without hesitation. "Whatever you need."

"I'm sure you heard what happened out in California with Jimmy."

Joe slammed a balled fist down on the table. "Of all the fucking stupidity, going after a Byrne."

"I don't think they'll be hurting anyone else," Tommy said, "but Jimmy… he's not in a good place right now. I know him and Alex were close once."

Joe looked over Tommy's shoulder as he fiddled with his perfectly knotted tie. "Yeah," he said as their eyes met once more. "Yeah, they hung out for a bit. I think it's been a while though."

"Yeah, I think it has been, but… I think he needs someone out there that's family… that he can relate to."

Joe looked suddenly resigned to something he would rather not have faced. "Yeah, I'm sure it'll be fine. Those two can… you know… catch up and all."

Tommy nodded. The waitress soon brought over Joe's second beer, and Tommy ordered another for himself. As they waited, they engaged in light banter, Jimmy and Alex, and their unspoken bond, now in the past.

"How's business?" Tommy asked once his beer had been delivered and their empty glasses removed. They still had a few more minutes before the first of their associates arrived and the real work between the men began.

"No complaints," Joe said. "The men are happy. Things are quiet. People are behaving."

"Good," Tommy said. "Good."

"When can I send that cousin of yours back to New York?"

"What? You don't like him?"

"No offense, but the kid is a complete fucking dipshit."

Tommy laughed. "Yeah, he is a dipshit," he agreed. "I'll get him out of your hair here soon."

Joe paused.

"Something on your mind?" Tommy asked.

"No, not really. It's good to see you up here, I guess." He pointed his thumb over his shoulder at Sam. "You're always sending this ugly one. It's good to see you around."

"I try to get up here when I can."

"With all due respect, it'd be good to have you up here a bit more. It keeps people… you know… they like the attention."

Tommy nodded. "I heard you had other visitors today."

"Yeah, your pop came by… him and Moretti."

"They invited me, but I figured I'd let them have their fun."

"Your pop seemed pleased to be out," Joe said. "He asked about how business was. I told him it was good."

"I won't ask what Moretti said."

Joe roared with laughter. "That prick? He just sat there. He's old school. If there isn't the thrill of getting caught he isn't happy about it."

"That's my father's man, all right."

"He likes to complain, that's for sure. 'Why do we need all this?' he would bitch."

"I think it's all the man has," Tommy said, a sadness in his voice. "This life is it for him, and we're slowly yanking it out from under him."

"No, I get it to a point, I do, but I've told him more than once, 'Ever heard of Capone and tax evasion, you dumb fuck?'"

Tommy laughed as Joe reached across the table and grabbed his hand. "Watch that slippery guinea," Joe warned in a low undertone that died before it could carry beyond the booth.

Tommy frowned. "Why you say that?"

"Just a hunch. I don't think he's ready to let go of the old days just yet."

41

With the sun setting between the office towers, Tommy walked among a sea of tourists and professionals as he made his way down Michigan Avenue toward home.

Sam was consistently dismayed by his boss's insistence on walking to his apartment on the Gold Coast. Tommy would have none of it, rarely thinking of his personal safety, the family's boundaries and interests well established and respected. No one in the family had been targeted in many years, and the mile-long walk cleared his head, especially after the string of meetings he had just completed. Beginning with Joe Mullens and their silent agreement not to discuss the relationship between the younger men under them, and ending hours later with a city alderman angling for support with a zoning variance, the day had taken its toll. Tommy's legs ached from being parked in that booth for the better part of an afternoon. He needed to move about for a while.

Not that he was complaining about his day. With the exception of that first meeting, it allowed him the momentary luxury of setting the past few days aside. He found peace in the routine he often failed to fully appreciate until events like those in San Diego reminded him of all the brutal ugliness bubbling underneath the surface.

As he wended through tourists milling on the sidewalk in front of one of the street's vertical malls, he spotted a father and his teenage son coming toward him, the older man constantly scanning their surroundings as the boy carelessly walked beside him. *You said they would never hurt me again* rang once more in his head, that broken promise now threatening to damage the last close relationship he had with his family.

Tommy was barely twelve when Enzo initiated the rivalry that would define them both. Tired of living in the shadow of the heir apparent, his younger brother had instinctively seized an opportunity that cemented his future role as the force behind the family and its concerns.

Tommy hadn't known how old the man was, though the gray hair and lines only age could award suggested the poor bastard was well into his seventies. He had been strapped down to a chair by his wrists, chest, and ankles, and his elegant suit had been torn and rumpled during the beating that had put him there.

Tommy, Enzo, and their father had arrived at the warehouse only moments before. The last car to arrive was the beaten man's Bentley, which was driven by Joe Mullens. Tommy had never seen anything like it, a bright-red car with a large grill that screamed for the attention its owner demanded.

"You think I wouldn't find out?" Ciaran yelled as Tommy and Enzo stood off to the side, spectators in their father's arena. "You come to my fucking house, meet with my fucking wife, and you think I would miss that? You think I'm that fucking stupid?"

The man didn't answer, his head bowed, his hair disheveled and matted with blood. Ciaran held a metal baseball bat in his hand, but it had yet to be used. The old man's torture had been performed with fists, knives, and a small billy club. The weapon his father held, Tommy knew, would be for the grand finale that would finally put him out of his misery.

"You don't have anything to say?" Ciaran continued. "Huh? Nothing?" Still no movement from the man, who hadn't spoken since they had arrived. His defiance had been removed easily enough, but with the exception of crying out on a couple of occasions, he had remained all but silent. The man only looked toward Tommy and Enzo once, quickly flashing a gentle smile before the impassivity returned.

Ciaran frowned, appearing deep in thought. He flipped the bat in his hand, holding it by the barrel and extending the handle toward Tommy.

"Finish him," he ordered.

Tommy couldn't move.

"Tommy, this is yours."

"I'll do it," Enzo offered.

"Tommy—"

"I… I can't," Tommy said, his voice barely above a whisper.

"Goddamn it, son," Ciaran bellowed as he shook the bat handle. He tapped it against Tommy's chest to reinforce his command. "Do it."

"I'll do it," Enzo repeated.

Ciaran looked at Enzo, who was almost jumping out of his skin in anticipation, before looking back at his eldest. "Fine," he said as he handed Enzo the bat.

The younger boy, smiling broadly, took it in both hands and walked behind the man. He raised the bat as he sized up his target, taking one practice swing before twisting from his heels with a blow that rang with metal and broken bone.

"Good evening, Mr. Byrne," said the doorman at the entrance to Tommy's building.

Tommy blinked his eyes a few times to clear the image and forced a smile. "Good evening, Eduardo," he responded before passing through the doorway and into the lobby.

"Have a good evening, Mr. Byrne."

"You too," he said without looking back.

WEDNESDAY

42

"Enzo, come on… enough," Jimmy pleaded after absorbing another punch to the temple, Enzo's boxing gloves scarcely muting the impact of the blow.

"You've had enough when I say you've had enough," Enzo answered as he slammed his fists together. He swung once more, barely missing Jimmy's jaw as the younger man leaned back. "See, you're getting the hang of it."

"I hate this."

"Because you're a goddamn pussy, that's why."

The two had been sparring for the better part of an hour, the downstairs den empty save the two combatants at its center. To create their makeshift boxing ring, Enzo only had to shove the square cherry-stained coffee table—normally positioned between the broken-in leather couch and the flat-screen television bolted to the wall—toward the battered pool table at the far side of the room.

Enzo found himself irritated with his father's directive to wear gloves, the unfortunate result of an overzealous bout during Christmas break that left the youngest Byrne slightly more marked up than usual. Their mother, as always, had never flinched, but Ciaran rolled his eyes and warned Enzo not to make it a habit. With a house full of guests upstairs this evening he would comply, but next week, when it was only the two of them, Enzo would have his way. His responsibilities to the family had cut into their time together over the past few years, and with Jimmy leaving for college in a month, Enzo needed to get in what he could while the opportunity still existed.

He despised softness. He thought Tommy spineless, and had for some time. Ever since his elder brother flinched from putting that pathetic old man out of his misery, Enzo could never view him with the admiration he once felt. Tommy was sentimental and weak in a position that demanded ruthless brutality. The prince in his penthouse along the Chicago River who concerned himself more with how many stars his worthless restaurants were receiving than their true endeavors could never be the man their father was, and Enzo knew instinctively that the family and its interests would never survive with Tommy at the head of the table.

Enzo thought once more of the old man tied to the chair in the warehouse. He would always cherish the memory, the day when he awoke to his true calling. And now, looking at his brother, he felt the same clarity. The skill that his father and others displayed—the careful balance of pain that kept a man awake and aware—were inspiring. He had to push down his own excitement to study how they exacted the suffering he desperately wanted to inflict, observing and mimicking in the air as they utilized the simplest of tools to bring forth the most agony.

Even now, a basic four-and-a-half-inch high-carbon steel utility knife was what he favored. He liked cutting people. The dozen or so scars on his body—short, shallow, deliberate—were experiments, nothing more. His victims, without exception, feared knives. The looks of terror, the tears, the pleas for mercy... none ever answered. Of that he was incapable. Then came the screams.

They found themselves opposite him for any number of reasons: information, to send a message, or simple retribution. From time to time, they were permitted to live, if he had been ordered to spare them, though even those survivors were left scarred for life in both body and mind.

He delivered another blow to Jimmy's chest, his brother's trembling gloves halfheartedly attempting to block the successive punches beyond pitiful. How the two could even be related, Enzo would never know. His attempts to toughen him up, to make him the man he could be with the right guidance, had up until now failed, and miserably. Jimmy was hopeless, destined for failure in this world that their father and grandfather had built.

Enzo swung again, knocking Jimmy back a few steps with a blow to the elbow. "I saw you staring at Alex Mullens," Enzo remarked. He had always assumed their closeness came from growing up together, but it was hard not to see how peculiar the two had become around each other. The passing facial tic of Jimmy's eye seemed to confirm it.

"Fuck off," Jimmy said, his composure regained.

"You blowing him or what?" Enzo asked as he launched another salvo, battering Jimmy's ribs with both hands.

"Fuck off," Jimmy repeated, his voice ragged.

Enzo pointed a glove at him. "You're a fag, aren't you?"

"I said fuck off."

"Answer the goddamn question!"

"No! And fuck you!"

Enzo glared. "You're a goddamn liar," he said, almost in a whisper, then grabbed Jimmy by the neck, shoving him backward until they slammed into the wall, Jimmy's head breaking the smooth surface of the sheetrock, blood staining the light-yellow paint.

Then steadily, methodically, Enzo battered his brother with punches to the ribs, and then to the face when his brother dropped his arms. This would not go unanswered. He would not have a fag for a brother.

Jimmy's legs gave out, and Enzo grabbed him by the neck again, hurling him to the floor. "You're a fucking pussy and a fucking faggot," Enzo barked, delivering a kick to Jimmy's stomach that left him coughing and gasping for air. "You are a goddamn…"

He took off his gloves, hurling them across the room, then walked to the pool table and picked up a cue stick. He struck Jimmy with it again and again, the teenager crying out with each hit. "Take it like a goddamn man," Enzo ordered, swinging the cue so hard that it snapped in two.

"Enzo, please," Jimmy begged, tears running down his face.

"Please what?"

"Please stop."

"Are you a little faggot?" Enzo asked, hitting him in the back of head with the bumper end of the broken stick. "You a little faggot who wants Alex to fuck him? Huh?"

"No!"

"You *are* a little faggot, and I'll show you what faggots like." He crouched down, forcing Jimmy onto his stomach with his knee. He then climbed on top of his younger brother, wrapping his left arm around Jimmy's neck and tightening his grip to near strangulation.

"You scream, you little bitch, and I swear to God... I will break your fucking neck. And if you say a goddamn word about this, I will kill you, and I will kill your fucking boyfriend."

As James wept, Enzo slid the stick under the younger Byrne's gym shorts and underwear. He squeezed Jimmy's neck a little tighter. "Here you go, faggot. Here's Alex coming to fuck you."

Eddie snapped his fingers in Enzo's face, dragging him out of the memory. "Yo, Enzo—you want a fucking drink or what?"

Enzo looked around the confines of the small private jet, Eddie sitting opposite him, his cousin Michael poring over some documents at a table toward the back of the plane. "Huh?"

Eddie pointed at the flight attendant, who stood patiently, his hands clasped together in front of him. "A drink. You want one?"

Enzo sneered at him. Another fag giving him the eye. "No. Fuck off," he said before turning to look out the window.

43

Tommy reclined his seat as the Gulfstream lifted off from Chicago Executive Airport. Across the narrow aisle, Sam idly flipped through a magazine.

His head still ached from last night's indulgence—a bottle of Barolo keeping him company as he sat alone in the dark and considered Jimmy and everything that had befallen him over the past year. Having endured two horrific attacks, Tommy doubted that a phone call to check up on him would suffice. It was probably the wine talking when he called Sam and proposed the flight to San Diego, but they were en route, nonetheless.

He pictured Sabrina standing over him earlier this morning, a glass of water in one hand and a fistful of pills in the other. She was his only true friend, a thought that often crossed his mind at times like these. Outside his immediate family no one ever really told him no, never tried to dissuade him from anything he decided to do. If Tommy wanted it, Tommy got it, his life lacking all the normal boundaries of friendships, the give and take that made people human.

Sam had once been something to a real friend, but that ended when the boys became young men, as playmate transitioned into right-hand man. Though they still shared a sense of camaraderie, it was always tempered by the business relationship that sat foremost in both men's minds. His father had warned of the loneliness of being king, but it wasn't until Tommy took power that he finally and fully grasped what that meant.

There was one other person who would tell him no, though he would hardly call her a friend. Alongside Moretti, his mother had almost overnight become viscerally opposed to his plans and could barely hide her contempt for his new endeavors if any came up in conversation.

She had yet to overtly undermine his efforts, but he suspected that she would make her move soon enough. She was adamant that going legitimate invited weakness and tempted others with a steelier resolve to want to take that power for themselves. All the towers and restaurants in the city would be for nothing once Tommy found himself under another's thumb as others were now under his.

"Fuck," he muttered to himself.

"Huh?" Sam asked as he looked over the top of his magazine.

Tommy shook his head. "Nothing. Tell me about this pain-in-the-ass detective in San Diego."

"He's asking a lot of questions."

"Where?"

"Chicago. The Bureau," Sam answered. "Our friends downtown said it would get lost in the bureaucracy."

"And our friend in DC?"

"He said they'll play dumb, but it needs to go away. Our arrangement only buys so much leeway. And I'm not sure the detective is ready to give this up."

"I'm sure he'll go a couple more rounds," Tommy said. "As long as he keeps getting the brick wall we should be good."

"He also pinged Vegas apparently."

"Oh, fuck."

Sam nodded. "Yeah… that will be an issue."

"A dead cop does not make this go away."

"Not with their plans for down there. Your uncle is going to want to break them in sooner rather than later."

"Sounds like we have a detour then," Tommy said, looking out the window at the clouds below.

■ ■ ■

Paul Anderson had been an avid scuba diver since he was in his early twenties, an addiction he had no intention of ever giving up.

He and his son Clay had only been diving together for the last year or so; his wife worried about her baby's safety, never mind her husband's. But the boy had kept insisting, so after some heavy persuasion and a set of large diamond earrings, Clay got lessons and the two had been going out practically every week since.

This was Clay's third trip to the HMS *Yukon*, his father's twentieth. The 366-foot Canadian destroyer rested in about 105 feet of water off Mission Beach in the northern area of what San Diego-area divers called Wreck Alley. It had been intentionally sunk in July 2000 by the San Diego Oceans Foundation as part of an artificial reef project, and had been prepared for divers with a number of entry and exit holes to increase both accessibility and diver safety.

Despite having been there twice before, Paul was still a little hesitant about taking Clay to the *Yukon*. It was part of a three-dive package that included the former Coast Guard Cutter *Ruby E* and finally a dive in the kelp beds off Point Loma. The *Yukon* lay on her port side and could be a little disorienting to inexperienced divers. And Clay, like many teenagers, had very little fear of death, and Paul constantly had to remind him of the potential for disaster when it wasn't taken seriously.

After taking a local charter, they and eight other divers began their descent. Clay always preferred to quickly dump the air out of his BC and sink as quickly as possible, but with the potential for strong currents and low visibility, Paul insisted that his son descend slowly, and to use the chain between the buoy and the bow of the ship to guide himself down. They could both feel the thermoclines—changes in the water temperature brought about by increasing depth—as they descended deeper, and as their dive watches read forty feet they could see the ship, the visibility surprisingly good enough that they could just make out the bridge.

They were approaching the forward guns—which were actually replicas—when they came upon what looked like two bundles of plastic, each about six feet long, resting on the sandy bottom. Both were secured with ropes and attached to several concrete cinderblocks.

Paul looked over at his son, who immediately pointed down to where they lay, a gleam in his eyes which always portended trouble. It certainly couldn't hurt to have a closer look.

44

Carlyle entered the bar, standing in the entryway until his eyes adjusted to the dim lighting.

It was strangely empty—the sole occupant, other than the bartender, a thirty-something man in a tailored suit, seated midway down the long row of well-worn stools. His forearms rested on the bar, his right fingers surrounding a rocks glass with a half inch of bourbon puddled in the bottom.

Less than a half hour earlier, Seegars had greeted Carlyle as the latter stepped off the Harbor Police patrol boat onto the dock, walking over and having to lean in to relay the news over the commotion around them.

Carlyle furrowed his brows. "You're shitting me, right?"

"I wish," Seegars answered. "Want me to tag along?"

Carlyle now slowly made his way over, the man never turning to look as the detective approached and stopped two stools away. He could see the family resemblance between the two brothers. "Mind if I sit down?"

"Please," the man answered, lifting his glass.

The bartender started to walk over but Carlyle waved him off. "I was wondering if we'd get to meet."

The man finished off his drink and nodded to the still attentive bartender, who hurried over and refilled the glass. He turned to Carlyle. "I thought this would be a good place to do so."

"You seem to know a lot about me if you picked it."

"I know enough."

"I take it I have you to thank for our privacy?"

"I thought it'd be better this way."

Carlyle nodded. "I assume that's Sam Dorgan parked out front?"

"Speaking of knowing a lot about someone."

"I'm familiar enough with the top end of the org chart," Carlyle said. "What are you doing in San Diego?"

"Visiting my brother."

"Of course," Carlyle remarked. He paused as he watched the younger man. There was something in the pose, in his tone, that compelled him to reconsider his approach. "You're something of a reluctant don, aren't you?"

"Excuse me?" Tommy asked.

"Your father would have never arranged something like this. He would have just had me killed for the insolence of harassing his youngest son."

"That wasn't very bright of you."

"It got your attention. That was the point."

"What?" Tommy asked. "That you're going to try to come after my family?"

"Yes," Carlyle said. "I am. But still... at least we're having a conversation about it."

"Times change."

"Based on the overtime they're putting in at the county morgue, not all that much."

"Mistakes happen."

"Mr. Byrne. With all due respect, what are we doing here? You want to look me in the eye or something?"

"I want to talk."

"About?"

"Coming to an understanding."

"About?" Carlyle repeated.

"Putting this behind us."

Carlyle scoffed. "I'll make it simple for you. Give me the men who killed those people and we can very much put this behind us."

"You know I can't do that."

"Then you're wasting my time. This isn't Chicago, and I don't take bribes."

"I wasn't offering one," Tommy said. "I came here to warn you."

"So, now we get to the heart of the matter."

Tommy shook his head. "I'm not threatening you. You can make all your information requests with the city of Chicago. Hell, you can even keep calling the FBI if you're naïve enough to think it'll do you any good."

"You know I can't comment on an ongoing investigation," Carlyle answered, permitting a tinge of sarcasm to seep into his tone.

"If I were you, though… I would not call Las Vegas again."

"And why is that?"

"I may not be my father, but my uncle very much is. I would dare say doubly so when it comes to matters such as this. This is his territory—"

"This is *my* town, not his."

Tommy put up a hand. "He will do whatever it takes to keep things running smoothly. Be very careful before you poke that bear, because I can't control him."

Carlyle reached into his jacket and tossed an evidence bag onto the bar between them. Tommy studied it a moment, then picked it up. "What's this?"

"OxyContin, Percocet, and Vicodin, according to the lab."

"And?"

"They found it on your brother when they brought him into the hospital."

Tommy felt his face turn pale as he nodded slightly.

"I've heard an ugly rumor about how the Byrnes… 'address' those who deal in these sorts of things. I'm curious… does that extend to family?"

"I wouldn't worry about it."

"Perhaps I will," Carlyle countered. "You see, Mr. Byrne, I'm going to get my scalp one way or the other. Either you give me whoever caused this mayhem or I'm going to push a felony drug distribution charge on your brother—and I'll make sure he gets plenty of face time on the local news so everyone back in Chicago—*and* Las Vegas—knows what he's been up to. He may *want* to go to jail after that, although I don't think he'd do too well in there. A little too young and pretty for his own good."

Tommy scowled as he pictured his brother, dazed and bloodied as he lay on the couch in his parents' basement. "You son of a bitch."

"Not usually, but when I'm forced to spend my morning on a boat off Mission Beach because a couple of locals found two bodies on the bottom of the ocean, it tends to put me in a bit of a mood. And you know who was down there? Your brother's missing friends, one of whom happened to be the only son of a state senator up in Sacramento. Are you getting a picture of the shit I'm swimming in right now? Do you really think I'm in the mood to let your family slither out of here unscathed?"

Carlyle took back the evidence bag and returned it to his jacket pocket. "It's time for you to sack up and deal with this. I don't really give a shit who you decide to throw overboard, but I will get my way. You understand?"

"You threatening my family?"

Carlyle smiled. "Maybe you are a bit like your father."

Tommy said nothing.

"You know where to find me if you decide to send your friends back out," Carlyle said. "Someone has to clean up this mess, and I don't think you're up to the task." He stood up. "Now if you'll excuse me, I have work to do."

■ ■ ■

Sam was mid-text when the detective stepped out of the bar. Dropping his phone into the cup holder, he watched as Carlyle got into the passenger seat of the Jeep Grand Cherokee before it pulled away from the curb.

Tommy came out moments later, and after glancing for traffic, walked toward him. Sam already knew what the look on his boss's face meant. It took a few moments after Tommy sat down beside him before he would even look over.

"And?" Sam asked as their eyes met.

Tommy shook his head. "Not good. He's got me by the balls."

"How so?"

"Jimmy's been dealing scripts. He was carrying a whole fucking pharmacy when they found him. I want to know who his dealer is."

Sam nodded. "I'll take care of it. We can't bend this guy?"

Tommy snorted. "No, not this one. Brute force can't fix this."

"What's he so pissed off about?"

"Enzo fucked us. He killed a state senator's son, some innocent kid, and they just found the body."

"Fuck me," Sam muttered. He paused a moment. "I got something to tell you… and you're not going to like it."

"What could possibly make this day any fucking worse?"

"Your cousin Michael. He's in Chicago."

45

"I'm sorry my son couldn't see fit to join us this evening," Isabella said.

She was seated at one end of the table, which could accommodate ten, with Ciaran at the other. To her left was Enzo and then Moretti, Michael to her right. At her request, an empty chair and place setting rested between Michael and Ciaran—a subtle gesture to the others of the slight she felt at Tommy's absence.

She had told Moretti to invite Tommy, who hadn't bothered to even answer the call. Isabella had wanted almost desperately to have him here, to see the look on his face when he saw Michael, the beautiful comeuppance to the arrogance he had displayed this past year. She would have to wait, but she would see it soon enough.

"I heard just before dinner," Michael announced as he looked around the table. "Tommy was in San Diego today."

He could see from their reactions that none of them had known beforehand. Ciaran was, as his father had told him, not altogether there, so the old man simply nodded in acknowledgement before returning to his meal. The advisor across the table seemed momentarily surprised but masked it well. Conrad Moretti, Michael had been advised, was a man to keep close—if only to watch his actions carefully. A man with his own agenda, and though he had always acted with the family's interests at heart, Michael suspected that Moretti's own would rule the day should push come to shove.

And then there was his aunt with her pursed lips, whom his father had no illusions of controlling. There would be no need to—at least not immediately—as she and Liam were of like minds about how Chicago should be run. It was only a matter of getting their foot in the door and waiting her out. The only remaining issue would be Tommy, but unfortunate accidents happened with enough regularity. Their partners in New York, who had always viewed the friction between the two sides of the family as an internal matter so long as business was not interrupted, would learn to appreciate the new status quo in time.

"Oh," Isabella said with a forced casualness. "I didn't know that. Do you know what for?"

Michael shook his head. "Maybe to visit Jimmy?"

"Perhaps. Those two are… they're very close."

"Couple of faggots," Enzo muttered as he held up his glass of wine.

"What was that?" Ciaran asked.

"Nothing, Pop," his son said, taking a sip and then returning his glass to the table.

"I did get this, though," Michael said. "He apparently met with the lead detective down there who's looking into—" He glanced over at Enzo; he too would eventually be of no use, not as sloppy as he was. "—what's going on down there. He threatened him—to back off, or else."

"And how do we know this?" Moretti asked.

"A friend of ours in the department down there."

Moretti nodded. "Well, that certainly is an interesting turn of events," he said, looking from Michael to Isabella, who seemed indifferent to the news. "Don't you think, Isabella?"

"We'll see," she said as she picked up her glass of wine.

Ciaran stood, allowing the napkin in his lap to fall to the floor. He looked over the table a moment, frowning slightly as if attempting to recall why he found himself looking down on them. "I'll be back," he announced before walking away.

Isabella forced a smile. "Bathroom," she clarified smoothly once he had departed. "Now… where were we?"

Michael grinned. "There's one more thing I heard that I think you should know about."

46

"*Tommy?*" James asked as soon as the door opened. He had expected the return of the two detectives, or perhaps Ben, who had been determined to drag him out for drinks. "What are you doing here?"

James had spent most of his day on the couch, his attempts to sleep in his own bed returning to him the nightmares he had wanted to forget. For some inexplicable reason, he could close his eyes there without worry, his body slowly healing from his latest wounds. The hidden scars would be added to those given to him by Enzo, but with his last name, he knew they would not be the last.

Matt and Tim were both dead. Ben's Facebook had blown up after it had come across the local news, although James felt nothing at finally confirming what he instinctively already knew. His family had removed them as they had those who attacked him, no distinction made between the guilty and the innocent. No, his friends were just another mess to clean up, his lifestyle, even in California, a stain to be removed as best they could.

"I've been knocking for like two minutes," Tommy said, looking past him into the apartment. "What the hell took you so long?"

"Sorry," James said. "This reporter won't stop harassing me. I thought it was her again until you called out my name. What are you doing here?"

Tommy reached out and hugged him, and his brother flinched in his arms. "You okay?"

"Yeah," James answered as he stepped aside so Tommy could enter. "Just a little sore."

Tommy walked to the center of the room and looked around. "Nice place."

"When'd you get here?" James asked, ignoring the comment as he closed the door.

"This morning," Tommy answered as he examined his brother. He looked good, showered and dressed to go out. "Sam and I flew in."

"Where is he?"

"In the car."

"And you came out just to see me?"

Tommy shook his head. "No."

An unease washed over James. "What else you here for, then?"

Tommy sat down in the leather chair by the couch and pointed to the latter. "Sit down. We need to talk."

James placed himself on the middle cushion about five feet away. "What's up?"

Tommy rested his forearms on the arms of the chair as he crossed his legs, his right knee now resting on the left, his foot hanging in the air. "You on them, or do you just sell them?"

"Fuck."

"You think I wouldn't find out?"

"I was taking them, I needed them, after—"

Tommy knew the deflection would start with Enzo. "Don't blame him for this."

"I needed them. It just… it got out of hand, that's all."

"You're a drug dealer."

"No. It's not like that."

"I had a nice little chat with your friend Detective Carlyle," Tommy said. "He's got the bag that they took off you from the other night."

James remained silent.

"He's given me a choice: I can either give up who tracked down those animals that did that to you, or you go to jail on a felony drug distribution charge."

"No, Tommy," James pleaded. "Please."

"Do you realize the fucking mess you've caused?"

"Tommy—"

"This is what you've brought me. I can turn into a rat, or I can watch you go to jail."

"Tommy, *please.*"

"I need to know right now… who's your supplier?"

James froze. "I can't. I—"

"Who is it?"

"Tommy…"

"Is it Sean Dillon?" Tommy asked, and James's nervous smirk betrayed the answer.

Tommy had feared that was the case since Sam first posited the theory over drinks a few hours ago, that it was their former employee—now his uncle and cousin's primary man on the ground in Southern California—who was the supplier in question. His relatives in Nevada were all too happy to profit handsomely from the never-ending stream of addicts Las Vegas attracted, and no doubt looked the other way if someone like Sean decided to partake in an extracurricular side business of similar interest as long as they got their part of the transactions.

"No," James said.

"How long you been dealing?"

"Tommy—"

"I'm not in the fucking mood for this. You have put all of us at risk. Answer my fucking question."

James paused. "A while."

"How long? Since you got out here?"

"I don't know. A while."

Tommy slapped the arm of the chair. "Goddamn it, answer the fucking question!"

James put his hands together to steady them. "Yes."

"Yes, what?"

"Since I've been out here."

"Why?"

"I just did."

"Why, Jimmy?" Tommy pressed, his voice raised once more.

"I don't know. I guess because I like the attention," James answered, his voice rising. "No one fucking cares about me in Chicago. Here, though… I matter to people."

"Because you're their dealer, you fucking idiot. That's all you are to them."

"I don't care. It's better than anything I ever had back home."

Tommy paused. His connection to his parents had frayed almost to nothing, and there was none with his other two siblings. Aside from his wife, Jimmy was all he had left. "I need to know… is this whole thing over a drug deal gone bad?"

James violently shook his head. "No. I swear. I didn't know those guys. They just… it came out of nowhere."

"Do you understand what Dad would do to you if this ever got out… that he would go to war with Vegas over something like this?"

"Yes."

"And you did it anyway."

"I. Don't. Care."

"I don't know if I can protect you if he hears about this," Tommy warned. "You know how he is. There are no second chances, even if you're family, even if you're out in California. He will show no mercy."

"Like he ever did."

Tommy took a deep breath and let out a long sigh. "I wish I could fix what happened to you."

"You can't," James said before he stood up and walked to his bedroom door. "No one can."

He closed it behind him.

47

Her husband had been home for several hours, in bed since just after eleven, when Sabrina found herself in his chair in the living room, a nearly full glass of merlot beside her as she took in the evening skyline.

Seated on a barstool at the island, she had been aimlessly flipping through one of her cooking magazines when he came through the front door and entered the room. His expression, the mixture of exasperation and relief that he had been wearing as of late, was once more upon his face.

"How's Belize sound?" he asked after the two kissed.

"I thought it was Costa Rica?" she asked, closing the magazine.

"No, definitely Belize," he said as he opened the refrigerator and pulled out a beer. "You want anything?"

Sabrina glanced down at the empty wine glass before her. "Another glass of merlot." He brought over both bottles. "How's Jimmy?"

"He's fine," Tommy said. "Physically, anyway. I just don't…" He never shared this part of his life with her, and was hesitant to now, even if it involved his brother. "There's something I have to tell you—and it does not leave this room."

The wine glass shook in her hand, and she set it down. "What?"

"He's been selling scripts to his friends."

"Oh, God. What are you going to do?"

"I…" He let out a long sigh. "Fuck. I have no idea."

"Who else knows?"

"Here? Sam. Just him."

"Where's he been getting them?"

"My cousin's point man in San Diego."

"Do they know?"

"I don't think my uncle would knowingly put up with using his nephew to move product. They may be trying to provoke us, but to what end… I can't see it."

"What are you going to do?"

"It gets worse," Tommy said. "My cousin Michael is in town."

"Michael? Here? In Chicago?"

He nodded. "And I believe staying with my parents."

"Why?"

"It has to be my mother," he said. "David would make more sense. He runs things out there now, but Michael? He's worthless. He's not a halfway-decent emissary, if that's what he's even out here for."

"You going up to your parents to find out?"

"At some point, yes." Tommy sipped his beer. "Although… I hear Sydney is nice this time of year."

"There are like fifty kind of spiders that can kill you."

"I have a friend down there who owes me a very deep favor. My dear brother-in-law can arrange things financially. You and I can officially disappear."

She took his hand and squeezed it. "As if they'd ever let us go."

"You could go and get away from this."

"We're in this together," she said. "I knew what I was signing up for when I said yes. We'll weather this like everything else."

He put the bottle down on the counter and pulled her to him, kissing her deeply as their bodies merged. "And that is why I love you," he said, both hands now on her waist as he guided her backward.

"And where do you think you're taking me?" she asked.

His lips lightly caressed her neck as he moved slowly toward her ear. "I think you know where," he whispered.

He had been muttering in his sleep when she left the bedroom and walked to his chair, his body twitching as he endured yet another nightmare. He always had them during strenuous times, but until these past few days it had been so long that she had almost allowed herself to believe that they would never return.

So, she sat in his chair and worried about the man in the room down the hall, and the younger man half a country away. They were her only concerns now; the rest of the family had long worn out its welcome. She knew her husband would be fine. He had a resolve that would see him through. Jimmy, though, had been overwhelmed by his demons if he had turned to working for the Byrnes of Las Vegas.

She thought back to the day that had set all of this in motion. They had been at one of an endless stream of parties the family had hosted that spring, a chance for Ciaran to reward those who worked so diligently for him and the family. Up until then it had been a good summer, Tommy having just officially taken the helm after several years of increasing responsibility. They should have all known it would be too good a time to last for very long.

She had been in the family room talking with Isabella, the two having grown somewhat closer as the older woman seemingly came to accept her into the fold, finally setting aside their drawn-out passive struggle over the man who would be king.

Tommy appeared in the doorway. In his eyes Sabrina instinctively saw that something was amiss, and the few drops of blood on his right shirtsleeve confirmed it.

"Sabrina," he said as he attempted to mask his unease behind a casual tone. "Can I borrow you for a second, dear?"

"Sure," she agreed, patting Isabella gently on her knee. "A wife's duty is never done, is it?"

"Never," Isabella agreed. She turned back to Tommy. "Is everything all right?" she asked with a slightly raised eyebrow. She was not a woman who overlooked subtle changes in people.

Tommy nodded as Sabrina joined him. He slipped his arm around her waist and pulled her close. "Oh, sure. I just need to steal her away for a second."

Isabella smiled. "Hurry back."

"What is it?" Sabrina asked as they rushed down the hall. He had dropped his feigned look of calm, and she was now truly alarmed by whatever it was they were headed to.

"It's Jimmy."

He was on the couch when the two descended the stairs, partially covered with a blanket as he lay curled up on his side. She had never seen anyone so white without actually being dead.

Sabrina went to him and crouched down. He made no acknowledgement of her as she rubbed his face, his hollowed gaze staring at nothing. She turned back to Tommy. "What happened?"

He shook his head. "I don't know. I found him on the floor, but... he didn't say anything. I put him on the couch and went to get you."

She looked back at Jimmy, gently tapping his cheekbone as she called out his name. He met her eyes briefly. She took his wrist to check his pulse, which barely registered under her fingers. Only when she placed his arm back on the couch did she notice the blood.

She pulled back the blanket, revealing the dried streams between his legs. Then she saw the broken pool cue lying on the floor. Her hand went to her mouth. "Oh, God," she muttered as she grabbed Jimmy's chin with her hand and tilted his head. "Jimmy?" she asked again, a new urgency in her voice. His eyes slowly met hers once more.

"What?" Tommy asked.

"We need to get him to a hospital."

"What the hell are you talking about?"

Sabrina pointed toward the cue stick. "That. Enzo is a sick, sick fuck."

"What do you—" He stopped as everything came together, his arms now folded across his chest, one hand across his mouth. "He cannot go to a hospital. You realize what will happen if this gets out?"

She looked back. He had never seen her so angry, so desperate before. "Fuck you."

"Sabrina—"

She stood to face him. "Tommy, he's going to the goddamn hospital, and fuck you about your stupid family's reputation. I don't care if I have to do it myself, but he will die if we don't. Is that what you want?"

"No."

"Then do something."

His mouth tightened as he grasped for options that were not there. "Get the car and bring it around back," he finally said, his voice barely a whisper.

She leaned in and kissed her husband, then stepped away as Tommy crouched down to scoop Jimmy up into his arms. At the foot of the stairs Sabrina turned. "They'll never hurt you again," she heard Tommy whisper before kissing the top of Jimmy's head. "I promise."

THURSDAY

48

"Wake up."

"Hmm?" Tommy asked from the comfort and quiet of the bed, his face against the cool sheets, a pillow strategically placed to block the rising sun.

"Wake up."

He rolled onto his back and squinted up at her. Sabrina stood above him as she had untold times before, pills in her right hand, a glass of freshly squeezed orange juice in her left. As always, a scarcely veiled look of displeasure accompanied the relief she brought with her. She was too good for him, he thought.

He sat up, took the pills, and washed them down with the juice. "You don't have to do this, you know."

"Sure, but it's this or my spin class, and I wasn't up for Gail's eternal happiness this morning."

Tommy pivoted in the bed and pushed himself up. "You could go have lunch with my father for me if you're looking for something to do."

"I'd almost rather have lunch with your mother."

As she started to walk away, he reached out and gently pulled her backward, wrapping his arms around her waist and resting his head on her shoulder. The familiar scent of her shampoo brought to mind better, calmer days. He kissed her gently on the neck, feeling her shudder as he did. He smiled, happy to elicit the reaction after all their years together. "I love you."

She put a hand over his. "I love you too, but how does this end?"

"When you run away with me to Belize."

Sabrina laughed, but joylessly. "For a weekend, but that's it."

"Not even a whole week?"

"I'll give you two if you get this taken care of. I hate what it's doing to you."

"You and me both," he agreed before kissing her neck again. He paused. "My father would be handling this differently."

"And that's better?"

He shook his head. "I don't know."

"Hon… your father, and your brother—and I think to a certain extent your mother—all have the same response to a crisis: lash out until people bend to their will. I don't know if that's what this will take, but you can't always just go in and kill people to get your way." He remained silent as she turned and put a hand on his chest. "I know you'll do what's best. And sometimes it's okay to not be your father."

■ ■ ■

Isabella looked across the table to her guest, watching as he mindlessly shoveled in eggs and hash browns as he scrolled through the phone that held his full attention.

She didn't trust Michael, nor find him particularly bright—his father's puppet, no more, no less. A means to an end, and so long as she secured the family's legacy, she was willing to dance with that particular devil out in California. Liam understood what she hoped to achieve, to retain, and despite their differences, they were in alignment. She knew she could trust him just enough to see it through.

"What has your father told you?" she asked.

"Huh?" he grunted without looking up.

She wanted to slap him. "What has your father told you about what's going on out here?"

Michael set down the phone, then placed his fork on the plate. He leaned back in the chair, raising his chin ever so slightly. "He said there might be an opportunity for us to do more business together."

"Is that all?" she asked, resisting the temptation to comment on his arrogant posture. Her sons knew better than to preen like peacocks.

"He thought that David and Tommy could, you know, maybe have a better relationship than he and Uncle Ciaran do."

"I don't know about Tommy."

"Yeah, he said something about that too."

"My son doesn't have an appreciation for what we've built here," Isabella clarified. "He's content to let it weaken until someone takes it from him."

"Enzo doesn't want to step in?"

"He isn't suited to that role. He's better behind the scenes."

"Is that what I'm doing out here then?" Michael asked.

"That has yet to be determined. I would consider this visit as an opportunity to take it all in." She sipped her coffee. "Are you and Moretti going to Wrigleyville?"

"Yeah. He's coming up to get me and Uncle Ciaran. We're supposed to drop him off to see Tommy, and then he's going to take me up there to meet some people."

"I'm embarrassed my son hasn't shown you the proper respect and welcomed you to town himself."

Michael sneered. "Yeah, well, I guess he's too busy with that other crap. I'm sure we'll cross paths here soon. He's on my list now." He picked up his fork and started back in on his eggs.

■ ■ ■

"Sam?"

"Yeah?"

"Meet me downstairs in ten minutes," Tommy ordered, then ended the call.

49

She hated waking up anxious. There was an unease at the back of her mind that she could not shake, despite repeated assurances that everything was fine. Regardless, she refused to attribute it to her call with Carlyle the night before.

"Susan?" he had asked after she hastily answered the phone, fearing he would change his mind.

"Detective Carlyle, how nice of you to finally return my calls," she said, keeping her voice down so she wouldn't disturb her partner in the next room. Edie was paranoid enough about this story.

"Don't look a gift horse in the mouth," he said.

"And to what do I owe the pleasure?" she asked, continuing to lightly goad him. "You finally going to answer some of my questions?"

"Not hardly," he admitted. "I just wanted to ask if you've had any contact with James Byrne."

Carlyle wasn't sure why he was even bothering with this call. He could have told her he was monitoring James Byrne's phone, but Tommy Byrne's visceral reaction to the idea of something harming his younger brother had stayed with him. Whatever the source of it, Carlyle knew he'd backed the man into a corner. And he didn't want any civilians—even Sue Hendricks—caught in the crossfire. Too many people had already died this week through no fault of their own.

"And why would you ask me that? You monitoring his phone records—or mine now too?"

Carlyle snorted. "I would never do something like that."

"Then how would you know I've been trying to speak with him?"

He wished she could see him smirk. "*You* just did."

"Goddamn it," she blurted out.

"Do you think that's a good idea?"

"I'm a reporter. It's my job to ask questions."

"Are you bugging that kid?"

"I've called him a few times," she admitted.

"You think it's wise to keep pushing him?"

"I won't know until he starts talking."

Carlyle sighed. "Look, the kid doesn't know anything."

"Are you sure?"

"My gut tells me he's not involved in any of this."

"He's right in the middle of all this."

"As a victim," he argued.

"Victim or not, he's connected to a mob family, and six bodies connected to that boy have turned up already."

"He hasn't killed anyone."

"Detective, is there a point to all this?"

"Look, Sue… we don't always get along."

"I don't think we've *ever* gotten along."

He ignored the comment. "I would stop calling him if I were you."

"Are you actually concerned about me, Detective Carlyle?"

He sighed once more. "Yeah, if you want to call it that, I am, a little."

"Nothing's going to happen to me. They wouldn't dare touch a reporter."

"Just watch your back," he said, then ended the call.

Sue had been threatened on a number of occasions, even on the most mundane of stories, the result of a social media environment where every embittered misogynist with a Twitter account felt it necessary to attack whatever angered them, and they were a crowd in a perpetual state of irritation. It was a race to the bottom yet one without end; there was always something new to draw their attention and fury.

This, she told herself as she finished packing her shoulder bag, was no different—no matter how hard the words tried to stick in her throat. The Byrnes might have Chicago and Las Vegas cowering at their feet, but she had no patience for bullies. She would keep pressing. It was the least she could do for all the people they had trampled.

"I'm off to work," she called out to Edie as she entered the bedroom, her partner finishing up in their bathroom. "I've got to work on this story and see if Charles will let me go to Chicago… maybe Las Vegas."

Edie stopped applying her makeup and walked to the doorway. "No."

"I could get a Pulitzer."

"You could also wind up dead," Edie said. "Just let this one go."

"I can't."

"For me. Just this once. *Please*," she pleaded.

"You know I can't do that."

Edie sighed. "No, I suppose not," she said. She walked over to Susan and gave her a kiss. "Just be there for dinner tonight."

Sue nodded, even as she wondered if she'd just agreed to something she couldn't keep. "Shit. What time?"

"I knew you'd forget," Edie said. "I think six. Call me at noon and I'll let you know. Now have a good day and try not to get too many people pissed off at you in the process."

"Love you, Edie."

"Love you too, hon. I'll see you tonight."

■ ■ ■

Sam looked down at his phone and tapped the number. "Alex?"

He was still a little wary of sending this kid out to California. Sam knew him well enough as Joe's son and right-hand man, but from what he'd observed the boy didn't even have the motivation to fill that role that correctly, much less be groomed for greater responsibility.

There had been one too many stories about Alex being a little off somehow. Sam had casually excused it to the boy doing what he did only to please his father, but there was a hidden layer beneath he couldn't quite wrap his head around. The drinking he understood—especially at that age—but there was something else. Alex moved through his life like an observer, present but uninvested, with no girlfriend, no boastful stories of his sexual conquests, no visible wants. For all Sam knew, the kid could have been a virgin.

But a social visit from an old friend Sam could understand, even if those two together came off to him as slightly peculiar. He had certainly seen stranger friendships in his line of work. Something had occurred, for whatever reason, that meant Jimmy was never coming back to Chicago, so the trip certainly made sense to him even if the circumstances surrounding it did not. Tommy never spoke of what transpired, and Sam being Sam, didn't ask. If his boss wanted him to know he would have told him.

He had come to trust Tommy's judgment without question. His boss had articulated a clear vision for building up their legitimate concerns and followed through beyond expectations. Their other businesses he had completely restructured, decentralizing command and establishing firewalls to protect their legal enterprises, which Sam recognized as a first step to their exiting them completely. For the moment Tommy could still tolerate allowing the drugs to pass through for a fee, along with the importation and sale of every type of firearm imaginable, but he would be damned if either, or any of their other off the books activities, would bring down all he had painstakingly built.

"Uh… yeah?" Alex answered.

"You awake?"

"Uh, yeah. Yeah, I am."

"Good," Sam said. He closed his eyes and said a quick prayer for the success of the orders he was about to give. "I have some things I need you to do for me."

50

"Dare I ask for a status report?" Captain Scott asked as Carlyle took a seat across the desk.

The captain's perpetual scowl seemed to grow darker as the week progressed. Carlyle, though, had nothing to report, so he would take the reprimand as gracefully as he could and move on.

He shook his head. "I have nothing."

"Nothing?"

"Nothing. Nada," Carlyle said. "Well, I have four crime scenes involving who I believe to be the Byrnes, but they're still sorting through everything. Right now, there are no usable forensics, no witnesses, and they were smart enough to avoid surveillance. I don't know if they came from Chicago or Vegas, or if they called up one of their friends from south of the border to take care of it for them."

"No usable forensics? Really?"

"Those three apartments were a goddamn mess to go through. I have no fingerprints tied to anyone who could even remotely be involved. And for some convenient reason, no known Byrne associate is in any relevant DNA database to compare against the stacks of samples we have. It's like they don't even exist."

Scott pursed his lips. "Have your team look at those apartments again."

"What would be the point?"

"Because I told you to."

Carlyle nodded, resigned to carrying out the futile request. "Yes, sir."

"What about the Feds?"

"Do you really want me to extend that invitation?"

Scott scowled. "I suspect not," he admitted. "What about the Byrne boy?"

"Nothing there."

Scott frowned. "*Nothing?*" he asked, his skepticism bordering on mockery.

"Something tells me the gay kid studying philosophy at UCSD doesn't get the family memos."

"You'd be surprised."

"I don't think so."

"Take another look at him. Find something that we can use. Get some leverage on him."

"I can always arrange witness protection."

Scott glared. "Don't get cute with me," he said. "Just find out what he knows, and don't take no for a goddamn answer."

Carlyle glanced out the window into the bullpen. "Okay," he said as he looked back at the captain. "I'll take another look."

"You're being awfully agreeable today."

Carlyle shrugged. "What can I say? You caught me in a good mood."

Scott picked up his coffee cup, an old blue mug with the City of San Diego seal on two sides, a vestige of a time when budgets weren't so restrictive. He drank slowly, never breaking eye contact with Carlyle. "I get the feeling you're not telling me everything."

"I'm telling you what you need to hear."

Scott set the mug down on his desk. "For my own good?"

"For your own good," Carlyle agreed.

Scott nodded slowly. "So, I need to call the assistant chief and tell him we have to suck up six unsolved murders, including the son of a state senator."

"I'm not going to give up, but I don't know how any of this is going to turn out."

"*This* being whatever it is you don't want to discuss."

"Correct."

"I want a report I can send upstairs first thing Monday morning, you got it?"

"Understood."

"I don't care what kind of bullshit is in it as long as I don't look like a total asshole. Now get the fuck out of my office."

■ ■ ■

The phone still on his chest, Alex stared once more at the ceiling as he reran the conversation in his head.

His new assignment could be managed, Sam's gruff instructions simple enough to be tackled within the requested timeframe. Annoying distractions, he thought—but they would fill the time while he went about completing his original assignment.

He didn't know what he should expect when he finally got to see Jimmy for the first time in almost a year. Alex knew what Enzo had been putting him through for most of their time together, but he had been helpless to stop it and hated himself for that. He had mentioned it to his father once, hoping he could somehow intercede, but Joe just scowled at him. "Stay out of their fucking business," he ordered. "If Ciaran wants Enzo to toughen up the boy, then that is what happens." Shortly thereafter he and Jimmy had talked about running away together but acknowledged it for the fantasy it was.

Alex briefly closed his eyes, still regretting his decision to get so drunk on his first night in town. His only respite from the pain of their abrupt separation and what his life was becoming was to be found at the bottom of a bottle. That and other distractions.

The shower running in the next room had stopped a few minutes before, and the door finally opened.

"Hi," the young man said as he stood in the doorway and seductively ran a hand through his mop of wet hair.

"Hi."

"You don't remember me, do you?"

"Enough," Alex lied.

The guy laughed. "Okay. Well… I'll be going now?"

"You asking me or telling me."

"Telling you, I guess."

"Okay," Alex said. "I'll see you around."

"Sure," the guy said. And Alex, once more, was alone.

51

"So… where you taking me to lunch?" Ciaran asked as he sat across the desk, the one he had once occupied when they moved what had once been their shell corporations into the heart of the Loop.

He almost didn't recognize the place when he entered the lobby one floor below. Physically it appeared the same, but what was once a place of quiet respite when he wanted a few hours to think, or to meet with city officials at a place more convenient for them, had become a bewildering hive of activity. Even in his old office, his eldest son now occupying his chair, the hum of activity could be heard through the opened door behind him.

He had seen Tommy's plans for their new and significantly expanded offices up State Street on the other side of the Chicago River, although he had no desire to walk through the nearly completed space that they would be moving into within the next few months. Traditional offices would give way to open floor plans, dark wood paneling and eighteenth century–style furniture to glass walls and modular fixtures. Very little of what currently surrounded him would be coming along, the past remaining where it was as Tommy forged ahead with his future.

Despite his reservations when Tommy had first been presented his ideas, he was proud of his son and his accomplishments, especially in so short a time. Like Isabella and Moretti, he worried that their past would not be honored in this new future—that Tommy's fixation would leave their interests vulnerable to those eager to use them as leverage, his elder brother chief among them. His nephew's arrival brought Ciaran a renewed apprehension of his sibling's intentions, no matter Isabella's assurances. The man could not be trusted, even as he tended to his grapes.

"I don't know," Tommy answered. "Couple good restaurants downstairs if you're not up for going far."

"Get me out of the goddamn Loop," his father commanded. "I don't need this white tablecloth shit. Take me somewhere good."

Tommy smiled. "I think I know a particularly good burger joint up in Wrigleyville."

"Where you should be going anyway," Ciaran added. He leaned forward in his chair. "These relationships need to be nurtured, my son. Constantly."

Tommy nodded. "I know."

"Then show them some respect. This isn't a game where everyone plays by the rules." Ciaran pointed toward the window. "They're fucking animals out there, and you cannot get complacent, you hear me?"

"Yes," Tommy said. "So… how are things at home?"

"Your cousin is in town."

"So, I hear."

"You planning to pay him a visit?"

"Eventually."

"It looks disrespectful for you not to meet him."

"How long is he here for?"

Ciaran shrugged. "I don't know. He's come to break bread on David's behalf. Your mother thinks you and your cousins need to work more closely."

"And what do you think?"

"I don't trust my brother," he answered as he slowly shook his head. "Maybe his sons are better, but I don't think the apple falls far from the tree."

"How is everything else?"

"If you came up to visit more you wouldn't have to ask."

Tommy nodded, accepting the rebuke. "I know."

"You know, your mother knows… no one bothers to tell me what the fuck is going on, so I… *I* do not know. Care to enlighten me a little?"

Tommy looked away, that day when his relationship with his mother forever changed resurfacing as if the year since then had not passed.

"Where is my goddamn son?" Isabella had yelled as she burst into the penthouse, her wrath on full display for the small audience before her.

"I'm here, Mother," Tommy answered as he stood from the couch, turning to face her as she stormed into the living room, Sabrina on her heels.

He knew this was coming. Her calls ignored—you didn't ignore Isabella Byrne—it was only a matter of time before she came downtown in search of answers.

"You know I meant Jimmy," Isabella snapped.

Tommy thought of the outpatient surgery at a small private clinic with doctors and nurses threatened to within an inch of their lives, and of a teenage boy recovering for several weeks in the guest room down the hall until he had been put onto a plane to San Diego just two days before. The one suggestion that they call home was met with a visceral reaction that it took Sabrina more than an hour to calm him. The idea was never revisited.

"He left for school," he said, feigning confusion. "I thought you knew."

"I didn't," she said. "He wasn't supposed to leave for another few weeks."

"I guess he was anxious to get himself set up," Tommy said, momentarily breaking eye contact to watch Sabrina walk over and stand beside him.

Isabella looked from one to the other. "He hasn't been home since the night you three so abruptly left, and now you're telling me he's gone."

"Yes."

"Without his phone? Without his clothes?"

"He wanted new."

"And who's paying for that?"

"I am," Tommy answered.

"We are," Sabrina said.

Isabella glared at her. "I am talking to my son."

"Mom," Tommy interrupted, "he wanted to go so I sent him."

"And why would he want that?"

Tommy paused. This was a necessary argument, but one he could never win. He glanced over at his wife, her unspoken support given in a barely perceptible nod. "I think he was done with Enzo."

"What goes on between the two of them isn't your concern."

"I made it my concern. He doesn't feel safe at your house."

"You need to stay out of it," Isabella commanded.

"That won't happen."

She pursed her lips. "So, he's never coming back? Are you keeping him away from us now?"

"I'm keeping him away from Enzo."

"So, he plans to remain in California?"

"At least until that rabid dog is brought to heel."

He felt Sabrina go rigid beside him as he watched his mother fill with rage. "Don't you talk about your brother that way," she said.

"He's a goddamn animal," Tommy yelled, "and it will not happen again. Do you hear me?"

"Son?" Ciaran asked, his voice raised. His prior two attempts had garnered no response.

Tommy closed his eyes and shook his head before looking back across the desk. "Sorry, Pop. My mind wandered."

"What am I doing here if all you're going to do is ignore me?"

"Sorry," he repeated. "What were you asking?"

"I'd like to know what the hell is going on with our family."

"What do you mean?"

"What do I mean?" Ciaran snapped. "Why haven't I seen or heard from my youngest son in almost a year? The boy couldn't even bother to come home for Christmas. Why are you and your mother barely on speaking terms? Why do you and Enzo only communicate through Sam or Moretti? Should I fucking continue?"

"No, Pop. I get your point."

"You get my point?" he asked. "Well, if you get my point, how would you like to fucking answer one of those questions?"

Tommy sighed. "It's complicated."

"Son, I didn't get to where I am by being a fucking idiot. Why don't you try me instead of sitting behind that desk like a pompous ass?"

"Pop—"

"Don't fucking 'Pop' me. Answer the goddamn question, Tommy. I'm tired of this shit. I know I'm not well, but I don't need to be treated like a fucking child."

Tommy paused. "There was a problem between Jimmy and Enzo. I picked one side, and Mom picked the other."

The older man sat back in his chair. "Why does there have to be sides in this? We're family."

"Pop… I'm keeping Jimmy out of Enzo's reach."

"Over what? Their sparring matches?"

"It was a little more one-sided than that."

Ciaran waved a dismissive hand. "Oh, fuck… it wasn't that bad."

"Yes, it was."

"Enzo was trying to toughen him up."

Tommy tapped his desk. "You can call it whatever you want. He will not get anywhere near Jimmy again. Over my dead body will that happen again."

Ciaran nodded, acceding to his son's command. For the first time since relinquishing the office, Tommy did not look like a frightened child pretending at authority. Finally, he was coming into his own. "I know he's a… well as Moretti would say… a fanook," he finally offered as the silence wore on.

Tommy winced. "Did Mom tell you that?"

"A father knows." Ciaran tapped his temple. "I may not be all there sometimes, but some things I can still figure out on my own."

Tommy laughed, the tension removed. "Fair enough. And?"

"And what? I have bigger problems than that right now. Just… does it have anything to do with San Diego? Are we dealing with this because of what he's doing out there?"

"No, I don't think so."

"What *do* you know?"

"It's being… handled." Tommy said. "You really want the details?"

Ciaran shook his head. "No, I suppose I don't," he said, sounding regretful. His days numbered, his wits not always about him, he spent too many lucid moments worrying about secrets long since buried finding new light as his mind slipped away.

"At the moment it's under control."

"At the moment?"

Tommy sighed. "It's out of our jurisdiction, so to speak. I can't control what happens out there."

Ciaran stood up. "You'll figure it out, my son. Now let's go break bread with our friends to the north."

52

Coffee in hand, Alex stepped out onto the side patio and into the bright sunlight, the sounds of baristas busily filling orders replaced with the din of the city around him. Even in San Diego, the ants dutifully marched, each of them intent on keeping their lives in order.

He found his target sitting alone by the railing at one of the half-dozen iron mesh tables with matching chairs, dressed in a distressed t-shirt, jeans, and flip flops, fingers dancing over his phone. The two were alone, the other patrons content with the air conditioning and cushioned seats that the interior offered.

Remaining at the door, he watched Jimmy focus on his screen, his gaze never wavering, the world passing him by unnoticed. Alex didn't know what to say, doubting that he could do anything to bridge this rift between them. Their time had passed, and though he hoped for a closure of sorts, he wasn't sure if even that was available.

Even with the large aviator sunglasses and a light application of foundation, Alex could make out the mild swelling and bruising on the left side of James's face. He could feel the rage inside him begin to build, even with the knowledge that those fuckers had been dealt with in the cruelest possible way. He only wished, bitterly, that he had been there when it ended.

After taking a deep breath, Alex slowly walked over and sat down across the table. James looked up but registered no emotion, his gaze immediately returning to his phone.

"What are you doing here?"

"Tommy sent me."

"You shouldn't wear a suit," James said, his voice monotone and distant. "You stand out too much."

"You don't like it?"

"I didn't say that. It's just… you stick out. A lot."

"Okay. Thanks for the tip."

"How'd you find me?" James asked, finally finishing up with his phone and sliding it into his pocket.

"I wouldn't be very good at this if I couldn't track you down."

James smirked, unconvinced. "What did he tell you?"

"He wanted me to check up on you."

"Why?"

"I don't know. I assumed with… with everything, that he—" Alex laughed. "I really have no fucking idea, to be honest."

A grin finally appeared. "Smooth."

Alex held up his palms. "I know. I know. He told me to come out, and I did. I didn't ask why. I just wanted to see you again. I didn't care about anything else."

"I wish he hadn't done that."

Alex paused. He understood that it wasn't meant for him, that there was a reason for this façade, but it stung regardless. "Do you really mean that?"

"Yes."

"Well, what am I supposed to tell Tommy?"

"You can tell him I'm fine."

"Goddamn it, Jimmy—"

"James," he corrected.

"James?"

"Yeah."

Alex shrugged. "Fine, *James*. What the hell happened to you?"

"Nothing."

Alex sighed. "You want me to go back to Chicago and say that everything's great in your world, I will. But you owe me an explanation."

"I don't owe you anything."

"My fucking God," Alex snapped. "You're still such a brat." He tapped the top of the table once. "It's a simple deal—answer my one question, and I'll leave you the fuck alone."

He watched as the blood drained from James's face. "Enzo," came the response, barely above a whisper.

Alex could see the fear on James's face, could feel it emanating from across the table. He watched as James gripped the edge of the wrought-iron chair. "What happened?"

"He put me in the hospital," James said. "He threatened to kill me. And you, too."

"How did he know?"

"I don't know. He came after me, and… I don't remember much. I woke up at Tommy's, and I was gone within a few weeks."

"I wish you had said goodbye. I could have handled Enzo."

James scoffed. "He would have killed you and not thought twice about it. And no one, not your father or mine, would have done a damn thing about it."

Alex slowly nodded, his ego checked. "Would you go out to dinner with me tonight?"

James looked confused. "You asking me out on a date?"

Alex smiled. "Yeah, I am."

"I answered your question. Now you need to hold up your part of the deal."

"Oh, for fuck's sake, it's only dinner." He put up a hand as James tried to protest. "And then I can report back that you're doing okay without getting killed for lying to your brother."

James let out a sigh. "Okay. Fine. Whatever."

Alex stood up. "Well, I guess it's time to get out of this stupid suit." He walked over to James and placed his hand on his shoulder, feeling him flinch at his touch. He paused, waiting for the tension in the shoulder to subside before he leaned down to gently kiss James on the head. "Pick you up at seven?"

James nodded. "Sure."

■ ■ ■

"Who the fuck is *that* leprechaun?" Seegars asked as he lowered the digital camera with the extended lens.

"I have no fucking clue," Carlyle said. "What is that family up to? Those two..."

"They're a couple."

"Or were."

"I'm more worried about the suit," Seegars said. "The idiot looks ten in that thing."

Carlyle shot him a look. "Seriously?"

"Just observing," Seegars answered with a shrug.

"Forward me those pictures. I owe Lubbock anyway, and I'd like to see what he knows. They've got to be tracking this kid."

"What are you thinking?"

"I want to know if he's out here just to entertain the kid or..."

"What?" Seegars asked.

Carlyle pointed to the woman slowly walking by the coffee shop patio, her attention fixed on the two young men. "Do you know who that is?"

"No. Who?"

"Susan Hendricks."

Seegars shook his head. "Dyke doesn't know when to leave well enough alone, does she?"

53

Isabella looked across the table as Enzo shoveled the last of his lasagna into his mouth, her own salad left mostly untouched.

Her appetite this week was off, the result of a stress that would not abate until the issues surrounding San Diego were resolved. The status quo needed to be upended, and the second of her two agents of change now sat across the glass patio table as they enjoyed a favorable break in an otherwise cold week.

Enzo had always been her favorite, her eldest his father's son since shortly after he was born. Tommy was the heir, while Enzo would be the one to ensure that his older brother would have an empire to govern. Their bond was not based on a mutual intellectual curiosity, as Tommy had with Sabrina, or one of protégé and mentor as Tommy had with his father. No, Isabella and Enzo bonded over what they both prized most: family and survival. Each did what needed to be done when needed, one with influence, the other through brute force.

"So, good to be back home?" she asked after Enzo, napkin tossed aside, finished off the last of his beer.

"Yeah," he answered as he stood up and walked over to the small refrigerator built into the grilling station, retrieving another bottle before returning to his seat. "It was okay, but I'm glad to be back."

"Moretti was concerned that it didn't necessarily go according to plan."

"What the fuck does he know?" Enzo snapped. "He wasn't even there. We got the job done. Like he or Tommy could do any better from their ivory fucking tower."

"He is your father's closest advisor," Isabella said. "You will show him the proper respect."

Enzo sighed loudly. "Fine."

"What about Jimmy's friends?"

"A couple of fags," Enzo said with derision. "They knew too much anyway."

"It's not your fault," Isabella said. "Jimmy is to blame for all this. It's his mess we're having to clean up."

"Yeah."

She picked up her wine glass. "You know, Enzo…"

"Huh?"

"More drastic measures might have to be taken out there. Your brother Tommy is fiddling somewhat, but in the end he and your father are going to have to understand what you and I do, that this family cannot be threatened by Jimmy carrying on the way he does. You understand me?"

He grinned. "Absolutely."

■ ■ ■

"We're not publishing the name," Dana, a reporter and close friend who worked down the street at San Diego's progressive weekly newspaper, informed her after pleasantries had been exchanged.

"What do you mean you're not?" Sue asked, her tone bordering on the belligerent. "You've published all the others."

"We're just not going to."

"Why not?"

"Because."

Sue let out a long, frustrated breath. "You've got to be kidding me."

"I'm not."

"And you can't tell me why."

"No," Dana said. "It came down from up high, and they never get involved, so when they do we listen and don't ask questions."

"It's the goddamn Byrnes."

"Sue, I love you. I really do, but we're not allowed to even talk about it, that's how serious it is."

"Okay. Fine."

"Still meeting up for dinner tonight?"

"Absolutely. Sixish, right?"

"Yeah," Dana said. "Okay, I've got to get back to work, but—"

"What?"

Dana lowered her voice to just above a whisper. "I'd try Jake Rosenthal at *Windy Loafing*… their weekly. They might—*might*—bite at that."

"Love you," Sue said. "See you soon."

Jake Rosenthal, however, was much more succinct in his rejection, which came in the form of a very curt "not interested" when she had finished introducing herself and explaining the situation.

"Is there anyone else over there who would be?" Sue asked.

"No."

"How do you know that?"

"I just do," he said, and hung up the phone.

54

Tommy glanced up from his work as Moretti's shadow filled the doorway. He feigned a look of surprise. "Sorry… didn't see you standing there."

Moretti entered, closing the door. "How was your dad?"

"Fine," Tommy said as he leaned back in his chair. "Visit to the office, lunch with some of our friends, head back to the dungeon."

"Sorry we missed you up there."

"Yes, I heard you were giving the grand tour today. How's my cousin doing?"

"He's young," Moretti said as he seated himself across the desk, "and he's got a bravado that would otherwise get him into trouble."

"And my uncle, on a whim, just decides to bring about this détente with my mother?"

"Apparently so."

Tommy nodded. "Well… that's good, I suppose. It's probably long overdue. We're so intertwined in our interests that it certainly makes sense to be on better terms."

"Exactly," Moretti said. "If I might suggest something?"

"Of course."

"You should probably make an effort to get to Highland Park. He's been in town a few days now, and your uncle is a stickler for protocol."

"I'll come up tomorrow," Tommy assured him, growing weary of the etiquette lectures. "Perhaps dinner."

"It would go a long way."

"Of course. How is everything else?"

"It's fine," Moretti said. "I did get a call this morning from a friend of ours at the *Windy Loafing*."

"We have a friend over there?" Tommy asked. "They crucify us every chance they get."

"Who do you think feeds them their information? We've had that arrangement with them for years. We burnish their rebellious image in exchange for courtesies such as this."

"And what courtesy are we talking about?"

"It seems a certain reporter out in San Diego is trying to drum up the story here."

"Fuck," Tommy muttered. "You've got to be kidding me."

"Don't worry. It's going nowhere. But if she continues to press things, more may be required."

"I suspect, yes."

"Your uncle's man on the ground," Moretti said. "I could reach out, see if they could have him warn her off. I'm sure they wouldn't mind helping out with the new 'détente,' as you put it."

"Actually, have Sam tell Alex Mullens to do it," Tommy said, sure that Sam would play along as Moretti told him to do something already underway.

"*Alex Mullens?*" Moretti sneered. "Joe's son? Why would we do that? We've already got someone out there."

"He's already there, and I'd prefer not owing my uncle the favor."

"What's he doing out there?"

"I asked him to go."

"Why?" Moretti pressed.

"My brother. He's not doing well, and the two of them used to be good friends. I thought it might not be a bad idea to have someone out there."

"So, nothing you could help out with during your trip?"

Tommy grinned. He'd suspected that Michael would relay that piece of information. "No. Jimmy needs his space."

"I think he's been getting plenty of that lately."

"I think he needs a little more."

Moretti forced a smile as he stood. "I'll talk to Sam. Is there anything else I need to be aware of?"

Tommy shook his head as he turned his attention back to his laptop. He was enjoying cutting his father's man out of their plans. He would know soon enough. "No, that will be all. Thank you."

■ ■ ■

Sean had been on something of a spending binge as of late, the extra money earned for helping the Chicago Byrnes gnawing at his brain.

His work for the family allowed him plenty of spare time, which in turn allowed him to fill it in ways that his employer generally frowned upon. He could have easily taken up surfing, deep-sea fishing, or even scuba diving, but money was the primary motivator of Sean's activities, and playing in the water would only waste the time he could otherwise be spending it.

Selling coke and a wide selection of scripts to rich kids up in north county San Diego had started out as just a part-time thing, but had been profitable enough to pull him in further. After a certain bartender in Solana Beach had an unfortunate accident with a crowbar, demand immediately spiked. He couldn't help but fill the void, and after he became the main distributor for his new Los Angeles connection, the money was flat stupid. Who could have imagined how much cash these brats had to snort up their noses?

He treated himself well with his earnings. The Porsche SUV had probably attracted some unwanted attention, but he rationalized to himself that it was well deserved. Along with the designer clothes he wore, the car gave him credibility in his line of work, where image, and the perceived power behind it, were everything. The Byrnes were more subdued in their projection of authority, but it was a very different world out here. When he moved their products he adhered to their standards, but when it came to his side business, he did what needed to be done. What they didn't know wouldn't affect them anyway.

He only hoped that James had kept his mouth shut. Too many members of the family had been out here since the assault, and the Byrnes tended to be very quick with their retribution.

It wasn't even Sean's doing; James had suggested the arrangement at a pool hall in Solana Beach last fall. "I'll take it all," James had said after Sean pulled the large bag of pills from the black travel bag hidden in the wheel well of his Porsche.

"You getting a lifetime supply or something?"

"No, man," James said, sounding a little too forced. "My friends keep trying to buy them off me. It's a win-win."

"You don't need the money."

"So?"

"Kid, you know what your brother would do if he finds out you're dealing for me?"

"You're protected by my uncle. My brother can't do shit to you."

"I don't think your uncle would want me doing this either."

"Then don't say anything," James said. "You think I will?"

Even now, Sean recoiled at the thought of being blackmailed by a teenager with a pill addiction. He was sure the kid would say nothing, but it was cutting life a bit close to be involved in something like this. Chicago might not be able to touch him, but even his direct employee might not find this particular business arrangement to their liking.

He glanced once more at his gold wristwatch. He had received a call earlier this morning from Tommy Byrne's right-hand man about getting a handgun to one of their associates in the area, and quickly. Since he had already been told to accommodate Chicago as needed he immediately agreed, although he would call Las Vegas to confirm it on his way to the exchange. Something about the request seemed off.

■ ■ ■

Alex was still in elementary school when Sean worked for the Byrnes in Chicago, so tailing him around the open-air two-story mall had been relatively easy. His mark had been somewhat preoccupied with himself anyway as he bounced from one luxury store to the next, the roll of hundred-dollar bills in his pants at the ready.

Alex wasn't sure exactly what he had done to so anger Chicago, but he had his orders and they were not to be questioned. If Tommy wanted Sean removed, then that was what was going to happen. It wouldn't be a difficult task. This clown was too self-absorbed to see what was coming.

He had never killed a man, although had been witness to more than one murder while working for his father. He was still young, and there would be plenty of time for that. A mixture of fear and excitement propelled him forward, his father's words of advice lingering in his head: "Just get it done," Big Joe had told his son moments after shooting a man twice in the chest. "You don't linger. You do your business and get out," the gun in his hand waving through the air as he gesticulated. "This isn't a time to be macho, to make the other man beg or cry. A real man doesn't need that. It's business, and you treat it like business. Just get it done."

Alex's mind once more wandered to Jimmy—James, he reminded himself. Despite the wall between them there was still something there, an ember still burning despite Enzo's best efforts to stomp it out. What had once been lost had been rediscovered as the two reconnected at the coffeehouse.

He didn't know when, and he didn't know how, but Enzo would pay for what he had done. But in the meantime, there was the target at hand.

55

Sean was having yet another banner day. Or so he thought. He had landed a number of really good buys—the economy still wasn't all that good and half the mall was on sale, it seemed—and had also scored a phone number from a really attractive salesgirl. He would sometimes buy crap from one just so he could talk with her, to woo her with his wit and charm. This time it cost him a few hundred dollars for a shirt he would return next week.

He glanced at his watch. The exchange was coming up, though he had some business in Encinitas first. It wasn't Enzo or any of his crew, just Big Joe's son. While he respected the man, and had worked under him for a time before moving out west, Sean had been busting his ass since that kid was eating crayons. He had been a bit of a whiny child anyway, from what he could remember, so his stupid ass could wait.

■ ■ ■

Alex followed Sean toward the mostly vacant parking deck. He made sure to stay about ten paces behind lest Sean decide to abruptly turn around and take full stock of his surroundings. He dropped back even farther as Sean pulled out his remote and unlocked his SUV, which straddled two spots on the outer edge of the far side of the lot.

Sean was within a few feet of the back bumper when his phone began vibrating in his jeans. "Yeah?" he asked after clumsily answering the call, his other hand still holding the starburst of shopping bags he had accumulated.

"Sean?"

"Yeah? Who the fuck is this?"

"It's… Derek."

Another stupid fuck in North County. "What's up?"

A pause on the other end. "You coming to Cardiff today?"

"Did we not discuss that like two fucking hours ago?"

"Yeah."

"Has anything changed in the last two fucking hours?" Sean asked as he opened the back of the SUV and tossed his bounty inside.

"No."

"Then why the fuck are you bothering me?" he asked as he opened the door.

"Sorry."

"You *are* sorry, you stupid piece of shit. I'll see you in about an hour."

As Sean hung up, something moved in the corner of his right eye. Standing about ten feet away was some teenaged punk. "What the fuck do you want?" he demanded.

The kid held up his palms. "Sean? Sorry… didn't mean to scare you."

"Who the fuck are you?"

"I'm Alex. Alex Mullens. Joe's son. Sam sent me."

"You following me around the goddamn mall? What the fuck?"

"No man. Sorry. I was just killing some time, and I saw you when I was about to leave and thought, you know—we're both here, right?"

"You remembered what I looked like?" Sean asked.

"Kind of, but they sent me your picture."

"Who did?"

"Sam," Alex said. "Michael gave it to him so I would know who I was supposed to meet."

Fucking Michael, the goddamn idiot. "Why the fuck you sneaking up on me?"

"No, man. I wasn't sneaking up on you. I called out to you a few times, but you were on the phone. I was hanging out here until you hung up."

"Whatever, just—" Sean slammed the door and walked to the back of the SUV, reopening the hatchback. "Get your ass over here." Sean retrieved the weapon, which was wrapped in a kitchen towel, and handed it over.

"Thanks," Alex said as he started to unwrap it.

Sean's hand slapped his. "Not here. You a fucking moron?"

"Sorry."

Sean frowned. "How old are you?"

"Twenty-one."

"Twenty-fucking-one. Jesus Christ, they got toddlers doing this shit now?"

"I can handle myself," Alex said.

"Maybe with a pack of six-graders. Now get the fuck out of here before I call your father and tell him what a dipshit you are."

Sean slammed the hatchback door closed and climbed back into the SUV. He let out a long sigh, exasperated by a day full of frustrations. He looked down to start the car, then back out the windshield, catching a shadow on the left edge of his vision. He looked over to see Alex standing beside the car.

"And what the fuck do you want now?" Sean demanded after lowering the window. "You're a fucking creep, you know that?" Only then did he notice the Sig Sauer he had just handed over—towel gone, a silencer threaded on.

"Tommy Byrne sends his regards," Alex said, raising the weapon and pointing it toward Sean's left eye.

56

Sue looked over her desk, each haphazard stack of papers representing an uncompleted story, few of which would ever be. Not that she was complaining, she thought, picking up then dropping a binder-clipped stack of notes for a puff piece on a charity fundraiser in Balboa Park. As if she could ever go back to that inanity again.

She glanced at her left hand, the slight tremor she'd noticed a few hours ago still there. She wondered when it had started—probably after her short conversation with James Byrne the night before.

"Hello?" he had said in voice mixed with apathy and something else—something darker.

"James Byrne?" she asked, aiming for perkiness. "Hi, my name is Susan—"

"I know who you are, and you need to stop."

"I just have a few questions."

"Never call me again."

"But—"

"Or else," he said, and the call ended.

Or else, she thought as she continued to study her hand. He was just a boy, but one she suspected had been forced to grow up long before he was prepared to do so. She had seen it before—in her friends' adopted children, kindergartners so damaged by their short, tumultuous former lives that you had to lock the silverware drawers.

Her phone lit up. It was Edie.

"Didn't we just talk?" Sue asked as she glanced at the travel itinerary to Chicago and Las Vegas that had been placed on her desk only an hour before. She was still astounded Charles had approved it without question, although now she had no idea how to break the news to Edie without an ensuing argument.

"Yeah, but I'm in the neighborhood and wanted to see if you were in the mood to sneak out a little early for margaritas with Sharon and Julie."

"Sounds good. Where?"

"The wine bar at Fashion Valley we went to the last time. Fifteen minutes?"

Sue glanced at her laptop. "Give me twenty to thirty. I've got to get organized for tomorrow."

"See you then," Edie said.

■ ■ ■

"This is Sam," he announced after answering the call on the burner phone used for such occasions. It, like countless ones before, would be tossed and replaced by week's end.

He was in his office working on some contracts as part of a new mixed-use development they were hoping to break ground on before year's end. It had been a relatively quiet morning save a terse conversation with Moretti, who brought instructions on something already underway, Tommy's signal that he had been forced to bring his father's man partially into their plans.

Sam didn't particularly like Moretti, but respected his position and loyalty to the family. The old advisor was proud and stubborn, much like Ciaran, and it had to have pained him when the elder Byrne fell ill and Tommy assumed full control. Before long Moretti would also be out of the day to day, but until that time Sam would be polite and respectful, and ignore the bitterness directed his way.

"It's Alex," said the voice on the other line.

He forced a smile, though he was alone. "Alex... how's San Diego treating you?"

"Not too bad," he answered, somewhat surprised by the attempt at small talk. Sam had never given him anything more than a passing grunt of acknowledgement, and he chalked even that up to respect for his father. Most people Sam simply ignored, which was probably not a bad thing for them.

"And how's Jimmy doing?"

"Better. He's fine. We're going to grab some dinner tonight and catch up, but when I saw him today he was okay. He didn't say otherwise, and I think he would."

"Good," Sam said. "Let me know if that changes so I can tell Tommy."

"Absolutely," Alex said, looking down at the fist he'd made with his free hand, which hadn't stopped shaking since he shot Sean. "I got it under control."

"So," Sam began, concluding their pleasantries, "how's your homework coming along?"

"The first is done," Alex said.

"And the other one?"

"I'm on my way over there now."

"Okay."

"It's the easier of the two, anyway," Alex said. "It shouldn't take too long."

"Okay," Sam repeated. "Just call me back when you're done."

■ ■ ■

"Carlyle," he answered curtly as he continued to stare at his monitor, his grilled chicken sandwich unwrapped on his desk, the empty fry carton and mostly consumed Coke testifying to his culinary priorities.

He had spent the last several hours trying to stay busy by poring over reports, looking for a pattern in the noise he had gotten from those under his command. There was apparently nothing to go on, as no one had seen anyone who could be linked to the case. Who the hell even knew who the Byrnes had dispatched in the first place?

"I'm inbound," Seegars announced.

"Isn't that nice?" Carlyle said. "What for?"

"We're off to Fashion Valley. There's been a shooting, and we've been asked to drop by."

"I've got enough murders on my plate. Let it be someone else's problem."

"Just have your ass outside in five," Seegars said before abruptly hanging up.

57

"Susan Hendricks?" Alex asked as she crossed the parking garage next to her office.

"What?" she asked as she stopped and turned toward him.

"Are you Susan Hendricks?"

"I stopped, didn't I?" she snapped. She frowned. "I know you. You were at the coffee shop with James Byrne."

"What the fuck?" Alex asked. "How did you—"

"I don't have time for this. What do you want?"

"I'm a friend of the Byrnes."

Sue snorted. If they had wanted her dead, they wouldn't be talking. "*Yeah, no kidding.*" She looked him up and down with a sneer. "I guess they finally let you take the training wheels off your mafia kiddie bike—you stupid little fuck."

Alex raised his eyebrows, unable to hide his surprise. "Look, we don't want any trouble."

"Oh, really? You don't want trouble? I thought that was what you people were all about."

Alex put his hands up. This was not going anywhere near how he thought it would. Using the Byrne name had always elicited both fear and respect. "We don't want any trouble," he repeated.

"Bullshit."

"Look, I've been sent here to ask you to leave James Byrne alone, and to stop sticking your nose in the Byrnes' business. That's it."

"That's it? *That's* my job, you stupid shit. Too many bodies have turned up for me to walk away."

Alex took a step toward her. This had gone on long enough. "There's always room for one more," he said.

"Go fuck yourself," Sue barked as she dug into her purse, the farce of this aspiring mobster child angering her beyond reason.

He watched as her hand went deep inside the large canvas bag as it quickly moved from one object to the next in search of something. At the same time, she began to shuffle away, one foot then tripping over the other. She tumbled backward, unable to get her hand out of her bag in time to catch herself, the hand that had been holding it now tangled in the strap as she tried to yank it free to break her fall.

Seemingly in slow motion, he saw her drop. As she went down her head suddenly jerked forward before her chin hit her chest, the back of her skull having struck the ball mount of the raised pickup truck behind her. She appeared to hang there a second before her now limp body landed on the concrete with a muted thud.

Alex's hand covered his mouth, his face shocked white. His heart pounded as the small canister of mace rolled out of her relaxed grip, stopping a few inches from her fingers.

"Oh, God," he muttered to himself. "Oh, God. Oh fuck."

A car horn in the distance startled him. He quickly looked around, but they were still alone. Turning to the staircase that had brought him there, he quickly walked toward his escape.

■ ■ ■

"Did he tell you why he wanted us to join this little party?" Carlyle asked as Seegars guided the sedan into the Fashion Valley Mall and toward the east parking garage. He now felt somewhat guilty for sending his friend's repeated calls to voicemail.

"No," Seegars answered. "He just said he needed our help with this one."

"He didn't tell you who the victim was? Fuck, the last thing I need is getting involved in a goddamn narcotics investigation."

"Technically it's a murder investigation now."

"Don't be an asshole."

"You're such a killjoy," Seegars remarked as the car climbed the ramp to the second level. "I don't know. He wouldn't tell me."

As their car came to a stop Carlyle looked through the windshield at the red SUV roughly thirty feet away, both its front doors ajar, the rear tailgate opened. Boslin was standing off the back of the driver's side and holding an evidence bag as he stared into the opened rear of the car, where the spare tire had already been removed and now rested on the concrete a few feet away.

The two detectives climbed out of their sedan, and were almost to Boslin before they finally spotted the bagged body on the gurney alongside the driver's side.

"Gentlemen," he said as they approached.

"Don't you 'gentleman' me," Carlyle said with a smirk. "Every time you show up my life gets that much more complicated."

"That's what you get for taking my call."

"I didn't."

"Oh yeah, that's right," Boslin said as he held up the clear plastic evidence bag. "We've got the murder weapon."

"Where was it?" Seegars asked.

"Tossed onto the floorboard and left for us. Definitely a planned hit."

They went to the driver's side door and glanced in, the driver's headrest and passenger seat both spotted with blood. Carlyle stepped aside and looked over the hood at the assembled crowd now gawking as best they could from forty feet away, slowly scanning their faces. Twice in his career the perpetrator had remained on scene to watch, but these bored housewives and kids out of school didn't warrant a thorough review.

He turned as Boslin motioned toward the back of the SUV. "There are enough drugs in the trunk to keep the kids at Torrey Pines tweaking for a month."

"This just keeps getting better," Carlyle said.

"You don't know the half of it."

"And what would that be?" Carlyle asked as he and Seegars walked to where Boslin stood, peering in at the four large bags of cocaine and dozen or so bottles of pills that had been uncovered, the tire iron already in an evidence bag beside them.

"I sent the MEs on a coffee break so you could see this," Boslin said as he pointed to the gurney. "Guess who the victim is?"

"Who?"

"Take a peek."

Carlyle and Seegars stood on either side as Carlyle grabbed the zipper and opened the bag. He didn't recognize the young man, one bullet hole in the left eye socket, a second by the left cheekbone. "Well... that answers a few questions," he said.

He glanced up to see Seegars, his face almost as pale as the victim, before his partner covered his mouth and bolted for the corner.

Boslin appeared beside him. "Is he okay?"

"Fuck if I know. Never seen him do that before."

"Hmm." Boslin patted the bag by the victim's thigh. "Any guesses?"

Carlyle looked back down, noticing the dried streaks that ran down to his chin and had stained the top of the shirt when the head was slumped forward. "This one I don't know."

"Sean Dillon."

Carlyle shook his head. "A dead Irishman with a trunk full of drugs," he said. "What are the odds?"

"His name came up in a database as a known associate of your dear friends from Las Vegas, which is why I called you over here."

"The coke is definitely Vegas," Carlyle said as Seegars returned. He looked over at him. "What the fuck's wrong with you?"

"Nothing," his partner answered, his voice low, as he wiped his mouth once more.

"Then what the fuck's your problem? You were fine around burnt-up corpses the other day and now you're hurling in a corner?"

"I just… I don't know."

"It's got to be a hit," Boslin theorized once more. "With a drug deal gone bad you don't get to keep the drugs, not unless both sides get shot."

Carlyle snorted as he closed the bag. "Well, I guess someone has finally sacked up after all."

58

Carlyle paced as the techs started their work, hands on his hips as he scanned the secluded corner of the garage for something—anything—that would give him a lead. He glanced back over at the onlookers, who still numbered near two dozen, most of their faces hidden behind a wall of phones recording a stranger's murder for their social media pages.

He had been the one who triggered this event, he knew. Tossing the bag of drugs in Tommy Byrne's face, making that threat had given him no choice but to burn off any loose ends. Now a man had been murdered, and it gave him no solace that he was a drug dealer who had no doubt been involved in what had transpired over the past few days. Even the worst of them deserved a day in court. At least the brother, he assured himself, would not meet the same fate. That Tommy would never do. He just prayed that he hadn't started an intrafamily feud that would bring more violence to his city.

Carlyle looked up at the ceiling. "Why the fuck doesn't a mall parking lot have any security cameras?"

"They're too cheap?" Seegars asked from his concrete perch, smoking a cigarette that he had bummed off one of the officers on scene.

The two looked toward the opposite end of the structure as Patterson approached. Carlyle hadn't seen him since they'd found the charred bodies of Harvey and Estrada, having relegated the junior detective to chasing down leads with the others still pouring in on the city tip line. It was an utterly useless task, but one that kept the boy busy, which was all Carlyle wanted until he could figure out how to better utilize him. "I see you got my text," he said as the two shook hands.

"You lovebirds are texting now?" Seegars asked.

"Yes, sir," Patterson said, ignoring the taunt. "What's going on?"

"Homicide that might be related to our case," Carlyle said. "A Byrne associate who's based here—Sean Dillon."

Patterson shook his head. "Never heard of him."

"You're still green," Seegars remarked, and Carlyle shot him a look.

Patterson continued to ignore him. "What do you need me to do?"

"Why don't you take my partner and get me the surveillance video from that department store for the last two hours or so," Carlyle said.

Seegars stepped on his cigarette. "And why do I get that shit assignment?"

"Because I need you to show him what to do, so he can hit the rest of the stores and do the same. I need a lead, so go get me one."

■ ■ ■

Carol Strickland had been a copy editor with the *Times* for nearly six years, and as she always did, the forty-year-old single mother of two walked straight to her late-model Toyota Camry after another long day at work. A creature of habit, she always parked in the same spot, or if some bastard had stolen it from her, as close to it as possible.

She paused at the driver's side door and glanced over the roof towards the building. She immediately recognized Susan Hendricks's aging Subaru a few rows over—hard to miss with its gay-pride and assorted themed stickers—parked caddy-corner to the hideous lifted pickup truck driven by one of the new salesmen. She didn't even know how he managed to fit it through the entrance, much less into its own space, but her eyes drifted back to Susan's colorfully decorated car.

"Hmm," she muttered to herself, knowing that she had seen her leave about an hour beforehand, the car still sitting there seemingly out of place.

She retrieved the keys from her purse and unlocked the car. Before climbing in she looked back to Susan's, a dark mass on the concrete between the bumpers of the Subaru and truck catching her attention. Her first thought was an oil leak, but whatever it was, it was three dimensional.

Her brow now furrowed, she closed her car door and headed over to investigate.

59

"What happened?" Sam asked.

His contracts done, he looked down at the perfectly timed first pour of gin, his index finger circling the rim as he awaited the answer. The short, quickly paced breathing on the other end of the call had not subsided. Sam had expected problems—only not after the more difficult task had already been completed. Of course, hindsight reminded him, it would occur with the simpler of the two.

"I tried to warn the fucking bitch—just like you asked me to."

"Alex, I'm going to need you to calm down and take a few deep breaths for me, okay?"

"Okay. Yeah."

"Now what happened?"

"She's dead."

Sam picked up the glass and emptied it in one swallow. "What do you mean she's dead?" he asked, forcing calm into his voice as he stood and walked toward his office bar.

Alex hesitated, his mind attempting to recall a moment he still could not comprehend. "I, uh… it happened so fast."

Sam retrieved the bottle and headed back to his chair. "What did you do to her?"

"Nothing."

"Then how is she dead?"

"She fell."

"How did she fall?"

"She tripped."

Sam poured the glass halfway full, leaving the bottle on his desk. "I'm not playing twenty fucking questions with you, Alex," he snapped. "Just answer the fucking question."

Alex paused once more as he gathered his thoughts. "We were talking," he began. "She kept arguing with me. She just wouldn't listen."

"Okay. And then what?"

"I took a step towards her. I mean, we were still like five, six feet apart. I wasn't anywhere near her. She freaked out, went for mace. Bitch was going to spray me with it. She... she tripped, and her head hit this truck."

"And you didn't touch her?" Sam asked.

"No! Fuck no. I didn't lay a hand on her."

"And you're sure she's dead?"

"There was blood. Her eyes were still open."

Sam exhaled slowly. "Where is she now?"

"I left her."

"You left the fucking body behind?"

"Yeah," Alex said. "Shouldn't I have?"

"A missing person is better than a body. That shouldn't be a difficult concept to grasp."

"I've never done anything like this before. How am I supposed to know what to do?"

"Pick up the fucking phone and call someone," Sam said.

"That's what I'm doing now."

"Go back down there now. Put her in the trunk. Leave the scene. Then call me back."

"Okay."

"Can you at least do that fucking much?"

"Yeah," Alex said. "I'll call you in fifteen."

■ ■ ■

Carlyle looked up as Seegars strolled across the lot. He seemed much more relaxed than when they had first arrived on the scene.

"What are you doing back?" Carlyle asked. "I thought you had video to get."

"They're working on, and I left the kid to deal with it. He can manage."

"Hey guys," Boslin interrupted. "There's an eleven-four-six that just came over the wire that you'll probably be interested in."

Carlyle raised an eyebrow. "This shit is just never going to end. Where is it?"

"The *Times*."

60

It wasn't supposed to be like this. He had dreams of a triumphant return to Chicago, with more responsibility, prestige, and power, having earned the opportunity to rise to what his father had accomplished. It had all been his for the asking, but in an instant that dream had been smashed beyond repair by a clumsy, middle-aged lesbian.

There would be repercussions. There always were. This was too big a screw-up, even if it was completely out of his control, for it to go unanswered. His only hope at salvaging the situation, and his life with the Byrnes, would be getting to her body before anyone discovered it. They could suspect the Byrnes all they wanted, but without proof he was home free. That was how it always worked. In time, his reputation could be salvaged, and this blunder would subside to nothing more than a joke among friends.

The garage was just ahead as the flashing lights appeared in his rear-view mirror. Two police cruisers, lights blazing, were racing up from behind. His heart immediately tried to leap out of his chest, his hands shaking uncontrollably as he strangled the steering wheel. They flew past him in the left lane. She had been found, and his life as he knew it was over.

He pulled the car over to the side of the road. Shutting the engine off, he took a few deep breaths before reaching down to his phone in the center console.

"Yeah?" Sam asked.

"They already found her."

Alex could hear Sam take a deep breath followed by a long sigh.

"What kind of phone do you have?"

"Why?"

"Answer the goddamn question," Sam snapped.

"An iPhone," Alex said. "Why?"

"You didn't get a burner?"

"No."

"Oh, fuck me," Sam muttered. "Power it down and get rid of it. Somewhere wet and deep. Now."

"Why?"

"You think these cops are so fucking dumb they're not going to figure out who the hell you are?"

"The phone was off at both locations," Alex protested. "They can't put me anywhere near there."

"They can put you in San Diego, so kill the fucking thing now."

"Anything else?"

"*Anything else?* No, but you're in a fucking load of trouble."

"I already know that," Alex replied, but the line was already dead.

■ ■ ■

"Detective Carlyle," he answered, Seegars at the wheel.

"Well don't you sound official?" Lubbock said.

"Just showing respect for your office, *Special Agent*," Carlyle said as Seegars glanced over. "What do you got for me?"

"Never any foreplay with you, is there?"

"You want foreplay, I'll put my partner on the phone," he said, which earned him another look.

"I've met your partner," Lubbock said. "No thanks."

"So, what you got?"

"His name is Alex Mullens. His father is Joe Mullens, one of their captains."

"What you got on him?"

"Not much. One arrest… bar fight last year. Charges dropped, of course. Father manages their alcohol distribution on the North Side. Mostly on the up and up."

"Mostly?"

"Eh, a few of the usual rumors involving organized crime and money," Lubbock said. "Nothing we're too concerned about."

"That doesn't concern you?"

"*Too* concerned about," Lubbock repeated. "Priorities, my friend."

"Got a cell phone we can track?"

"Yeah," he said, then recited the numbers as Carlyle wrote them down. "So, he's out there?"

"Yup," Carlyle said. "We took that picture while he was with James Byrne."

"Hmmm."

"I think I know where you're headed."

"We never pursued it."

"If they had urgent business to take care of, they wouldn't send this Alex Mullens, would they?"

"Oh God, no," Lubbock said. "Kid's as dumb as a box of rocks—and not the fancy ones. He helps collect for his father, but that's about all he's good for. Why? You got another body pop up recently?"

"Yeah. About an hour ago, and I don't think those assholes who rolled through earlier are still around."

"I can't imagine it's him—but fuck if I know what they're up to."

61

"This can't be good if you came in person," Tommy said, climbing into the car outside his building for their second meeting of the day.

It wasn't ideal, but some things couldn't be said at the office or over the phone. He was fairly certain that neither were being actively monitored, at least not in the office, which was swept regularly for bugs, but in here the two could talk candidly about their business interests to the north, orders given and received, then disseminated as needed.

Sam paused. "The first task was handled without incident."

Tommy reclined into the seat a bit more. This wouldn't be one of their brief exchanges. "But?" he reluctantly asked.

"The reporter is dead," Sam said.

Tommy paused. "How?"

"She tripped and hit her head."

Tommy didn't move. "How."

"She stumbled trying to get a can of mace out of her purse."

"Fuck me." Tommy took a deep breath and exhaled loudly. "What'd he do with the body?"

"He ran."

"He *what*?"

"He left, called me to find out what to do."

"What'd you tell him?"

"What do you think I told him?" Sam asked, insulted. "I said to go back and get the fucking body."

"Well? What'd he do with it?"

"Nothing. Someone had already found it by the time he got there."

"Jesus fucking Christ," Tommy said. "Where is he?"

"I'm not sure. Still in San Diego somewhere. I told him to ditch his phone. Dumb fuck didn't bring a burner."

It had been a calculated risk to have involved Alex at all, Tommy knew. Even under the best of circumstances, their exposure could be significant— depending on how hard Carlyle pushed the supplier's murder. Tommy didn't think he would have, but the death of the reporter, however inadvertent, would force the detective's hand. It was only a matter of time before they linked Alex to both crime scenes.

"I think he's fucked on the phone alone," Sam said, and Tommy nodded. "This Carlyle prick isn't stupid."

Tommy sighed. "Get with Joe on this. He needs to know."

"And Highland Park?"

"Probably," Tommy said, "but let's just try to get this mess cleaned up beforehand."

■ ■ ■

"You got my ten bucks?" Seegars asked as Carlyle approached the crime scene.

"Jesus fucking Christ," Carlyle muttered as he stood over the body, ignoring his partner's comment. "Will this ever fucking end?"

He looked down at the spirited journalist, now a wilted version of her former self, lying on her side, her head tilted to the right. Her graying brown hair partially covered her face as her lifeless eyes stared off over the pavement. A small can of mace lay by her open hand, and a small pool of blood extended roughly six inches from the back of her head.

"What's this? Number six?" the forensic pathologist asked as he watched the two detectives study the scene.

"You tell us," Seegars said. "It's your morgue."

"This is the eighth," Carlyle said as he tried to recall the man's name, the last, Hampton, all he could recall. "So, what do we have?"

Hampton crouched beside the body as he pointed to the ball mount extending from the raised Silverado, a deep maroon mark along the top. "She hit her head here."

"How'd it happen?" Seegars asked. "Was she pushed?"

Hampton shook his head. "Hard to say. It's certainly a possibility." He pointed to her left black dress shoe. "I did see this, though. The shoes, as you can see, are otherwise pristine."

"That's a lesbian for you," Seegars commented.

"There's a scuff along the inside left, though, by the ankle. It looks like the heel of the right rubbed against it, and you can see it here," he said as he carefully lifted her right leg and pointed to the back of her shoe.

"Are you saying she tripped?" Carlyle asked.

"She definitely tripped backwards, I'm just not sure what caused it." Hampton answered as he stood up. "If I had to guess, she was standing about here," he began as he pointed about a foot in front of her feet. "Whatever happened, I don't know, but she stepped back when she was going for that mace over there," he said as he then pointed toward the small canister. "She tripped backward and—" Hampton pointed towards the truck. "—hit the ball of the trailer hitch at the base of her skull before her ass touched the ground. If the truck hadn't been raised, she would have been seated before she impacted."

"You're fucking shitting me," Carlyle said.

Seegars looked up. "Oh," he said. "We've got a camera. Let me get on that."

62

James opened the door. Alex stood there with his hands thrust deep into his pockets, his face tight with worry. "What's wrong?" James asked as he stepped aside to let him into the apartment.

"Nothing," Alex said. "It's nothing."

James closed the door. "It has to be something."

"It's just one of those days," Alex said as he headed to the couch, James on his heels. He sat down in the far corner, knocking his head back into the soft leather.

James sat down on the middle cushion, tucking his right leg under him, careful to give Alex his space. He had never seen him so visibly upset. Something had transpired that afternoon—enough to expose the lie about why Alex had really come to San Diego.

He pictured himself back in the bed at Tommy and Sabrina's while recovering from Enzo's assault. He would spend most of the few hours he was awake staring through the blinds out the window. Sabrina said very little, accepting his silence and feeble nods in response to her questions, which she limited to inquiries about food and assistance to the bathroom. And on those few times he found himself curled up on his side crying, she would climb into bed next to him and hold him until the wave subsided. Only when it was time for James to leave for California did the two finally share more than a few words, although the assault was never discussed.

"Why do you stay?" James had asked.

Sabrina was sitting in a chair by the window with her iPad. "What?" she asked.

"Why do you stay? Here. With my family."

She set the tablet down on the side table beside the chair. "Because I love your brother."

"You know what my family is."

Sabrina nodded. "Yes, I do. But I love him enough to look past that."

"How can you?" he asked.

"I just do. And I know that things will eventually change for the better."

She stood and walked over, sitting down beside him. Their eyes met briefly, then his gaze quickly returned to the window. "Is this about—"

"No," he said. "I don't want to talk about him."

"What are you going to do?" she asked.

A tear fell from his left eye, across the bridge of his nose and dripped onto the pillow. It hadn't quite been a day since he confessed his deepest secret, and he prayed once more that it would stop with her. Alex's life could very well depend on that, he knew. "I have to end it," he whispered. "They'll kill him."

"Tommy would never allow it."

"Enzo doesn't care about what he says. My mother—"

"Jimmy, it's going to be all right. I promise you. Everything will be fine."

She was wrong, James thought as he patted Alex on the leg. "What happened?" he asked.

Alex groaned. He couldn't shake the image of the dead woman on the pavement, her blood slowly trickling from the back of her head. He imagined her twitching involuntarily—his mind playing tricks on him—though she never flinched after she struck the truck. "It's nothing. I don't want to talk about it."

"Are we going out, or…?"

Alex raised his head and their eyes met. "Can we just stay in?"

"Sure," James said. "Whatever you want."

Alex raised his hands. "Come here." James crawled over and into his arms. Alex gently kissed James's head. "I'm sorry. I know you wanted to go out."

James rubbed Alex's forearm. "It's okay," he said, content just to be held by him once more.

...

It had been roughly an hour since they'd returned to the office before Seegars had the screenshots of the surveillance video printed and taped to the whiteboard behind Carlyle's desk.

The two said nothing as they studied each of the ten photos, the first five from the mall, the others taken from where Susan Hendricks had been discovered. In both were the same person, dressed in jeans, a black hooded sweatshirt, and a Yankees cap, first following Dillon as he made his way around Fashion Valley, then at the parking garage with Hendricks. In none of them was a clear face shot, although on build alone Carlyle knew it was Alex Mullens. Proving it, however, would require more.

They could watch as Dillon was shadowed through various areas of the mall, even exiting the last building before being gunned down moments later, but there was nothing to prove that the person trailing him pulled the trigger. For all they knew, one of the Byrnes had returned, sending the younger man only to alert him that Dillon was exiting the mall.

And then there was Susan Hendricks. The video was being reviewed to get a transcript of what she said—whoever was with her had his back to the camera, of course—but it was clear from the body language that her life wasn't in danger, that the man meant her no physical harm. Carlyle could only watch the video of her demise once, and even then, he instinctively turned away as her head struck the truck and fell lifeless to the ground. They'd be lucky to get the DA to agree to an involuntary manslaughter charge, and even then a halfway decent defense attorney would laugh it out of court. Assuming, of course, they could even prove who was standing in front of her.

"What's with the Yankees cap?" Seegars asked.

Carlyle looked over at his partner. "Huh?"

Seegars nodded at the screenshots from the mall. "What sort of douchebag from Chicago wears a Yankees cap?"

"A smart one."

"That kid is slap happy stupid."

"He's smart enough to evade a million fucking cameras."

"I wouldn't be too sure of that," Patterson said from the doorway. He reached into the file folder he was holding and brandished a photo. It was a clear face shot of Alex Mullens as he walked through the mall. "I *knew* he'd have to look up at some point."

Carlyle motioned him over and took the photo. A smile crept onto his face. "Well, we got the son of a bitch. Let's get a warrant out for him," he ordered as Seegars stood. "And make sure our friends in Chicago know he's a wanted man."

■ ■ ■

She walked into the darkened living room, lit by only the city lights below, her husband in his usual seat, holding an inch of bourbon as he looked out on the world through the floor-to-ceiling windows. She quietly walked over with her glass of merlot and sat down in the chair's twin a few feet away, a small round table the only physical barrier between them.

He was thinking of a night last August, when he stood in his parents' living room fixing one last drink, his meeting with his father and Moretti having concluded only a few moments before. Both of the older men had departed, one for Lincoln Park, the other upstairs. His mother, still enraged by their confrontation over Jimmy, had once more shown her displeasure with her absence.

Tommy had just finished pouring himself a bourbon when Enzo entered the room from an evening out. He could feel his body stiffen as his younger brother sauntered over, the two watching each other as Enzo stopped on the other side of the ornate mahogany bar. Enzo glanced down only long enough to grab a glass and the decanter of whiskey to pour himself a drink. With a sneer, he turned and sat in the middle of the sofa.

Tommy remained where he was, taking a sip from his glass. He watched Enzo, who stared across the coffee table toward the unlit fireplace as both hands cradled his drink.

"I know what you did," Tommy said.

Enzo scoffed. "I do a lot of things," he said without looking over.

"To Jimmy."

Enzo slowly turned his head. "And?"

"You're a sick fuck."

"And?"

Tommy didn't answer.

"That's what I thought," Enzo said. "How many men have you ordered me to kill since you took over? I'm sorry—have *Sam* order me to kill, since you like to pretend you're above this. Not even a year since Pop put you in charge and I think we're up to what—eight? Nine? I've lost count."

Tommy looked down at his drink as Enzo continued: "I just beat an alderman's nephew half to death—and for the record he'll never walk right again—all because your dear friend the mayor didn't like how his uncle voted on some stupid education bill. Before that I tossed a fucking Teamster in front of a Metra train so you could—"

"Things are going to change around here."

"Yeah? Good luck with that."

"And what you did to Jimmy… you will answer for it."

Enzo leapt up from the couch. "What the fuck are you going to do about it?" Again, Tommy remained silent as Enzo walked back to the opposite side of the bar and refilled his glass. "You couldn't kill that old man back when we were kids, and you don't have the balls to do anything about this now. I gave that little faggot something to think about, and you *will* accept that and let it the fuck go."

The two watched each other from across the bar. "That's what I fucking thought," Enzo said. "Fuck you, you douche."

"Hon?" Sabrina asked.

"Huh?"

"Are you okay?"

Tommy nodded. "Yeah." He knocked back the last of his drink. "Sorry."
"You were out there."

He forced a grin. "A bit," he admitted.

A silence fell between them as they looked out at the skyline.

"When did you know about Jimmy and Alex?" he asked.

"Last year."

"Did you suspect, or…?"

"No. He told me. Why? What's happened?"

He sighed. "It's nothing."

Sabrina, not wanting to press him after his most recent confession, one
she was sure he regretted, managed a smile. "Whatever it is, I'm sure you'll
find a way through."

Tommy's phone buzzed, and he quickly answered. "I'll be right down."
He looked over at her. "Sam and Joe," he said as she stood up.

"What are they doing here so late?"

"Joe requested a meeting."

Sabrina gently kissed the top of his head as she picked up his empty
glass. He stood up beside her, leaning in to steal a kiss.

"I love you," she called out as he walked into the foyer.

He turned, a grin on his face. "I love you too."

FRIDAY

63

It was bitterly cold, a typical Chicago winter night where the wind cut through you as you cursed yourself for having to be outside and envied those who had chosen better, now safe and warm. He had retraced these steps countless times, déjà vu tickling at the edges of his mind as he rounded the corner. Across the street, only yards away, was the convenience store he had been seeking.

As he entered, he crossed his arms tightly across his chest, taking in the linoleum floor streaked from dirty mop water, the painted metal shelves showing wear with nicks and scuffs, the sparsely stocked merchandise velveted with a thin layer of dust. The exposed fluorescent tubes, arranged in parallel rows above the small aisles, flickered feebly. Several of them were already dark, no one having bothered to replace them.

He found himself standing in line behind an elderly woman, watching her grope her tote bag for loose change, a cold bottle of water heavy in his hand as he tapped his foot.

The chime of the door announced a new arrival. He continued to fixate on the woman in front of him, shaking not with impatience but the cold—the bottle now a block of ice in his hand.

"Everyone on the floor! Get on the goddamn floor!" He turned to look, only to be struck across the face with a handgun, his body spinning around with the impact. Another blow to his back sent him to his knees, his hands briefly arresting the fall before a boot stomped him face-down onto the linoleum.

He looked over at the old woman, who now faced him in a similar position, terror in her eyes as she struggled to keep from crying. He could feel his breathing become labored, his heart seizing as he desperately grasped at a composure teetering on the edge.

Dirty black work boots paced between them. Whoever lorded over them was speaking, but their words were muffled by the ringing in his ears. They were speaking quickly, the staccato of their sentences conveying both urgency and anger, but he could not tell who they were, nor what they were discussing or deciding. He thought he recognized one of the voices, but not well enough to give him a name.

The feet stopped and turned, the toes now pointed at his head. He heard the chambering of a bullet, and he found himself floating above his own body—as he had countless times before—watching the man above him direct the weapon toward his head. The loud bang and flash jerked him upright in his bed, unable to catch a breath as he dripped in sweat.

Tommy looked around the room as the terror slowly dissipated. He was alone, save for the morning sun illuminating the drawn curtains.

He glanced at the alarm clock on the other side of the bed, which read 7:34. He rubbed his eyes before lying back down, resting his hands on his chest as his breathing slowly returned to normal.

He didn't know why that particular nightmare visited him at times like this, or what it symbolized. If only he knew who the masked men were, what they represented, then perhaps he could see what they foreshadowed. Tommy Byrne was a man who believed that dreams eventually came to pass.

The phone on the nightstand began to vibrate.

"Yes?" he asked.

"Eleven," Moretti announced before the call ended.

64

Carlyle awoke suddenly, Susan Hendricks immediately coming to mind. His dream faded as he pictured her once more on the cement parking deck.

Not in many years had he found himself emotionally dwelling upon a crime scene, even the most gruesome. How he handled each death over the past few days was a living testament to how he normally faced such things—even the water-damaged bodies of Foss and Clark, even the burned corpses of Harvey and Estrada. But her death had somehow touched him in such a way that he had no longer believed possible.

He thought back to a time when he was still vulnerable, his first case as a detective—the murder of a four-year-old girl and her mother at the hands of their father in South Park. All were illegal immigrants, and the bastard had made it back over the border before they had been able to catch up with him, and getting Mexican authorities to track him down was about as likely as convincing his ex-wife to lay off the alimony demands.

They had been beaten to death with a hammer, and the images of their shattered corpses had stuck with him for several years after the case had been filed away. The nightmares had long subsided, the visions of the child's collapsed skull faded to a dim memory, but every so often he thought of those two poor souls who would never see justice served.

As his breath slowed and the adrenalin receded, he found some humor in the irony. He hadn't even liked Susan that much.

A new thought intruding, he reached over to the phone sitting in its charger.

"What's up, partner?" Seegars asked as he pulled the phone from his ear to check the time. It was early even by Carlyle's standards, and the man was obsessive to a fault.

"James Byrne," Carlyle said.

"What about him?"

"You think he knows what his coffee-shop friend has been up to?"

"Uh... I don't know. Probably not," Seegars answered.

"And why do you think that?"

"I think your theory was correct. They're two lovebirds. Mullens was sent out to check on the kid and keep him happy."

"And then they send this punk kid to kill a guy?" Carlyle asked. "That make sense to you?"

"Sure, why not? Maybe it came up quick. And maybe your friend Tommy didn't want anyone in Chicago or Las Vegas to know what he was up to."

"Why do you think that?"

"Just seems to make sense to me," Seegars said. "Or they'd have gotten someone who knew what the hell they were doing."

Carlyle sighed. "Come get me in thirty. We need to pay James Byrne a visit. And let's pray he isn't alone this morning."

■ ■ ■

James lay on his stomach near the center of the bed, his right arm outstretched, his fingers under the pillow where Alex's head should have been resting.

He stared at the empty side of the bed a few moments, thoughts of their evening together replaying in his head as he slid his hand down the sheet. It was cool to the touch, his guest having seemingly departed some time ago.

He shivered as he reached down to retrieve the partially discarded top sheet. The duvet had been kicked to the floor, beyond recovery without the effort of getting out of bed. He curled up with the sheet, continuing to stare at the vacant spot beside him. If he could have willed Alex back to his side, he would have.

In the meantime, he thought as he closed his eyes, he'd sleep with the hope that Alex would return before he awoke.

65

When Tommy entered the kitchen, Sabrina was at the island, bent over the countertop as she aimlessly swiped through her iPad.

The sight of her husband in a suit—tie and pocket square included—was surprising, but not unexpected. As she was passing their bedroom she'd heard him talking to himself, mostly a random string of profanities. "Goddamn full fucking meeting," was one such muttered outburst—and it made her stop cold.

Full meetings were what Tommy used to distinguish those gatherings held for matters of grave importance. Always were Ciaran, Tommy, Enzo, Moretti, and whichever of the captains were involved. As of late, with Ciaran's condition and Tommy's ascendency, Isabella and Sam were also usually in attendance.

"I thought you had casual Fridays at the office," she joked.

"Yeah." He leaned down and the two quickly kissed. "I wish that's where I was headed."

She watched as he went for the coffee pot, his favorite cup already on the counter. "I wish your father would just let you take care of things."

He came back with his coffee and sat on the stool beside her. "He does… mostly. But I kind of made a mess. I suspected this would be coming."

"Is everything okay?"

"Yeah, oh yeah," he said a bit too casually. "We just need to discuss things, that's all. Everything is fine."

She sighed. "You mean your mother wants to bitch."

Tommy laughed.

"Am I wrong?"

"No, dear," he said, and the two kissed once more. "That's just my mother. She's going to have her say, and he's going to let her do it." He paused. "This isn't going to be any different from any other time."

As always she spotted the lie. It had become routine to ignore them, but since he had already brought up Jimmy and the drugs, she decided to push the conversation. "What happened?"

Tommy stood up and stepped away, stopping in front of the refrigerator before turning to face her. "Don't ask me that."

"I'm asking."

"Whatever it is, I can handle it."

"What is it?" she pressed.

"You know better than to ask me about my work."

"I'm asking."

Tommy paused. "Goddamn it, Sabrina. I knew I shouldn't have said anything. You need to let it go. This doesn't concern you."

"Fuck you," she said. "You know it does."

He stopped. She never probed on such things, but he realized it involved Jimmy. She was as protective of his younger brother as he was, but despite her feelings, he had no choice but to protect her at all costs, no matter the fallout.

He put his coffee cup down on the counter before their eyes met once more. "I'll take care of it," he said, already turning away.

■ ■ ■

"Hello, Mr. Byrne," Carlyle said after James opened the door. The two detectives were wearing their badges around their necks, a gesture they employed with those they thought might fear their position and the power that came with it. "I'm Detective Carlyle—"

"I remember," James said as he shook his hand.

"I assume you also remember my partner, Detective Seegars." James nodded after glancing over at the younger detective. Carlyle cleared his throat. "May we come in?"

"Oh… yes, please. Sorry," James said, stepping aside.

The two detectives entered the apartment, their second visit of the week. Ordinarily Carlyle would have combed through it while James was still in the hospital, seeking clues among the personal effects that could link attacker and victim. These assaults, however, hadn't required this, and he had stopped bothering after the third attack.

He recalled, when they arrived the first time, how he had been surprised by what he found. The furnishings were expensive, though not overly showy, more in line with a mid-to-late twentysomething professional's than a teenage college student's. Framed prints on the walls, tables decorated with candles and photos, a row of copper cookware hanging on the kitchen wall. Almost as if he were living in a model home rather than his own apartment. Perhaps, Carlyle thought, James was creating a space for the life he believed he would eventually occupy if he willed it into being, one far from his family's intrusions.

He looked back at the lanky teen in a hoodie and baggy, well-worn khaki pants, standing there barefoot. It was unmistakably Southern California in appearance, no trace of his Chicago heritage apparent. Even his accent, now that he thought about it, was nonexistent, a contrast to his older brother's distinct Midwestern drawl.

Their first visit had been more subdued, the three sitting down at the small round dining room table to the right of the front entryway to go over what they had found at the Foss and Clark apartment. Carlyle loathed having to further traumatize the victim with those particular details, as well as the probable outcome of the discovery, but it was a calculated risk to see what he could either get him to disclose, or to provoke a response out of the family. He would call his subsequent visit from Tommy Byrne a validation of the effort.

Today, though, the tension was that much more palpable, James Byrne exhibiting an unease which to both detectives meant there was something, or someone, he was trying to shield from them. Carlyle watched as Seegars slowly cased the room, glancing into the kitchen before ending his path in front of the opened bedroom door. His partner's hand was on his stomach, his fingers hidden behind the distressed jacket, his firearm within easy reach.

"You alone?" Seegars asked.

James looked over at him. He had been staring toward the kitchen, avoiding eye contact with either officer, his hands shoved into the front pocket of his hoodie. "Yes."

Carlyle stepped toward Seegars, putting James equidistant between the two detectives and the front door. He also glanced into the bedroom, the unmade bed the only thing out of place in the entire apartment. "You expecting anyone?" Carlyle asked.

"No."

Seegars picked up one of the picture frames on the end table beside the couch. In it was a photo of James, two other young men on either side of him. "Who are they?"

"Just friends."

Seegars put it down. He glanced at the others. "Any of family?"

"No."

"Why's that?" Seegars asked.

James looked down at the floor. "I just don't."

"Damn," Seegars remarked. "I wanted to see the infamous Ciaran Byrne."

It was time to get to business. "Do you know Alex Mullens?" Carlyle asked as his partner stopped his browsing and faced James.

"Yes."

"And how do you know him?"

"We're friends," James said.

"That's all?" Seegars asked. Carlyle shot him a glance.

James paused. "Yes."

"That's not what we heard," Seegars remarked.

"Where is he?" Carlyle asked.

"I don't know."

"He's in town though, isn't he?"

Another pause.

"Son, I'm asking you a question."

James knew that he shouldn't even be talking to them. That was part of the family code: say nothing and ask for your lawyer. He had visualized the scenario a thousand times before but never imagined he would ever face it. He had run too far for this to happen.

He glanced over at his phone on the dining room table. He could be talking with Sam, his only direct link other than Tommy without the rest of the family being involved. He didn't know what else to do, how to answer without putting someone at risk.

"Where's your boyfriend, James?" Seegars snapped. "Where the fuck is he?"

Carlyle turned to his partner. "Can I speak to you outside?"

"Are you serious?" Seegars asked.

"Yes," Carlyle said, pointing to the door. "You. Outside. Now."

James backed out of the way, the two detectives both clearly angry as they passed him. He didn't know whether this was an act or whether the two were truly at odds, only that he wanted them gone.

Carlyle stood in the doorway and looked at James. "You stay put," he ordered before slamming the door.

66

Alex watched from the newly acquired car as the two men exited the apartment, their badges glinting in the morning sun. He'd ditched his rental in Pacific Beach and pulled this one from a beachside lot the day before. Even at this distance he could see the agitation on their faces.

His mind spun with the possibilities. Were they looking for him? Did they even know he was in town? Or were they just stopping by to check on James after the attack? No, he immediately thought. There was too much anger between them for this to be a routine house call. Something more serious was happening.

Fearful that they might have spotted him, he leaned forward and reached for his makeshift ignition switch. His hands brushed the exposed wires as he continued to watch them through the gap between the steering wheel and dashboard, realizing that a quick escape would not be necessary. The two could not have cared less had he been standing at the base of the stairs to James's apartment, so preoccupied were they with whatever argument they were about to have.

■ ■ ■

The two stopped by the railing about five feet from the front door before Seegars turned back to his partner. "What the fuck is your problem?" he demanded.

"*My* problem?"

"Yes, your problem." He pointed toward the apartment door. "Don't you know who the fuck we're dealing with?"

"He's a kid," Carlyle said.

"He's a goddamn Byrne. If you think he's not as dirty as the rest of them, you're delusional."

"He's not one of them."

"Robert," Seegars began, a rare use of his partner's first name, "I don't know what the fuck's going through your mind right now, but you got to get your head straight. At the very least he's harboring a murder suspect, and you know it. We need to ride him like any other asshole out there."

Carlyle shook his head. "No. Not that hard."

Seegars nodded. "Yes. He'll crack. He's a bed wetter."

"Up to that line only, but he's not going downtown—it's not necessary. You can crack him in there."

"His ass needs to be in jail."

"Not yet," Carlyle said. "We don't need to go there. I also don't need the *Times* on my ass because we locked up one of the Hillcrest assault victims."

"Well at least your favorite lesbian is on vacation at the morgue."

"Not funny."

Seegars scoffed. "Look… it's an unrelated charge. Fuck them."

"Then think about your career. Even if you're right, it's shitty optics. We can wait."

"Why? So you can drag it out and let him walk from a felony drug distribution?" Seegars asked, Carlyle having finally confessed to the contents of the padded envelope after his meeting with Tommy at Lucky's. "Let's do that… make it cushy for the don's son and encourage the behavior."

"If we take him downtown on that, do you know what his family will do to him?"

"I don't give a shit."

"They'll kill him," Carlyle said, "and they'll do it without blinking."

"I somehow think your good friend Tommy won't let that happen."

"You assume that's his call to make. Do you really want to take that risk and wind up with blood on your hands?"

"Don't lecture me on the Byrnes and blood."

"We're not doing it. I'm not willing to take that risk," Carlyle said.

"Goddamn it!" Seegars raised his arms and locked his fingers together behind his head, elbows pointed outward, as he began to pace. His face flushed, his breathing hurried, he began to loudly exhale, as if gasping for air.

Carlyle watched as his partner went back and forth to the other side of the porch, refusing to make eye contact. He waited until he was walking away once more. "Well, if you're going to pout—."

Seegars stopped and turned, jabbing a finger at his partner. "Fuck you, you piece of shit. You're letting him goddamn walk. I can't believe it."

"Craig, he's not going downtown. End of discussion." He motioned toward the door. "Do I make myself clear?"

"Perfectly."

67

His first call had been to Sam, but it rang to voicemail. When the door opened, he had just gotten through to Moretti.

"Who the fuck are you talking to?" Seegars barked as he stormed over.

"My—my lawyer," James stuttered.

"Who is that?" Moretti asked.

"The cops," James said before the phone was ripped from his hand.

"We're thinking of taking your boy downtown," Seegars said as he looked towards Carlyle. "He'll have to call you back later."

"For what?" Moretti asked.

Seegars continued to look at his partner. "Oh, a few things. Possibly harboring a fugitive. We're also considering felony possession of illegal narcotics with intent to distribute, but we haven't committed to that one yet."

"Goddamn it!" Carlyle snapped.

Moretti smiled broadly in the empty foyer he had just entered as he made his way to the meeting. Of all dumb luck, he thought. "Well, officer… you do what you have to do."

Carlyle watched as Seegars tossed the phone onto the dining room table, then grabbed James's hoodie in his fist. "What the fuck were you doing? Are you a fucking idiot or something?"

James didn't answer, the color drained from his face.

"Answer me, you little fucking prick."

"No," James whispered.

"Get on the ground," Seegars ordered.

"What?"

Seegars shook him back and forth by the hoodie. "Get on the fucking ground—on your stomach."

James lay down, his cheek against the carpet, hands above his head. Seegars knelt, placing one knee squarely on James's back, the young man gasping under the weight. "I want to know where Alex Mullens is."

"I don't know."

"Bullshit."

"I don't know," James repeated more forcefully.

"Was he here last night?"

A pause. "No."

"You lying sack of shit," Seegars said. "I want to know where he is or I will take you downtown, and I will charge you with those fucking drugs we found on you."

"I don't know," James said, his voice cracking. "I don't know. I don't know."

Carlyle watched as Seegars grabbed James's left hand and yanked it behind the young man's back, his other hand retrieving a pair of handcuffs from his right pocket as the boy's body went rigid with shock.

"Do you know what they do to young guys like you downtown?" Seegars asked as he locked the cuff around James's left wrist. "Do you?"

"No, no, no," James chanted, tears streaming down his face.

"Oh, yeah," Seegars said. "They're going to have a fucking field day with your lily-white ass."

The boy's almost rhythmic chanting of "no" became louder as he squirmed under Seegars's knee, and Carlyle could see that he was no longer with them. "Craig—" he said.

"You go downtown, and you won't make it through the night," Seegars continued, ignoring his partner.

James began to thrash uncontrollably, now screaming "no" repeatedly as he nearly knocked Seegars off his back. Still holding James's wrist, he grabbed at the boy's right one, but he was bucking too much. He had never seen a kid this size put up such a fight.

"Craig!" Carlyle yelled. "That's enough."

"Fuck that," Seegars said as he continued to wrestle with the boy. "This little fucker is going downtown."

Carlyle stepped forward and shoved Seegars hard onto the carpet. Seegars, momentarily startled, started to get up but Carlyle gripped his shoulder. "No," he ordered as James frantically scrambled away on his hands and knees, his protestations now a raspy wailing as he vanished behind the kitchen counters.

The two partners exchanged looks as Seegars stood. "What the fuck was that about?" he demanded.

"Did you not fucking see that?!" Carlyle shouted as he pointed toward the kitchen. "What you were doing to him?!"

"That was the point," Seegars said. He held his thumb and index finger a half inch apart. "I was this fucking close to breaking him."

Carlyle glanced once more to the kitchen as the moaning on the other side of the counter continued. "You just broke him—broke him real good. Now call a fucking ambulance and let's try to clean this mess up the only way left."

68

"This is completely out of control," Isabella announced, her steely gaze settling on Tommy.

The grandfather clock behind the closed door to the foyer ticked as they waited for Ciaran to speak. The elder Byrne seemed lost in thought as he stared intently at the table before him, his forearms resting on the dark wood, a coffee—no doubt fortified with a splash of whiskey—sat a few inches from his right hand.

Tommy had seen the look before, the slightly furrowed brows, the fixated gaze. It was his father's effort to once more anchor himself in the present, to reaffirm who and what he was in that moment. It usually only took a moment or two, but with each beat from the muffled clock Tommy knew that the odds of his father successfully navigating the approaching pitfalls of this hastily called meeting were quickly slipping away.

Of all the worst possible times, Tommy thought as he too fixated on where his father's eyes fell. He slowly looked over at Enzo, who was inspecting his nails. Once just a boy, ordered by their father to kill a man with a baseball bat. If he asked, would his father even remember that day, and all the repercussions that had stemmed from it?

Tommy glanced back at his father, searching for what had caught the elder Byrne's attention. Somewhere in the empty space between his coffee and small bowl of grapes he had been picking from, he stared into the abyss.

The dining room table suddenly felt smaller as Tommy turned from one to the next. His mother and Enzo flanked his father, while Sam sat to his own left and Joe, sitting in for all the captains, sat to his right. Moretti occupied the middle; between Sam and Isabella sat Michael, who had practically lunged at Tommy when he entered the room minutes before.

"You son of a bitch," Michael had snarled, jumping to his feet as Tommy, Sam, and Joe entered the room. Moretti, Enzo, and his mother were present, but his father still hadn't arrived.

Tommy couldn't help but smirk. "And you must be Michael," he said, Sam now between them and Joe immediately behind, both at the ready.

"You killed my man, asshole. You think my father and brother are going to put up with that? Huh?"

"I'm not quite sure what you're talking about," Tommy said as he made his way to his seat.

"You know exactly what I'm talking about, you fucking prick!"

"You better watch your goddamn mouth," Sam warned. "You're a long way from your daddy, boy."

"Gentlemen!" Isabella snapped as the door leading from the kitchen opened and Ciaran entered the room with a small glass bowl of grapes. "We can discuss it soon enough."

"Discuss what?" Ciaran asked as he pulled back his chair.

"We'll get to it, dear." Isabella reached out and grabbed Michael's forearm. "Michael, please—sit down so we can get started."

"You're fucking done," Michael muttered to Tommy. "Done."

Now here they were, Tommy thought, taking a deep breath to try to steady his nerves, his mother's announcement setting the tone for what would follow. He had never been prone to panic, but at that moment the weight of life pressed against his chest. His tie felt as if it could strangle him at any moment, and he could easily picture either Michael or Enzo leaping out of his chair to do just that, one hand yanking at it as the other forced the knot into Tommy's throat.

He ignored Michael altogether and glanced once more toward his brother, then Isabella, careful not to make eye contact with either of them lest they detect any fear. They were both very adept at sensing and then leveraging any weakness. His mother figuratively, his sadistic brother in an all too literal manner.

Tommy now saw them as gargoyles, aggressively perched by Ciaran's shoulders, ruthlessly eager to serve as protectors of the status quo—their status quo—where she ruled with unquestioned authority and he slaughtered anyone who dared challenge it. With Michael and Moretti beside them, acting as an additional buffer between Tommy and his father, he understood how today would transpire. Michael's threat would ring true, and with or without him they would force a return to their way, unfettered.

69

Ciaran slowly picked up the pen that rested on a small notepad between him and Isabella, rolling it between thumb and index finger. "What, exactly, is going on?" he asked as he continued to study the pen.

Tommy had rehearsed the answer any number of different ways, but he didn't know where to begin: with the attack on James, Enzo's incursion, or his own orders to take out his uncle's man and threaten the reporter, the latter two now in the process of blowing up in his face. He could not bring himself to speak. He couldn't bring himself to give them the satisfaction, not yet.

Ciaran dropped the pen onto the tablecloth as he finally looked up and stared at his eldest son. "Well?" he asked.

"I'll tell you what happened," Michael began, not bothering to hide his disgust. "Your son took out one of my men yesterday without any fucking courtesy towards my family."

Ciaran glanced over at Michael, then back at Tommy. "Is this true?"

"Pop—"

"Yes, it's fucking true," Michael said. "One of my police informants says your man did it."

"Who the hell do we even have out there?" Ciaran demanded.

"Alex Mullens," Tommy said.

Ciaran looked at Joe. "Your kid did that?"

"Well—"

"Pop," Tommy said, "I don't know what he's talking about."

"Bullshit," Michael snapped. "You're a fucking liar."

Ciaran looked over at Isabella. "I still can't believe Joe's kid here is all grown up. My God, just yesterday, he was—" He held his hand about three feet off the floor. "The boy was this tall, and now look at him."

"Yes, dear," she agreed.

He looked over at Joe. "Your boy… all grown up, huh?"

"Yeah."

Ciaran turned back to Tommy. "What the fuck was he doing out there in the first place?"

"I sent him to look after Jimmy."

"And what a great job he did with that," Isabella sneered.

"Why?" Ciaran asked. "What's going on with Jimmy?"

"He hasn't been himself since the attack," Tommy explained. "The two were friends. I thought it would help him to get his bearings."

"What about my man?" Michael asked.

"Your man was a fucking drug dealer," Joe blurted out. "It was probably one of his customers that did him."

"Bullshit."

Joe scoffed. "He got what he deserved messing with that shit."

Michael looked over the table. "Like you all don't profit from it."

"We tolerate it coming through," Ciaran said. He tapped the table with his right finger. "But this side of the family? What you do out there is up to your father, but that shit does not go on here. Ever."

"I don't think your youngest son got that memo," Michael said.

Ciaran frowned, his steely gaze fixing on his nephew. "What the fuck are you talking about? Is this about Jimmy?"

"I don't know," Michael said as he glanced towards Tommy. "I just heard he was helping my man out… dealing to people at school."

"If you were any other man I would kill you with my own bare hands," Ciaran said. "The next time you open your mouth, I suggest you choose your words more carefully."

Michael nodded. "I'm sorry, uncle," he offered. "We didn't know. I didn't mean to make a joke of it. Of course it's a very serious matter."

Ciaran turned to Tommy. "What do you know about this?"

"It's been handled."

"Is it true?"

"He got into some shit, Pop," Tommy said. "I've dealt with it."

"By killing our man," Michael added.

"Get his ass back here," Ciaran ordered. "Now."

Tommy looked first to Enzo, who was smirking. Isabella was staring at the coffee cup that she cradled in her hands. He looked back at his father. "Pop, I think it's better if he stayed out there. It's been handled, and it won't happen again."

"You're goddamn right it won't happen again," Ciaran said. "I want his ass back here. Now."

"Pop—"

Moretti cleared his throat. "I'm not sure that's possible right now."

"And why not?"

"Because he's with the police," Moretti said.

"For what?"

"Felony possession of a controlled substance with intent to distribute, and harboring a fugitive."

Ciaran looked down to the pen he had dropped. "Why the fuck am I hearing about this now?"

"I was entering the house when he called. I just found out myself." The room remained silent. "The fugitive," Moretti continued, his voice deliberately softened, "is related to the warrant issued for Alex."

"For what?" Joe demanded as Tommy and Sam briefly made eye contact.

"Murder." Moretti nodded at Michael. "His man Sean."

Michael slammed his fist against the table before pointing at Tommy. "And fuck you, cousin."

Ciaran turned to him. "Michael," he began, his voice low. "I think it's best if you leave the room."

"Yes, Uncle," he said before standing. He stepped back, sneering at Tommy as he slid the seat back towards the table.

Ciaran looked to Tommy once Michael had exited. "My God, what have you gotten us into?"

"Every time I think it can't get any worse with that boy he keeps proving me wrong," Isabella said to the table before turning to Ciaran, her audience of one, Jimmy's judge and jury. "He is an abomination, and even after all we have done for him this is how he repays us? Selling drugs behind our back? Getting beat up in one of those… neighborhoods… probably a drug deal gone bad. Who knows what else he's been doing. This has got to stop. This has absolutely got to stop. The shame is too great."

"I said I've taken care of it," Tommy said.

She glared at him. "You clearly haven't if the boy has just been arrested," she countered. "And the other one… his 'friend'? Murder? We could be looking at war with Las Vegas over this if Liam decides to retaliate, or worse… cut off the entire supply chain to both us and New York."

Ciaran looked at Moretti. "Your thoughts?"

"If they actually arrest him it will get out," he said, "and by this evening the entire city would know that Ciaran Byrne's son is a drug dealer."

"He is not a drug dealer!" Tommy said.

"He was selling drugs," Enzo said. "That's a goddamn drug dealer in my book."

Tommy looked at Ciaran. "Pop, I've taken care of this."

Isabella snorted. "We can all see how good a job you've done."

"He's a fag and a drug dealer, Pop," Enzo said. "I don't know which is worse."

"And you torture people for sport, you sick fuck," Tommy snapped.

"Your brother does what he needs to do to protect this family," Isabella said, "which is better than I can say about you. You're enabling that boy to drag us through hell because you'd rather hide out downtown than tend to what matters. How many more glass towers you think you'll be able to build in this city once people find out what you've been hiding? You think anyone is going to want to do business with you?"

"They do business with us now."

"Because they respect us," Moretti said.

"No, because they fear us," Tommy said.

"And how much longer do you think that's going to last?" Isabella asked.

"If people don't believe we have our own house in order, it can make us look weak," Moretti seconded. "If Liam decides to create difficulty for us, which I don't doubt he will, it will create extensive problems for both us and New York."

Tommy looked to Ciaran, who had returned to his pen, the conversation having slipped his interest. He wondered whether his father even knew what they were arguing over, the significance of the decision he would soon have to make.

"I want this to go away," Isabella told her husband, determination in her eyes. "He cannot come back here. He is an embarrassment and a disgrace, and we are all soiled because of his behavior. When this gets out—"

"We're fucked," Enzo sneered. "We're going to be the goddamn laughingstock of Chicago."

Ciaran looked up, and as his eyes met Tommy's, the son saw both resigned sadness and confusion, a struggle to process what he was hearing. The room went silent as father stared at son, a moment where all else faded away and the two silently acknowledged only the other.

This was Tommy's one opportunity to plead his case, to look his father in the eye without the distraction and tell him that all would be right in the world if he just trusted him to make the final decision on the matter. And as he leaned forward to speak, Ciaran turned to Moretti. "Your thoughts?"

"There is very little we can do with the boy now," Moretti said without hesitation. "And with all due respect to Joe, his son has also become a huge liability. At the very least Liam will insist on his head."

"I want you to make this go away," Isabella pleaded. "This has to go away."

Ciaran nodded as he once more returned to the pen in his hands. "Enzo, you need to go out there and take care of this."

"Absolutely, Pop."

"Why don't we reach out to Liam," Isabella said. "Give our blessing for them to resolve the matter."

"No," Ciaran said. "They've done enough involving my son in this in the first place, and I will address that in due time. We will handle it."

"*I* will handle it," Tommy said. "I will do this."

Enzo scoffed. "Bullshit you will."

"If it has to be done, I will do it," Tommy said. "Better from me."

Ciaran stood. He continued to look at Tommy as he pointed to Enzo. "You will take him with you. You will go out there and do as I have ordered—or he will, however he chooses to do so. Now make this fucking problem go away."

70

As he stood on the landing outside of James Byrne's building, Carlyle had watched the ambulance pull away, lights flashing but no siren. A small crowd had gathered on the sidewalk. His distaste for the public grew that much more as several of them recorded the scene with their phones, earning bragging rights for happening to be around when someone needed emergency services. If Carlyle fell down the stairs and broke his leg, he had no doubt most of those vultures would turn their phones on him, dreaming of increased traffic to their social media sites rather than helping.

He heard Seegars open the door to the apartment as he took a last drag of the cigarette he had bummed from one of the paramedics, stubbing it out on the railing and tossing it to the ground below. He turned to see his partner, a backpack in hand as he closed the door behind him, locking it with a set of keys, then tossing them into the front pocket of the backpack.

"What's that?" Carlyle asked.

Seegars glanced down at the bag. "Just some stuff to bring over to the hospital. A change of clothes, some toiletries."

Carlyle offered his hand. "Give it to me."

"That wasn't the reaction I expected," Seegars said as he handed over the bag.

"You threatened him with prison rape."

"Like you haven't," Seegars countered. "It works about twenty-five percent of the time."

"Not this time."

Seegars pointed back at the door. "You can't tell me you've ever seen that before."

Carlyle slowly shook his head. "No, that I have not."

"There's something going on there. I don't know what, but fuck, that was a first."

Carlyle said nothing, those final moments with James Byrne replaying in his head. The reaction had been so visceral—animal, reflexive—like a cornered animal fighting for survival. The boy had most certainly been there before.

The two walked down the stairs and climbed into their department-issued sedan. Carlyle slipped the keys into the ignition but didn't start the engine, his hand returning to his leg. "You sentenced that boy to death up there."

"I did what I felt needed to be done."

"You disobeyed a direct order."

"I'm your partner, not your little bitch," Seegars said. "Take it up with the captain."

Carlyle started the engine. "We're going back to the station, then I want you to stay the fuck away from me."

"With pleasure."

■ ■ ■

Tommy looked out the window, the passing homes a blur as Sam's car sped south.

He left his parents' house without speaking. The room remained silent after Ciaran stormed out, the five aligned against him awaiting his reaction to the verdict his mother had always sought. How she could conspire to see her own son executed, he would never know—could never understand—even as he held no illusions of what she was capable of to bend them all to her will.

He couldn't bear to look at any of them, not after that. His eyes fixated on the pen that had remained on the other side of the table. He would not give them the satisfaction of seeing his pain and desperation. No, they could watch him stare into the abyss instead as he contemplated what had just occurred, and what the result would be. Despite all the crimes he had committed, he knew he would lose what was left of himself when he completed his father's latest task.

He felt the firm grip on his arm as the warm breath touched his ear. "Come on… get up," Sam said as he pulled him to his feet.

"Sam—" Moretti began.

"Shut the fuck up!" Sam snapped as he directed Tommy toward the still-opened door, Joe on their heels, not stopping until they were at his car and then safely on their way.

"You okay?" Sam again asked as he glanced into the rear-view mirror, watching as Joe turned down the street toward his own home. This was his fourth attempt at conversation, but Tommy said nothing as he gazed mindlessly out the window.

Tommy forced himself to nod. "Yeah," he whispered.

"Did what I think just happened actually happen?"

"Yeah," Tommy repeated.

"Holy shit," Sam muttered. He replayed Ciaran's final command in his mind. The elder Byrne had seemed distant and confused up to that point. Only when his wife spoke that final time, and their eyes met, did he appear to have returned to the reality of the moment before issuing a command Sam could never have imagined to come out of his mouth.

"In all my years, I never…" Sam trailed off, unwilling to put it into words. It was too surreal even for him, a man schooled from a very young age in all the crimes that the Byrne empire was capable of, many of which he had partaken in. But now it seemed there could be no limit.

Tommy's elbow rested against the car door, his body ever so slightly slouched to that side, his hand absentmindedly massaging his chin. His left arm was across his lap, trembling even as it gripped the seatbelt. He had not felt this way in some time, since that unforgettable day when he had been asked to kill a battered old man tied to a chair, then watched as his demented brother performed the brutal act with glee. Ever since they had each played their part, the upstanding businessman and the butcher behind the throne, rarely crossing paths and keeping their disdain for the other hidden… until now.

"I know you want to help," he said, still speaking barely above a whisper as he finally acknowledged the unspoken sentiment from his most trusted adviser. Tommy relied on only Sabrina more, and there were things he would never burden her with.

"You're goddamn right I want to help," Sam said, the frustration evident in his voice.

"Time to visit my brother-in-law," Tommy ordered, reaching for his phone.

71

Tommy sat at the hotel restaurant's bar seven floors above the bustle of Michigan Avenue. No televisions to attract the typical Chicago sports fanatic—seemingly incapable of watching ESPN without a public fit of rage—the place was empty save him and Sam, who sat at a small table near the entrance to the room. That his sister and brother-in-law lived in the building across the street, and that it was within a mile of his own, made these sporadic meetings that much more convenient.

Andrew Beaman was a good man and a highly competent investment banker. He was also highly resourceful, with long-standing relationships that existed well outside normal channels. That he happened to be married to Tommy's sister didn't hurt, although as far as Sarah was concerned, his meteoric rise within the financial community had nothing to do with her family. That same discretion and reach—and his ambition to prove himself—made Andrew a natural choice to oversee the many cash accounts of Byrne, Inc.

Tommy spotted him as he entered, dressed in a pair of wrinkled khakis and a cashmere sweater, neither of which fit his bulky frame. He looked like he had just rolled out of bed, his hair a tousled mess and round framed glasses slightly off kilter as he crossed the marble floor.

He passed Sam as the two exchanged a cursory nod of acknowledgement, Andrew not pausing as he continued to the bar.

"Tommy," he said, his breath slightly labored from the trek. The two quickly shook hands before he took a seat.

"What can I get you?" the bartender asked Andrew as Tommy finished his bourbon. He glanced over to Tommy, who nodded slightly.

"Water, please," Andrew said as the bartender refilled Tommy's glass.

"Thank you for coming," Tommy said after Andrew's drink had been served and the waiter made himself scarce, the bottle on the bar should it be needed. "How are things?"

Andrew shrugged. "Eh, you know. Things are fine."

"And Sarah?"

"Your sister is your sister. Nothing has changed."

Tommy looked down at his drink, tracing the rim with his finger. He nodded. "Yes. I'm sure that's the case." The two never discussed his sister's abandonment of the family, and this meeting would be no different. He asked out of courtesy and Andrew answered in kind.

"What can I do for you?"

"I need a couple of favors."

Andrew nodded. "Of course," he said without hesitation. "Anything."

Tommy nodded at Sam. "He has the details, but this is critical. I don't care what it takes. I don't care what it costs—or who you need to bring in. These need to get done."

Andrew nodded fervently. "Of course. Absolutely."

Tommy extended his hand and Andrew shook it. "Thank you," he said before returning to his drink.

Their meeting over, Andrew pushed himself off his stool and walked to an already standing Sam.

■ ■ ■

Enzo was sitting on the couch, staring mindlessly into the roaring fire when Isabella entered the room.

They had not spoken since the meeting, each of the victors exiting in their own direction: Moretti across the foyer and out the front door, Isabella upstairs to check on Ciaran, and Enzo to the bar to pour the first of several drinks. After the second one he took the bottle with him back to the couch, carefully placing it between his feet where any passing by would not see.

She poured herself a cherry—an occasional indulgence that seemed appropriate given the evening—seating herself in one of the leather chairs flanking the massive fireplace and facing the couch. She had seen the bottle on the floor but said nothing, an argument not worth having with an ally much needed. There were still goals to accomplish, power to solidify, and her best hope for that sat only a few feet away. In time he too would succumb, but for now she needed him unleashed.

"I'm concerned about Tommy," she said in passing before glancing at the fire, a deliberate break in eye contact that she used with him on occasion. He still craved his mother's love and attention, and she would withhold it as necessary if it made him more compliant.

"He'll never be ready," Enzo sneered. "He doesn't have what it takes."

Isabella nodded in feigned reluctance. "I suspect you're right."

"He never did. Pop always did favor him, though."

"Your father did not always favor your brother. He was the eldest, and he was groomed as your father had been." She took a sip from her glass. "It's to be expected."

"It doesn't make it right."

"No, I suspect it does not."

Enzo waved a hand dismissively. "It's not like he even knows what the… what's going on out there," he said, stumbling over his words not just because of the alcohol—he tried not to curse around her, and he did so incessantly otherwise. "He's too worried about his… his stupid little projects."

She allowed his anger to fester for a moment. "You don't think he's the right man to lead?"

"Fuck no," he blurted out. "Sorry."

Isabella waved him off. "I understand your passion. And wanting to protect the family."

"He can't do it, Mom. Not without Pop to hold his hand."

She nodded once more. "No, I suspect you're right."

"Is that why Michael is here?"

She paused. "Your cousin is here to forge closer ties between the families. It has been far too long a time apart. He could do some good here with that."

"What about Tommy?"

"Something else is needed—and I'm not convinced your brother has it. These are different times, and they require a certain… a certain something. What your brother is doing… it's not in line with your father's vision."

"No," Enzo said as his gaze returned to the fire. "No, it's not—and it never will be."

72

"And what of things back east?" Liam asked.

He had returned to Las Vegas at his eldest son's request—the loss of their key man in San Diego, and at the hand of one of Ciaran's men of all people, prompting this unscheduled visit. As serious a matter as it appeared, it could have easily been handled remotely while tending to his vineyard, but his eldest son, with his flair for the dramatic, had a penchant for conducting business face to face. So now, he sat in his old chair behind his similarly old desk, reacclimating himself to the life he thought he had mostly retired from.

"Moretti told me that Tommy and Enzo head to San Diego in the morning," Michael said through the speakerphone. "Ciaran actually ordered them to kill the little fag."

"Quite a target," David mused as he sat across from his father.

"No," Liam said. "Don't even think it."

"Arthur can be down there in a few hours," David argued. "We could take care of those two before they knew what hit them."

"And what of New York?" Liam asked. "You think they'll put up with that?"

"They don't care as long as Aunt Isabella keeps them at bay and it doesn't affect them," his eldest son continued.

"Ciaran would think different."

"Uncle Ciaran doesn't know his ass from a hole in the ground," Michael said. "He's like a—"

"You shut your fucking mouth and show some respect," Liam barked. "That's my brother you're talking about."

"What's the point of me being here then?" Michael asked. "I opened the door for you to move in."

"And we will," Liam said. "But we'll do it my way." He rose from his chair. "Get Arthur in here, and then get your aunt on the phone."

■ ■ ■

"So," Isabella began before finishing the last of her drink. She yearned for her own bottle like the one between her son's feet, but had made no move to retrieve it. Not yet, she told herself. "How do we fix this?"

"What do you mean?" Enzo asked. He reached down and refilled his glass.

"With Tommy."

"He's not going to do what Pop told him to do, I know that. I'm going to have to."

"Yes, you will."

Enzo laughed as he glanced toward the fire. "Nothing I haven't done before."

Isabella paused. "What do you mean?"

"The one time he was given a chance to show that he was a man and he fucking froze, the coward."

"What? When?" Isabella asked.

"You know, the old guy... the one Pop got us with."

"When was this?"

"I don't know, like fifteen years ago?" Enzo said. "When Tommy and I were kids."

"Oh."

"He didn't tell you about that?"

Isabella shook her head. "I don't remember," she said lightly, and lied. "You know your father. He doesn't always tell me everything."

"Pop ordered Tommy to kill him, and he couldn't. I mean, the guy was taped down to the chair, beaten to within an inch of his life—but Tommy was such a… wimp… he couldn't do it. I had to."

"*You* killed him?"

"Yeah, that was my first," Enzo said. "You know, the one with the fancy car, the Rolls."

She looked away as she suppressed a shudder. "Which one was that?"

"I don't know. Just some guy. Pop didn't say. He was just pissed with him. Something about him coming into our lives, but I never met the guy before."

"You remember a name?"

"No," Enzo said. "Just some weirdo Pop wanted gone."

73

When he entered the house, Sabrina was in one of the twin chairs overlooking the city, a glass of red wine and a half-empty bottle of cabernet resting on the table between them. She said nothing, nor broke her gaze toward the sparkling lights of the towers in front of her as he shuffled into the room, discarding both tie and jacket on the couch before taking his seat beside her.

"Where have you been?" she asked, smelling the bourbon on him.

"Out," he answered as he picked up his glass and took a sip.

"It's bad, isn't it?"

Tommy stared down at his wine, now held by both hands between his knees. "It's not good."

"Do you want to talk about it?"

He took another drink. "No."

She said nothing. She had already pressed too hard once today, even if it was killing her that it involved Jimmy.

"My father gave the order to clean up San Diego," he confessed.

She wiped the tear that immediately fell from her left eye, taking a deep breath to steel herself. "You're not going to do it. Please tell me you're not going to do it."

He sighed. "Enzo and I are flying out there tomorrow morning."

"Tommy—" she began, pausing to keep her composure. She had never been an emotional woman, and she didn't want to add to his burden now. "You can't do that. You *won't* do that."

He glanced toward her. Her face was pink, her lower lip trembling. He knew she wouldn't look at him, continuing to gaze out into the night to distance herself from the conversation at hand. "My options are limited."

"No, they're not."

"My father wants it."

"Then he can go to hell."

He paused. "My options are limited," he repeated. He thought of Andrew, but he could not lead her on with false hope. "If I don't, Enzo will."

Now she turned to him, her face red with rage. "You're the goddamn boss."

"Yes, but… with him around, it's… it's complicated," he said, looking back down at his wine. "You know that."

Sabrina stood, taking one last sip from her glass. "Then I hope that son of a bitch dies soon. For your sake as well as your brother's."

■ ■ ■

After her call with Liam, Isabella came to check in on him as she always did, as she had countless times before with her four children. In many ways he had regressed into a child himself. She hated the way she had to talk to him when he was like this, as if tucking a six-year-old into bed for the night. He was better than that. She was better than that.

He was mumbling again, his eyes closed, as she sat down on the bed beside him. Small bubbles briefly appeared between his lips as he tried to speak, his chin almost touching his chest as the pillows behind him propped him up into a position that would be intolerable to anyone not in his condition. Here was the once-mighty Ciaran Byrne, as feared as he was powerful, now reduced to a babbling old man whose moments of clarity grew fainter as time passed, whose grip on the reality around him came and went, and who, she suspected, did not fully comprehend what he had ordered only several hours ago.

And she despised him. She had no love for the perverted father who had abandoned her and her mother, but he was still her father, and he deserved the dignity of a swift and merciful death, not to be tortured and then bludgeoned by a child. As sadistic as Ciaran could once be, never did she think him capable of exposing her children to something so brutal, not at that age. She knew both would face those trials in time, as they developed into young men capable of succeeding their father, but not then, not with her own flesh and blood, however loathed, as the target.

Isabella leaned forward and pulled one of the pillows out from behind him, gently laying his head down into a more comfortable position. She straightened back up with the pillow on her lap, her arms lying across it as she gripped the end with her hands.

"You had no right," she said, her voice cracking with the rage she felt.

Ciaran opened his eyes. He looked out across the room for what seemed an eternity before his gaze eventually found hers staring down at him, filled with unbridled hatred. She saw no life in his, not the fire that had once defined the man for the past few decades. "You had no right," she said once more as she rose to her feet.

He didn't bother to look up as she stood above him, focusing back to whatever it was that had captured his attention before. He didn't even flinch as she placed the pillow gently over his face, her hands shifting to the opposing ends before she brought her full weight down upon it.

She was momentarily surprised by how little he fought. His arms attempted to swat her away, but he was too weak, too disoriented to break free before his life quickly faded. She could feel the moment when it happened, an immediate release of the tension within his body, his arms dropping to his sides as his arched back relaxed into the mattress once more.

She remained fixed into that position a few seconds longer, not quite trusting that he would ever go so easily, before removing the pillow to examine her efforts. He looked peaceful, his eyes closed, the right corner of his mouth curled upward as if attempting a grin.

Tossing the pillow to the other side of the bed, she turned and strode out of the room.

SATURDAY

74

Tommy silently entered the darkened bedroom, the only light coming from the city below through the partially opened curtains along the outer wall.

Gently sitting down on the edge of the bed, he placed his hand just inches from hers, his fingers sinking into the soft cotton sheets as he leaned in, wanting to be closer without disturbing her—not after the night before.

He had always enjoyed watching her sleep. Usually while beside her, curled up on his right side as he watched her dream, her lips moving ever so slightly, her eyes darting behind closed eyelids as her chest slowly rose and fell. On rare mornings like this, when his schedule preceded hers, he would start his morning before returning as he did now, enjoying the silence of the moment as he looked over her while she rested.

After particularly troubling nights he would sometimes find her almost mumbling, her soft features tensed as the darkness of her dream surfacing. In those moments, lying beside her, he often brushed her cheek with the back of his hand, carefully guiding her hair away from her face, watching as she almost instantly relaxed. But no such nightmares had visited this morning, and he was thankful. He had burdened her enough in the real world without it following her there.

It was at times such as this when he reflected on the gift of her presence in his life, the flippant, sarcastic nurse who was unafraid to speak her mind from the first moment that they met, who did so when merited even to this day. Not that he would ever complain. He had wanted her before the first stitch went into his forehead.

Feeling Sabrina's hand on his, he glanced over to look into her eyes. She smiled gently, as if no trouble existed between them.

"I need to go," he said.

She nodded, her smile losing its joy but not its tenderness. "Okay," she whispered.

"I need you to do something for me. If you don't hear from me by midnight..." He watched as her mouth opened, but she remained silent. "If you don't hear from me," he repeated, "I want you to walk out of here and go downstairs. Andrew will be waiting."

"Okay," she said.

"Leave everything but the clothes on your back," he said. "Phone, wallet—everything. Walk out of here and don't look back. It's been taken care of."

He stood up, then bent over and kissed her. From her lips he sensed—should he return—the forewarning of a rift that would never fully heal. He was to do what he had to, and she would reciprocate in kind. He tried to look back into her eyes, but she was staring toward the window.

As he stood in the bedroom doorway, he turned back one last time. She was now on her side, her back to him, and he could hear her begin to cry. He hesitated, wanting to go back to her, but knew her instinctive reaction would be to push him away.

Tommy had seen her cry only once before, when her father died several years ago. The two had never been close, especially after she married into the Byrnes, but his sudden passing brought on a grief like nothing he had ever seen from his determined and resilient wife. Now she was grieving for his younger brother, and this time he could provide no comfort from the pain. She saw it not as an inevitable part of life, but a senseless killing to uphold a twisted version of family honor.

And as he turned to exit the room, he wiped the lone tear that had managed to escape to his cheek.

■ ■ ■

She held his hand in hers as she had done countless times before, when she would feel the feeble pulse as his chest barely rose and fell, so shallow that she often had to watch carefully to believe it did. Today though there was no pulse, no movement in his chest, only the rigid coldness of his hand.

The sunlight had started creeping in only a few moments before, the cracks of light between the thick curtains slowly illuminating the room. She could see the outlines of his face, a peaceful expression written upon it as if in a deep sleep, the pillow that ended his life now back under his head.

She gently brushed a few stray hairs off his forehead. It had to look perfect, a very ill man who had finally taken his last breath as he lay peacefully slumbering at the end of yet another ordinary day.

As those final moments revisited her, Isabella held no regrets. She rarely did. Hers was a life well scripted—one that knew what came with marrying into this family and manipulating that power to her advantage. She had done so for many years, a comment here, a suggestion in passing, each designed to gently nudge a doting husband to her will. More than one grave had been dug as the result of a casual remark at an opportune time. Yesterday might have been her most direct assault, but she had known it would come to this and never flinched from what needed to be done.

There were many years left in her yet, and she still had much to achieve. Inviting her brother-in-law and nephews into a closer alliance would change nothing in the end. She knew that Liam and his sons would at least consider taking advantage of the situation, but they had few friends elsewhere, at least not any who wanted to see him back in Chicago unfettered.

She stood and adjusted the comforter, placing Ciaran's right hand on his stomach just above his left. She stepped back to take in the scene, then tilted his head slightly to the right. There, she thought, a wry smile appearing as she admired her work.

75

James opened his eyes and looked around the dimly lit hospital room, the furnishings almost identical to those from earlier in the week. Glancing through the window to his left, the amber and orange of morning not yet beginning to illuminate the room, he watched the headlights as cars entered the parking lot below before vanishing under the windowsill.

His clothes had been removed down to his underwear, an ill-fitting hospital gown in their place. Both sheet and blanket had been perfectly folded at the waist; he immediately flipped aside as he swung his legs over the bed toward the window.

Feeling lightheaded, he winced as the memories flooded back to him. The two detectives, him calling Chicago when they stepped outside, the two returning, the younger one pinning him to the floor—then nothing.

"I see you're awake," said a deep voice from behind.

James jumped slightly, then turned to see a heavyset, middle-aged man at the door, dressed in royal blue scrubs and holding a medical chart. "What am I doing here?" he asked.

The nurse smiled and slid the door shut behind him. "You had a bit of a spell yesterday," he said as he walked to the foot of the bed. "How are you feeling?"

James nodded. "I'm okay."

"Good. My name is Gary, by the way. I'm one of the nurses here on the night shift."

"I can't remember what happened."

"That's to be expected, but the doctor will be in in a bit," Gary said. He patted James on the shoulder. James flinched as the hand remained where it was. "It's okay. I just need you to lie back."

James did as he was told, watching as Gary returned the covers to their original position, recoiling once more as the nurse's hand touched his arm.

Sensing the discomfort, Gary immediately pulled away. "Are you okay?"

"Yes," James lied as he felt his heart began to race. "Yeah, I'm fine."

He obviously was not fine, though Gary refrained from reaching out to comfort the young man as he normally might. He had reviewed the results from yesterday's examination only moments before entering the room, and he chastised himself for not being more mindful of the circumstances before making repeated contact as he had. "Okay," he said as soothingly as he could muster. He reached over and pressed a button on the bed.

"Yes?" a woman's voice asked moments later.

"Katie, I'm in seven twenty-four," he responded as he looked down at the boy, now pale and shivering. "Can you come down?"

"On my way," she said before ending the connection.

■ ■ ■

Carlyle sat at his kitchen table, staring down at the cherry-stained surface as he continued to dwell on the Byrnes as he had the better part of the night. Even now, despite their more recent blunders, he was at least two steps behind and seemingly unable to catch up.

If they ever caught him, he knew Alex Mullens was dead for what had already happened. He wondered if they would try to lure him back into the fold somehow, allow him a false sense of hope before one of their butchers slaughtered him, or would they hunt him down as relentlessly, as viciously, as they had the others? He was too much a loose end to permit him his freedom for very long. There was some slim chance that he would turn to the protection of the police, but Carlyle held no illusion of that happening. He wouldn't snitch, even on those who wanted him dead. They rarely did.

And what of the boy, the one who only hours ago was curled into a ball, keening with a hopeless terror that Carlyle could still hear as if he were lying on the kitchen floor beneath his feet? He was yet another that required as much attention, if not more, than Mullens. After what he saw yesterday, he had little doubt they would also want to ensure his silence, and Carlyle had little confidence that Tommy Byrne could protect his brother from a death that James obviously viewed as certain.

The EMTs had looked at Carlyle and Seegars as if they were monsters. Their first few attempts to calm James had agitated him that much more, if such a thing were possible. The older EMT, her shoulder-length brown hair streaked with gray, finally put her hand on her partner's shoulder. "I got this," she told him before working her magic on the patient. Within a minute he was bawling in her lap, her hand gently stroking his hair as she murmured reassurances. She gave a slight nod to her partner, who nodded back and injected the sedative. Moments later, it was over.

He chastised himself for getting emotional, but as he stood in the hospital room looking over James while he slept, the doctor beside him detailing the results of the physical exam as he flipped through papers affixed to the chart in his hands, he could not help himself. Thankfully the man was too engrossed in his notes to notice the detective wiping away a tear, but Carlyle had to look away to get it to stop.

He stared down at the table, his thumb pushing his untouched mug of coffee in a circle. He knew that his only lead had probably already fled across the border, but the case moved on regardless. And until something else opened for them, he had a patient to check on.

76

His already-jittery hand rested on the kitchen table beside what remained of his third cup of coffee. He was restless, but Moretti understood the need to stay occupied as the day progressed. For the first time he could recall, he found himself mostly sidelined as the struggle between mother and son played itself out, and he could find no better outlet than sitting here and attempting to work.

He had a home office but preferred the small kitchen nook at their round maple table, flower-patterned placemats that his wife had picked out years earlier in front of each of the four chairs. His back against the windows, he would spread out his paperwork and enjoy her presence as she went about her day in the kitchen, preparing a seemingly endless progression of meals, many of them for neighbors she had taken upon herself to look after when others would not.

But today he found himself a few hours into one of Tommy's contracts, his wife still upstairs and feeling a bit under the weather. He would probably make the deliveries she normally did, the food already organized and waiting to be retrieved from the refrigerator, post-it notes on each to remind her of who would receive what. He would ordinarily complain but this morning he welcomed the task, a reprieve from one of the endless mundane documents like the one before him that he had been burdened with since Tommy assumed control.

Tommy would obey, Moretti assured himself once more. All Byrne sons did, and he always had when he and his father had disagreed in the past. This was no different, even if the stakes had changed. Tommy preened like he was above it all, but Moretti could see through the façade well enough. He might not be the cold-blooded killer his younger brother had become, but there was Byrne blood in him yet. Moretti had seen him wield that power enough times to know that when push came to shove, he understood its importance. The greater good mattered more than Jimmy Byrne ever did.

His phone began to vibrate, shimmying toward the green candle in the center of the table. He reached over to stop its progress, "Byrne Home" on the screen below his thumb.

"Yes, ma'am?"

"I need you to come over," Isabella ordered.

"What's going on?" he asked.

"I need you to come over," she repeated in the same monotonous tone.

Moretti glanced at the clock on the wall. "Okay," he said. "I'll be there within the hour."

■ ■ ■

Carlyle walked into the office, the work laptop in his bag making a dull thud as he dropped it onto the floor beside his chair. He sat down and leaned back, propping his feet up onto the corner of his desk.

His visit to the hospital had been short. A nurse told him that James Byrne had an episode earlier in the morning, and they had no choice but to sedate him again. After standing at the foot of the bed for a moment and watching him sleep, Carlyle had departed. There were far better places to ruminate.

His workspace wasn't ideal, but he hoped his partner would uphold his end and make himself scarce. He usually vanished on weekends anyway when given even the slightest opportunity, so Carlyle was planning to enjoy the solitude before the rest of the office came to life around him. He could tune them out easily enough, he thought as he swung his feet off the desk and

THE NAME OF THE GAME 341

reached down to retrieve the computer from his bag. Only after he placed the laptop into the docking station below his monitor did he look up to see a dour Seegars standing before him.

"I thought we had come to an agreement," he grunted.

Seegars's hand appeared above the top of the monitor as he sipped from a Starbucks cup. "You're welcome."

"About?"

His other hand appeared, a folded piece of paper between his thumb and index finger. "A peace offering."

"A bit late for that."

Seegars thrust it at him. "Just take the goddamn thing."

Carlyle took the note and opened it, and his expression tightened. He briefly looked up at his partner, then back to the paper in his hand.

"You're welcome," Seegars said.

"You're shitting me, right?"

"It got handed to me as I was coming in the door. I thought you'd appreciate it."

Carlyle looked at his watch, then stood. "Let's go."

■ ■ ■

Isabella glanced at the watch on her wrist, a gift from her husband on their twenty-fifth wedding anniversary.

She wasn't sure why she had picked this watch from the shelves of jewelry in the walk-in closet upstairs. It was clunky on her petite wrist, the gold a bit too shiny, the diamond-encrusted face somewhat gauche against what she would describe as her muted elegance. It certainly did not match with the dark blue skirt and white silk blouse she had on. Perhaps she would take it off later.

Seated where Ciaran had been only the day before, she looked down the table toward the empty seat that Tommy had occupied. A place setting had been arranged there for Michael, who had yet to make an appearance this morning. He and Enzo no doubt had a late evening, which she surmised from the empty bottle on the bar in the living room she had passed through.

The watch shifted on her arm as she picked up her coffee cup from its saucer. After the funeral, and the proper mourning period, she would dispatch someone to dispose of it for her, all the better to be rid of those things that reminded her of him.

In the meantime, however, there were pressing matters to deal with. She was hesitant to do so, but to ignore what had happened would only invite more suspicion. It was done in anger, and those who reacted out of emotion could be sloppy. That was certainly Enzo's struggle, and would ultimately be his downfall without proper guidance, something her husband had provided but her eldest could not.

Placing the coffee cup back in its saucer, she reached over to pick up the small brass bell with the mahogany handle. Moretti would be there soon enough. She rang it gently, waited a few moments then rang it again. Not long after she heard the familiar sound of hurried footsteps approaching.

"Yes, ma'am?" the housekeeper asked.

"Please wake Mr. Byrne for me," Isabella said. "I think he's slept long enough."

77

The plane had been parked alongside the private terminal for only a few minutes when the black sedan hurriedly pulled up, Tommy still finishing his last cup of coffee.

Leaning back in the tan leather seat, he spied Carlyle behind the wheel of the parked car, another man beside him, the two holding a seemingly intense conversation as they lingered inside the vehicle. Gently rubbing the rim of the china cup before him, he began to second-guess the decision to announce his arrival so brazenly. Perhaps there was a safer way to save Jimmy from his sentence.

He glanced down at the business card wedged into the notepad on the table. "From Andrew," Sam had told him before Tommy boarded his plane. "He's got everything taken care of. This guy has what you asked for, and he's available if you run into any problems."

"Did I catch you at a bad time?" Tommy looked up to see Carlyle standing in front of the cockpit, the reinforced door ajar behind him.

"No, not at all."

Carlyle glanced toward the empty cockpit, then toward the back galley. "You alone in here?"

Tommy nodded. "Yes," he answered as he stood. He picked up the cup and saucer. "Would you like some coffee?"

Carlyle shook his head, briefly raising a hand, palm outward. "I'm good."

Tommy motioned with his free hand to the chair on the other side of the rectangular table. "Please, have a seat," he offered before walking toward the galley.

Carlyle sat down, reclining in the comfortable chair as he placed his right ankle on top of his left knee. He could get used to this, he thought as he looked around the cabin. "Nice big plane for just one person," he remarked. "*Business* must be good."

Tommy glanced over his shoulder as he poured his coffee. "It's not too bad," he agreed, ignoring the remark.

Carlyle watched as Tommy finished in the galley and returned to the table. "You do this often?"

"Fly private?" Tommy asked as he sat back down. "No, but I needed some time to think." He held up his cup. "So, Detective Carlyle," he began before taking a sip. "What can I help you with this morning?"

"You made it a point to make sure I knew you were here, so I thought I'd play my part," Carlyle said. "I'll start with a softball. Would you happen to know where Alex Mullens is?"

"I wouldn't."

"Of course not. I guess that's for others… keep you insulated from that sort of thing."

"I wouldn't know anything about that either," Tommy said. He paused, taking another sip of coffee. "Any other questions, detective?"

Carlyle allowed himself a tiny smirk. "Yes, actually," he said. "For starters, you can tell me more about the rape."

■ ■ ■

He loathed being summoned like a servant, but as Moretti guided his car into the circular driveway and killed the engine, he acknowledged that in many respects, he remained only that, even after all these years.

She had always been this way, the queen atop the empire who ordered her husband's associates as if her own. They all complied, for to anger one who could make your life exponentially more difficult was foolish. Even he, who shared that power as her husband's closest friend and adviser, accepted the order of their world. Isabella would come first, always.

He remained in the car for a moment before climbing out and making his way to the front door, the better to compose himself and remove any vestige of aggravation. Despite their closeness and shared affection for the man they served, he realized, as surely she did as well, that those in such close quarters occasionally found themselves at loggerheads. As always he would allow any resentment to fade into oblivion until the next slight occurred, the greater cause and his loyalty trumping all.

The house was seemingly empty as he entered the foyer and gently closed the door behind him. All the lights were off, and with the sliding doors to the adjoining rooms closed, the only illumination emanated from behind the thick curtains covering the sidelight windows flanking the heavy front door. His eyes traced the outline of the stairs until they faded into the darkness above. All the energy he normally sensed in this house had seemingly vanished overnight.

He looked toward the entrance to the great room at the back of the foyer, a sliver of light guiding the way as he tread carefully across the room. He shivered as he approached the slightly parted doors, an unease creeping over him as he pushed one aside and entered.

She was seated in the chair to the left of the large fireplace, one ankle crossed over the other, her hands in her lap. The room was illuminated only by a small floor lamp beside her, and another, its twin, next to the matching chair on the opposing side. The dark green velvet curtains, which were normally pulled aside to display the backyard through the French doors, had been pulled tightly closed. The air was cold, almost as if to recreate a Chicago winter despite the near balminess outside.

He stepped inside and closed the door behind him. She had been fixated on something near her feet but now their eyes met as he took a step toward her.

Isabella had always been an elegant dresser, a woman who believed that a person's character could always be surmised by how they carried themselves. Even at home, among family and close friends, she was impeccably clothed, never allowing a casual moment to interfere with appearances.

Today was no different. There was, however, a melancholy about her. He once more acknowledged his unease, something he rarely felt within these walls. This wasn't a mere social call, and with Isabella, he had no idea what to expect next.

She motioned toward the chair across the fireplace. "Please… sit."

"Where is everyone?"

She said nothing until he was seated, her hand now returned to her lap. "I sent them all home."

"Where is Michael?"

Isabella raised her shoulders ever so slightly. "Out. He took Enzo to the airport this morning and hasn't returned."

He nodded slowly.

"Ciaran is dead."

Moretti paused. "He's dead?"

"Yes. Maria found him in bed this morning."

"I'm sorry," he instinctively offered.

"It's fine," she said, her tone dismissive. "It was for the best. He was a very sick man."

Moretti nodded. "Yes, that he was. I assume you haven't called the police."

Isabella sneered at the inquiry. "No, I have not," she snapped. "He's not going anywhere. It can wait until all this is done." She paused. "And that's not why I summoned you here."

He almost flinched at that last verb, but he didn't want to give her the satisfaction of knowing it bothered him. "So… why have you summoned me?" he asked, repeating it.

"Next steps."

"Tommy is now head of the family," Moretti mechanically said. "It was Ciaran's wish. I can understand delaying things until that business in California is concluded, but—"

"I'm not sure my son is up to the task," Isabella interjected, her voice raised.

He raised a hand. "Enzo will see things through, if he has to."

"I meant in general."

Moretti looked down at his left hand, watching as the light from the lamp behind him reflected on his gold wedding band. He had tried many times to get Tommy to understand who they were and what they were trying to accomplish, but he would chart his own path, the common history, blood, and sweat that had brought them together be damned. Tommy would comply with his orders, but once back in Chicago, once news broke of his father's death, it would all be his to dismantle at will, and he would, if only to cleanse his soul from today's task.

She was right—if they wanted their way of life preserved something had to change. This, though… he knew there was a chance it could go here, but this was not what he had envisioned. Using the chaos to break Tommy was one thing. Removing him… how had they gotten to this point?

He looked up and their eyes met. He could see her anticipation, and knew she only wanted one answer from him. Despite his reservations, his anger at her warping his plans, he would not disappoint. "One piece of advice, if I may."

"Of course."

"When you go to kill the king—"

Isabella raised a hand to cut him off.

"Call Enzo," she said. "He'll know what to do."

■ ■ ■

Carlyle walked down the staircase from the plane and stepped onto the tarmac. His face void of expression, he walked toward the waiting sedan, Seegars waiting in the passenger seat as he stared down at his phone.

"And how did that go?" he eventually asked as he finished typing out his message, dropping the phone onto the seat between his legs.

"It went," Carlyle answered as he visualized his handshake with Tommy Byrne. Never in a million years, he told himself once more.

"That's it? You were in there long enough."

Carlyle looked out the windshield. "We're letting the boy go," he said.

Seegars snorted. "And why would we do that? Did he threaten you?"

Carlyle nodded. "Yes, just not how his father would. He's here to meet with an attorney, and I'm not in the mood to go into court and justify how things were handled at the apartment. Are you?"

"Yes, absolutely. You did that to spite me. You were never going to hold that kid accountable."

"I did what I thought was right."

"So did I."

Carlyle scoffed. "I'm sure."

"Just take me back to the fucking station so we can keep ignoring each other."

Carlyle started the car. "With pleasure."

78

James could still feel the pull of the sedative as his wheelchair rolled through the hospital lobby and out under the portico.

The detective said very little upon entering the room, James watching carefully as he approached and stopped at the foot of the bed. He reached down and gently squeezed his foot. "We're getting you out of here," he said softly, regret flickering as he forced a grin.

James said nothing in return. He closed his eyes, drifting back to sleep until someone came to dress him in the clothes from his backpack. Then an orderly appeared with a wheelchair. As he was taken out of the room, his backpack—spare clothes and toiletries packed inside—was placed in his arms. The detective reappeared moments later, exchanged a few quiet words, then grabbed the handlebars and steered them toward the elevators.

The detective helped him into the back of the cruiser, and after closing the door and depositing the wheelchair by the front entrance, they began their drive toward La Jolla.

∎ ∎ ∎

The two sat on either side of a small, round wrought iron mesh tabletop, the sun shining down on the patio. They were tucked into the far corner, where the brick exterior met an ivy-covered lattice. Except for a few other tables, all of whom had opted to be closer to those passing by on the sidewalk, they were alone.

Each had a small coffee before them, although neither had bothered with them. Tommy rested his right arm on the table, his right knee over the left; his brother slouched in his chair, his left arm over the back, his right hand gripping his inner thigh, legs spread wide.

No words had been spoken since they sat down, their only greeting a nod to the other before Tommy ordered their drinks and the two had stepped outside into the sunny San Diego day. They had their task and knew what to do. It was only a matter of waiting for the right moment, and even that had been arranged.

"We good to go?" Enzo asked.

Tommy shifted in his chair as he glanced over at the crowded sidewalk. It was just after one in the afternoon and masses were still out getting lunch. "He took the bait, but it has to look like an accident."

"I'm not a fucking idiot," Enzo snapped. "And I want to do the other one too."

"No. I told Pop I'd take care of it, so I'll take care of it."

"You sure you're up for it this time?"

Tommy pulled a folded sheet out of his shirt pocket and put it down on the table by Enzo's coffee. "I told him three. You do it soon after that. Wheels up around four."

Enzo nodded as he reached into his jeans and pulled out a single car key. "Here's your ride to La Jolla. It's parked in the alley around back."

"Thanks," Tommy said as he reached across to retrieve it. He stood up and looked down at his brother. "I'll see you at four."

Enzo smiled. "I'll see you then."

79

Alex continued to bounce his left leg, his foot thrumming against the car's floor—boredom and nerves in equal measure. His seat was reclined at an almost forty-five-degree angle; he slouched low, his arms folded across his chest, staring through the windshield at James' front door.

He was hungry, and the mornings were cold even here, so he'd bundled up with whatever he had—the clothes on his back and a hoodie found behind the seat that reeked of beer, weed, and body odor. The granola bars and Sprite that he'd bought last night were long gone, but after nearly two days camped out in the parking lot— ducking down with each passing car or person—the end of his wait was finally within grasp.

The black sedan had been there almost half an hour, yet the adrenaline still surged as he sank deeper into his seat, eyes just level with the dashboard as he watched through the steering wheel.

It was the older detective who had swung out of the car, dressed in the same ill-fitting, wrinkled gray suit from the day before. Without sunglasses, the detective squinted against the bright afternoon sun as he scanned the area, Alex shrank further into his seat as he felt the detective's eyes pass over him.

Seemingly satisfied, the detective had opened the rear door on the driver's side. James stepped out onto the sidewalk, and Alex began to shake. He imagined running toward them, shoving the detective aside, the two of them sprinting away—but he remained frozen as they climbed the stairs and disappeared inside, the door closing behind them.

What the hell was the detective still doing in there?

■ ■ ■

Enzo had seemed almost giddy as they parted ways, Tommy thought as he turned off the street and entered the alley behind the coffeehouse.

About ten feet in, a middle-aged man sat against the wall to his right, his filthy jeans tattered where they met a well-worn pair of brown work boots. Tommy paused to look down at him as the man continued to stare vacantly to the gray cinderblock wall across the way, no acknowledgement of his presence. Either high or stoned, he was a barely living testament to why his father hated the drug trade so much.

The two were seemingly alone, though as Tommy began to walk towards the older-model Camry parked along the left wall about a third of the way in, he made a quick scan further down as he looked for others between the dumpsters that lined the right side of the narrow road. Yet again, his brother's excitement—this time over killing the detective—crept under his skin, a reminder of the sadistic brutality Enzo brought down on those he targeted.

Tommy paused beside the driver's door and glanced back towards the alley entrance. He looked once more at the homeless man, still lost in his stupor, before lowering his gaze and sliding the key into the lock.

80

Enzo glanced at his watch then looked down at his untouched coffee, longing for the diner fare from back home. This pretentious, overpriced crap was for douchebags, and he would be thankful once the day's business had been concluded and he was well on his way out of here.

Seated beside the ivy-covered wall, he was shielded as the blast from the alley rocked the building. Fragments of glass and metal rained down onto the brick patio as people leapt from their seats or cowered in shock.

He had to force himself not to react—shouts of pure joy clawing at his throat. There would be time for that soon enough. He pushed the coffee away and watched the chaos unfold before him. One down, and a few more to go.

■ ■ ■

By the time Carlyle stepped out of the apartment, he'd spent the better part of half an hour getting the Byrne boy settled.

It went as easily as he could have expected, given the circumstances. James paused in the doorway and looked hesitantly toward the kitchen. As Carlyle rested his hand on James's back, he could feel him trembling beneath the blanket he'd taken from the hospital. "It's okay," he said softly.

James had showered and changed while Carlyle pieced together a meal, his hair a damp mop when the two sat across from each other at the small dining room table.

James hungrily consumed a bowl of tomato soup and a grilled cheese sandwich while Carlyle sipped from a bottle of water he had taken from the refrigerator. Both of Carlyle's hands rested flat on the table, the bottle centered between his thumbs, as he watched the young man eat until the last bit had been consumed, the final piece of the sandwich soaked in tomato.

James pushed his plate toward the center of the table, only then raising his head to look the detective in the eye. "Thank you," he meekly offered.

Carlyle smiled. "I never thought I would be thanked for my efforts in the kitchen," he joked as he leaned back in his chair.

"I have a lot of stuff, but I don't know how to do too much," James said. "It's the best home-cooked meal I've had in—" He paused, the mood once more turning somber. "The best in a while."

"Well, the chef thanks you," Carlyle told him, sincerely.

James sat back in his own chair, his shoulders slumped as he stared toward the edge of the table. Their moment had passed, Carlyle knew, and it was time to get to the business at hand.

"I need you to pack."

James looked up at him. "Why?"

"I can't answer that. I need you to pack up some things—a duffle bag, a backpack, whatever you can easily carry."

"Where am I going?"

"I don't know," Carlyle admitted.

James nodded. "Tommy," he muttered. "He's coming for me."

Carlyle pushed the chair back and stood. He glanced at his watch then down at James. "You need to get ready."

James simply nodded again as Carlyle headed toward the door. He paused long enough to grip the young man's shoulder, squeezing it gently before continuing on.

81

Enzo stood as the sirens rose and fell at the edge of earshot. Thick black smoke continued to rise into the blue sky, passersby streaming toward it, their phones held aloft like torches. *Fucking idiots*, he thought as he brushed some soot from his shoulder, grinning at the thought that part of it was his brother's ashes.

■ ■ ■

After their long embrace ended, Alex followed James toward the kitchen.

"Are you okay?"

James picked up a box of tissues from the counter and offered it. "Yes."

The detective had been gone only a few minutes when Alex finally exited the car. Even then it was still dangerous—the man was as likely to return as not. The risk, though, had to be taken, so after a few hurried glances, he slammed it shut and quickly made his way toward the apartment.

Once at the top of the landing, he knocked, then forced a trembling hum to clear his throat, the uncertainty of the moment, of his future, almost too much to process. What would he say once the door opened? What would they do? Where could they go? He hadn't considered any of those questions to their logical ends. He was barely one step ahead of fate, with only happenstance to thank for that.

He heard the deadbolt move and James appeared, and it was all he could do not to cry as the two quickly embraced, emotions he had kept buried so long he hadn't known they were still there. The two held each other, time slipping past unnoticed. At some point one of them had closed the door behind them, but Alex couldn't remember who. All he could recall was James in his arms once more, the world held at bay for those precious moments.

Alex took one of the tissues and blew his nose. "Thanks."

"I don't think I've ever seen you that emotional before."

"I don't think I've ever *been* that emotional. I don't… I don't know what came over me."

"I wasn't insulting you."

"I know," Alex said, smiling. "Are you okay? I saw them carrying you out of here yesterday."

James glanced nervously to the corner of the room where he had been curled into a ball on the floor only yesterday. "I'm fine. I just had a reaction, that's all."

"To what?"

"I don't want to talk about it," James said, striding toward his bedroom.

Alex followed him and stopped in the doorway as James, his back to him, picked up a backpack and dumped its contents out on the bed. "What happened?"

"It's nothing," James said as he rifled through the clothes. "Nothing. I don't want to talk about it."

"You going somewhere?" Alex asked.

James nodded. "Yeah." He sighed as he sat down. "The detective told me to pack light. Tommy is coming for me. For us," he added.

"To kill us," Alex said.

"No. He won't do that."

"Then what?"

James stared down at the T-shirt in his hands. "To take us away from here, maybe." He looked up at Alex and smiled. "What was that city you used to talk about? The one in South Africa?"

Alex tried to smile back. "Knysna. We could get a sailboat."

82

"Boom! I got that fucker," Enzo yelled into the phone as he stood on the sidewalk half a block away from the alley, basking in the rush his brother's death had given him, watching the scene unfold from afar.

"It's done, then?"

"Fuck yeah, it's done. Been done for half an hour... I'm just letting you know."

"All of it?" Moretti asked as he passed through his own front door, his trip to Highland Park concluded.

Enzo sighed, annoyed at the question. "The big part, yeah. The rest is just cleanup."

Moretti turned left and entered the front living room as he began to pace back and forth in front of the sofa. "What about the detective?"

"He'll be dead in another hour or two. It's already been arranged."

"And when do you plan on taking care of the other one?"

"When I get there. I'm not on a fucking schedule. That little fag is parked in his apartment waiting for Tommy anyway. He's not going anywhere. Jesus."

"What about Alex?"

"Fuck if I know where that shit stabber is. I'll hunt his sorry ass down at some point. That bitch can't hide from me."

Moretti paused. "Where are you?"

"I'm here watching," Enzo said. "I'm down the street a bit."

"Are you a fucking idiot?" Moretti snapped.

"Excuse me? What the fuck did you just say to me?"

"I'm asking if you're a fucking idiot. You're parading around in front of the police? Only a fucking idiot would do something that dumb."

"I said I was down the street."

"I don't give a fuck if you're two blocks away," Moretti said. "Get the fuck out of there and get back to work."

"Do you know who the fuck you're talking to?" Enzo shouted.

"A fucking idiot, apparently."

Enzo's jaw trembled as he thought through all the ways he could kill the man on the other end of the call. "When I get home, you and I are going to have a very long talk about respect. Do you understand me, you fucking—"

"Perfectly," Moretti said, and hung up.

■ ■ ■

He stared down at the mostly uneaten burrito, once more questioning why he had ordered it, although the bottle of beer inches from his right hand had been the objective all along.

Carlyle couldn't pinpoint what had left him so unexpectedly off-balance after leaving James Byrne's apartment, but the disquiet had unnerved him enough to want to silence it, something he rarely entertained at this point in the day, no matter how it had started. This time, however, felt different—he told himself it was because of what was still to come before the sun set, not what had already transpired. It was only beginning—the culmination of a week of mounting tension. At least it would be over soon, one way or another, he assured himself as he took one more sip of the rapidly vanishing drink, his second.

"Carlyle," he answered after the phone began to vibrate.

"Detective Carlyle, this is Mark Patterson, sir."

"Yes, detective. What can I do for you?"

"Tommy Byrne is dead, sir."

He took a few deep breaths, his heart now pounding. "He's dead?"

"Yes, sir," Patterson answered. "We found his body in a burned-out car behind a coffee house in Hillcrest. It looks like some sort of explosive took him out."

That wasn't possible, he told himself. They wouldn't do that to him, not now. It would be much more manageable to pull off something like this in Chicago. How could they be so stupid, he asked himself as he attempted to process the unfathomable, his best laid plans now burned alongside the man with whom he had only recently collaborated. "How do you know it's him?"

"The wallet," the junior detective said. "Burned but not enough."

Carlyle picked up the bottle with his left hand and finished his drink. "Where are you?" he asked. "I'm coming."

83

Carlyle stared into the burned-out vehicle, the charred body still strapped into the partially melted seatbelt. He thought he could make out the remnants of the suit jacket Tommy had worn on the plane, but the fabric was as scorched as the man wearing it.

He scanned the area around the dashboard and front seat, checking every inch of blackened, warped plastic and burned fabric, his eyes stinging from the acrid smell. Something might be determined once a forensics team was able to tear the car apart, but his presence was all but useless here.

Just hours ago, the two were seated across a small table, discussing how fate had brought them together, how it had created this path of destruction, and how they might work toward a solution amenable to them both. But there were others hell-bent on continuing the chaos, or at least bending the outcome of the past week to their favor instead. This, he knew, was a decisive step toward that result.

He stared at the face of Tommy Byrne once more, or what was left of it after the explosion had ended his life so abruptly. "Where'd you find it?" he asked Patterson, who hovered beside him.

"Tucked into the seat."

Carlyle looked back at the wallet in the evidence bag that Patterson held. "Now why would he do that?"

"I don't know, sir. Maybe he didn't like sitting on it or something."

"And that doesn't seem strange to you?"

Patterson shrugged. "I suppose so," he said. "I don't know."

Carlyle's phone buzzed in his right pocket. Holding it up, he read the message. "I've got to go," he announced. He glanced around to the small swarm of fireman and police around them. "Captain needs me. Do me a favor and finish this out?"

"Yes, sir."

"Be available if I need you, though. Got it?"

"Yes, sir," Patterson repeated.

Carlyle reached for the evidence bag. "I'm taking this."

"Sir?"

"I want to look through it."

Patterson nodded as he handed it over. "Yes, sir."

"I'll check it into Evidence when I'm done," Carlyle assured him before walking away.

■ ■ ■

Isabella took another sip from the glass in her hand as she looked once more to the cell phone on the table beside her.

"We're underway," Moretti had announced before the call ended.

Her eldest son, her baby boy, was dead. She had expected to have sensed it when it happened, believing in a mother's intuition when something befell one of her children. Nothing had registered—whatever bond had once existed between mother and son had been severed the year prior.

"Don't be silly," she muttered to the empty room, then angrily took another sip.

Her thoughts drifted once more to the man lying upstairs, of decades of marriage ending as abruptly as it had. He had it coming, she reminded herself as she visualized the pillow over his face once more, though he would not be the only one once today was concluded.

Sam would have to be removed as well, although she needed something less direct than California. Perhaps a mugging gone awry a few months into the transition… he would relax by then. Big Joe, she suspected, would be felled by an unfortunate heart attack shortly thereafter. The coroner, she knew, was malleable enough when sufficiently pressured to accommodate. There would be others, too, though they would see their comeuppance once the larger problems had been put to bed.

Sabrina would present more of a challenge. She certainly had a mouth on her, but Isabella knew she wasn't stupid, and would know better than to attract too much attention to what had befallen her husband. It would be a difficult conversation, but in the end her daughter-in-law would see that leaving the city and starting over were in her best interests. She would allow her at least that.

And then there was Enzo. There was no denying his nature. He was a vicious, sadistic killer, not a leader of an empire like theirs. No, that would be left to her and Moretti in concert with their new partners in Las Vegas, his role remaining the same as he continued to be guided by those better suited to take the helm.

She stood to refill her glass, then climbed the stairs to watch some television. It would be an early night, and tomorrow would be a very active day indeed.

84

Their hands were bound with the plastic police restraints he had been given, the two of them seated against the couch a few feet apart. Blood dripped from Alex's nose where Enzo had punched him as the door opened, stunning him long enough to take him down. The other one had been just as effortless to subdue as before. And now they were his.

Standing before them, he glanced at his watch. It was nearly three already, and he was supposed to be at the airport shortly, although that time had been set by a man now dead. Private planes took off when their passengers showed up. If this took a little while longer, so be it, although he understood the need to be out of town soon. He certainly didn't want to still be in San Diego when the detective was discovered, and that would take but an hour or two at most.

In the meantime, he had them in his hands; his only dilemma was who to kill first and who would have to watch the other die before meeting his own end. They both deserved to suffer for what they had done. He had already decided to kill them both by strangulation, wanting to be standing over them when the rope tightened and the fight went out of their eyes.

Neither looked at him directly, both choosing to stare down at the floor between their legs. There were dried tears on his brother's face, but his sniveling had stopped at some point. He appeared to be in shock, but Enzo recognized it as the same withdrawal he had seen when the two of them had last been alone. He had fought it then, but that had only made things worse in the end. His spirit already broken, he would go quietly this time. The other one looked more defiant than scared, but that would vanish soon enough.

"Put your head back," he ordered. They both glanced up at him but neither complied. Enzo bent down and pressed the knife into Alex's crotch. "Put your head back or I'll give you a goddamn reason to bleed."

Rage flaring in his eyes, Alex complied.

"That's right, you little bitch," Enzo said as he withdrew the knife and stood back up. "You will listen to me, or your shitty day will get a whole lot worse."

85

Carlyle sat at the bar, his forearms resting on the rounded edge, a glass of tequila in his hands. The bottle to his left was noticeably lighter than it had been half an hour earlier. He tapped his phone: 3:02.

He looked up at the dirty mirror across from him, his own eyes peering between the tarnished blotches on the glass. He looked from one bottle to the next—the cheaper brands of vodka and whisky lined up front, the bottles of Drambuie and other unused liqueurs in the back rows shrouded in a thick coating of gray dust. He picked up his shot glass, set it down, and sighed.

When he heard the front door creak open he did not move, continuing to look at his reflection. Footsteps made their way toward him then ceased—six to eight feet away. Close but not too close, he thought, just as he would have done had the roles been reversed. He picked up his glass and knocked it back, wincing as it burned him.

"I thought it would be you," he said.

"Did you now?"

Carlyle nodded as he continued to look forward. "That I did."

"Was I that obvious?" Seegars asked.

"Little signs here and there. Definitely when you threw the kid under the bus like that."

Seegars chuckled. "He was already a dead man walking. I just put the cherry on top."

Carlyle turned to face his partner. "You also signed out Tommy Byrne's car from impound under Patterson's name."

"It won't stick, but that little fag has been annoying me all week. I thought I'd fuck him for a bit, that's all." Seegars sat down, leaving two empty stools between them. "And you really saw me coming for you?"

"Not at first," Carlyle admitted. "I figured you would do Tommy at James's and Enzo would come for me."

"That was the plan that came down this morning—to kill Tommy, then wait for Enzo to finish off the kid."

"Then why the car?"

"Enzo changed his mind… wanted to kill them both. His cousin Arthur is in town, so he had him rig the car to take out Tommy, and…" He glanced at his phone. "He's probably working on the other one right about now."

"And you got the honor of killing me."

"It's better this way," Seegars said.

Carlyle returned to his reflection in the mirror. "Probably."

■ ■ ■

"Why don't you just get it over with?" James muttered.

Standing in the kitchen doorway, Enzo put the last of the peanut butter and jelly sandwich into his mouth. "Why don't you just shut the fuck up before I give you a little more of what you got before."

Enzo walked over and looked down at Alex, who continued to glare at him. "Your boyfriend here tell you what I did to him?" He smiled when neither answered. "Didn't think so."

"You son of a bitch!" Alex shouted, lashing out with his feet.

Enzo reached down and grabbed a handful of Alex's hair, yanking his head back. Alex muffling a scream as Enzo pinched his bruised and swollen nose. "Look, you little cocksucker... I will break this thing into fifteen goddamn pieces if you don't settle your ass down." He twisted Alex's nose with a violent wrench before he released his grip. Enzo straightened up and kicked Alex in the calf. "You stay where you fucking are. You move again and I will stab you in the fucking spine until those legs stop working. You understand me?"

Alex nodded.

"Jesus fucking Christ with you two." Enzo glanced at his watch before pulling a nylon rope from his back pocket. "I'm going to strangle you first," he said to James, "because I need some alone time with your boyfriend."

Enzo stepped over James and straddled him, draping the rope loosely across his brother's chest as he sat down. He tightened his grip, looking over at Alex. "Don't you worry, pretty boy. Once I'm done with this one you and I are going to spend some quality time together."

"Fuck you."

Enzo grinned. "I was going to make this quick," he said, "but you've really fucking pissed me off. I think I might have to get my pound of flesh first. Literally."

He tightened the rope around James's throat, his legs now pressed against his shoulders to hold him in place. "Alex," he sang softly. "Alex, I want you to watch this. I want you to watch the lights go out on your little fuck toy here." He waited, but Alex continued to look forward. "If you don't, Alex, I'm going to keep choking and releasing until you do. I've got plenty of time. Your great savior got blown into a million pieces today, and no one is coming to save you."

■ ■ ■

"And where the fuck do you think you're going?" the voice called out from the gray sedan as he hurried by.

The favor called in, Tommy had run the last few blocks after bailing out of Andrew's man's car, snarled in a construction zone, forcing himself to slow as he entered the parking lot to James's apartment. He stopped, startled both by the Glock pointed at him and the young man holding it.

Tommy felt his chest tighten. "Who the fuck are you?"

The man scoffed. "Is that any way to speak to a Byrne?"

He paused. "*Arthur?*"

"The one and fucking only," his cousin answered.

Tommy scanned the empty parking lot as he stepped back toward the SUV behind him. "No, no, no," Arthur said, menace in his voice. "You're really bad at listening, cousin." The Glock came up. "You move again and I will blow off one of your kneecaps."

86

The two detectives sat in silence. "Nice of you to arrange some alone time," Seegars eventually said.

"The owner's out running errands. He didn't ask questions. No harm needs to come of him."

Seegars glanced around the room. He had been waiting across the street for the better part of an hour, watching as Carlyle entered the building and the owner left, the neon OPEN sign having been shut off moments before. "I find it odd you're taking this lying down."

Carlyle picked up the bottle and poured himself another shot. "You want one?"

Seegars shook his head. "I'm fine."

"There seems to be a certain futility in running from the Byrnes," Carlyle remarked as the bottle returned to its spot.

"I suspect so, yes."

Carlyle sipped from his drink, weighing his options. "You've been with them a while now."

"A few years. I took care of things for Vegas. Small things, nothing too obvious. It was all for Sean. This week's when I really earned my pay."

Carlyle snorted. "Congratulations."

"You've seen what that family is capable of. I didn't want to end up on the wrong side of that."

"So, you were forced into it?"

"Oh, fuck off," Seegars snapped. "You know what I'm talking about."

"Not really, but you don't need to keep the confession going. It's going to be hard to remember all this with my brains blown across the bar."

Seegars forced a laugh. "You should be thanking me anyway. At least this will be quick. You'd rather be strung up and burned alive like the others? I can arrange for that if you're so hell bent on being an asshole."

"You don't have to do me any favors."

Seegars pulled his service weapon from its holster. "Fine then," he said as he leveled the gun at Carlyle's skull. "If you want this over and done with, then that's how we'll do it."

■ ■ ■

"And how the fuck are you not dead?" Arthur asked. "I don't like to waste C-4 if I can help it."

"Because I stopped trusting Enzo a long time ago."

They had been standing there what felt like an eternity, though Tommy resisted the urge to look down at his watch. However long it had been, be it five minutes or fifteen, was that much more time Enzo was torturing James. As long as Enzo remained in that apartment, James was still alive. If only he could get past his cousin.

"He's going to be one surprised fucker to find you here," Arthur said. "It might be a while though. He said he wanted his final moments with your brother to last as long as possible."

■ ■ ■

Carlyle stared at the barrel's end, expecting a burst of light before everything went dark forever, but none came. Not yet.

Seegars's finger stroked the trigger as if he was still contemplating the task ahead. They both knew that if he had any chance of retaining his freedom he would have to commit at some point, but the younger man continued to hesitate.

"You doing this or what?" Carlyle asked.

"You want it that bad?"

Carlyle shrugged. "Like I'll be around to care."

"I would prefer you wait," Patterson announced as he stepped out from the hallway leading to the bathrooms and walked deeper into the bar, his own weapon drawn and pointed at Seegars's head.

Not bothering to take his eyes off Carlyle, Seegars snorted. "Really? You got Justin Bieber here as your backup?"

"He's the only one I could trust with the information."

"And fuck you," Patterson said.

"You wish, faggot," Seegars shot back. He slid off his stool and backed away toward the opposing wall, Patterson pausing about ten feet to Carlyle's left, another fifteen from Seegars, beside one of the pub tables running the length of the rectangular room opposite the bar. "So, how you want to do this?" Seegars asked after Carlyle had spun himself around to face him, his gun still on him.

His hands in his lap, his fingers intertwined, Carlyle shrugged. "I guess surrendering and confessing everything is out."

"Probably, yes."

"Then I guess it's you shoot me and he shoots you," Carlyle said. "I'm sure that will make Captain Scott a very happy man, getting rid of his two biggest pains in the asses like this."

Seegars allowed himself to crack a smile. "Something like that." He paused a moment. "I take it letting me get a head start would be out of the question."

Carlyle nodded. "I think so, yeah."

"Even to spare your life."

"You aided and abetted an organized crime family, which contributed to at least eight deaths this week, and however many more since you started covering for them."

Seegars stiffened. "Like you're one to talk. What was your deal with Tommy Byrne about?"

He saw little point in telling his partner the truth. "Whatever it was went away when that car exploded, didn't it?"

87

"I said look at him, you son of a bitch," Enzo yelled, loosening his grip around James's neck once more.

It had been the fifth such cycle, Alex watching in short bursts before turning away. His eyes were wet, tears streaming down his face as he tried to wipe them away on his knees, now pulled tightly against his chest.

James was slumped between Enzo's legs, his chin on his chest. Alex would have thought him dead already had it not been for the sporadic rising of his chest.

"Is this what you want?" Enzo asked. "You want me to keep torturing your little bitch like this all night?"

"No," Alex mumbled.

"Then watch him die and let me put him out of his misery. The sooner I get this done, the sooner you and I get to work—and the sooner you can join him, okay, fuck face?"

Staring down at the carpet, Alex nodded. He looked up at Enzo who grinned broadly as he once more tightened the rope in his hands.

■ ■ ■

"So, what are we doing?" Seegars asked, their standoff continuing.

"You tell me," Carlyle said. He had a sudden urge for one last shot of tequila, but his partner was twitchy enough to mistake his turning for the bottle as a hostile act. Instead, he glanced over to Patterson, who was intently staring at Seegars, weapon still pointed toward his skull, his body perfectly frozen as he waited on the older two detectives.

"You really want me to shoot you?"

"Just do it already," Carlyle said. "I've lived a good life—and God knows, if you don't, cancer will at some point."

His mind registered the flash from the gun first—the concussion of the shot and the bullet shattering a bottle behind the bar to his right coming immediately thereafter. It had been a deliberate miss, and with an upturned palm he ordered Patterson to hold fire as he continued to look at Seegars. For the first time he could see the sweat running down his partner's face as the intense apprehension came pouring out of him. He had hoped Seegars could be talked down from the ledge, but that shot had gone out only to build enough courage for the second, the finger hugging the trigger waiting for the command to pull back once more.

Carlyle nodded slightly, as if to tell his partner not to miss a second time. He had considered this outcome as a possibility, but had thought at the time that he could head it off long before they reached this moment. He had failed to do so, but they would go out together if that was what it took to put all this to bed.

Grinning, Seegars nodded back. He opened his mouth and flipped the gun, sliding the barrel between his lips until it pressed against the roof of his mouth. Carlyle was only a few steps off his stool when Seegars's thumb found the trigger and squeezed.

■ ■ ■

Tommy didn't see the car Andrew's man had driven from Hillcrest to La Jolla until it was roughly fifteen feet from the back of Arthur's, slowly creeping up from behind. Arthur, still pointing the gun in his direction, only glanced away occasionally, not trusting his cousin, however inept he thought him, to not try something if given the chance.

"This better not take fucking hours."

"My brother is a sick fuck," Tommy said, trying to keep his attention focused on him. "I'd get comfortable if I were you."

"Yeah, well you're the dumb fuck who…" Arthur looked into the side mirror. "What the—"

The engine roared. The older Buick lurched forward and slammed home. The gun fired as the two cars slammed together, glass shattering and plastic crumpling as one pushed the other almost fully into the empty space in front.

Tommy raced forward to the driver's side door, grabbing Arthur's still outstretched arm and slamming it into the doorframe until the Glock dropped to the pavement. He bent down and picked it up, falling back from the car as the door violently swung open, missing him by inches.

"Fuck me," was all Arthur could say as Tommy—now seated on the pavement—raised the gun and pulled the trigger.

Tommy immediately stood, turning to see Andrew's man already out of his car. "You all right?" the man asked, his legs shaking underneath him as he held on to the door.

"Yeah," Tommy answered. "Thank you."

"You've been shot."

Tommy looked down, the deep red stain growing against the right side of his white dress shirt. He pressed against it, feeling the warm blood against his hand. Then he felt the pain, gritting his teeth as the first wave passed through him. "I'll be fine," he said.

"You need—"

"You stay here," Tommy ordered. "This I have to do alone."

88

Enzo's head jerked up at the front door opening. He dropped the rope and picked up his knife.

"Motherfucker," he exclaimed. "This is what I get for letting someone else handle my fucking business."

Tommy glanced away long enough to see the door closed before turning back to Enzo. "Yeah, you missed."

"Somebody didn't."

Tommy pressed his hand against his side. He could barely feel the pain, but he knew he wouldn't have long. "Our good cousin Arthur, although he's worse off."

"Who was in the fucking car then?"

"A homeless guy and the hundred bucks I gave him," Tommy answered.

Enzo grinned. "There might be a Byrne in you yet," he said. "Too bad I'm going to cut it out of you."

Tommy raised Arthur's gun, and Enzo pressed the knife against James's neck. "Don't even think about it," he warned, "or I will slit his throat wide open. Toss the fucking gun over. Now." Tommy looked down at James, whose ashen face and dead eyes took him back to the basement sofa, scooping him up, promising him he'd be safe—a promise now broken. Enzo cleared his throat. "*Today*, you dumb fuck."

Tommy's shoulders slumped in resignation as he tossed the weapon toward the doorway to James's bedroom, just feet from the chair where he had lectured him on this very outcome. If only he'd caught up with Enzo earlier, this might already be over. Now he faced the cold reality of his failures—to protect his younger brother, to end the violence wrought by his family, and to return safely to his wife.

Enzo shoved James aside and stood between him and Alex as he pointed the knife at Tommy. "You're going to wish you burned to death in that car by the time I'm through with you."

Tommy still stood by the door. The two were nearly fifteen feet apart, perfectly still except for the eager trembling of Enzo's blade. Alex glanced towards James's motionless body, then turned back as an out-of-focus gray blur filled his vision—Enzo, grinning down at him. "Don't you worry, lover boy," Enzo said as he pressed the tip of the knife into Alex's nose. "We'll still have our fun."

Out of the corner of his right eye Alex saw Tommy charge. Enzo, sensing movement to his left, instinctively turned, grunting as he began to lunge towards his brother, the knife now raised to meet the threat.

As Enzo stepped over him, Alex turned his left foot. The tip of his tennis shoe caught the top of Enzo's right boot as he moved away. Enzo stumbled, flailing his arms as his fingers splayed, the knife skidding across the carpet to Alex's feet just before Enzo regained his footing and collided with Tommy.

Enzo had lowered his head, his left shoulder impacting with Tommy's chest as he tucked his arms around Tommy's ribs and tightly hugged him before he could pull away. His momentum still carried them forward. Enzo twisted them around and hauled them both down, landing on his back with Tommy atop him. His older brother stunned, Enzo quickly slid out from underneath, rolled, and climbed on top, pinning him face-down on the rug. He hiked himself onto his knees, squeezing his legs against Tommy's sides as he raised his right fist and brought it down onto the back of his head.

"Take it, you bitch," Enzo snarled, driving his fist down while Tommy struggled to push himself up off the floor.

Alex was paralyzed, watching the battle unfold, the plastic binds biting into his wrists as his hands flailed uselessly. He glanced to James, who remained slumped against the sofa, his chin hovering just above the rope still draped across his chest, seemingly oblivious to the commotion as his two older brothers fought before him.

Alex didn't see the knife until Tommy's foot kicked it toward him as his shoes thrashed against the carpet. Still a few feet away, he lurched forward, rolled onto his back, and kicked out until the heel of his right shoe found the knife. He dragged it toward his hip before rolling onto his left side, writhing on the floor until his bound hands found the handle. He flipped the blade and forced it between his bound wrists, feeling it slice his skin as his fingers pressed against the end of the grip. He fumbled the handle into his right hand and began sawing away at the plastic.

89

"You should go, sir," Patterson finally said.

Carlyle had parked himself at one of the rarely used square tables that ran front to back—a parallel row between the bar and the wall, a kind of no man's land between those pretending to want company and those who preferred solitude. Slumped in the chair, mired in disbelief over what he had witnessed, he continued to stare at Seegars as he lay on the floor.

"Sir," Patterson said once more. "You should go."

Carlyle glanced over. "Hmm?"

"You need to go to La Jolla."

"I…" He paused as he turned once more to his former partner. "I have to deal with this."

"I can deal with this. You have Tommy Byrne." Carlyle remained seated. "Sir, you need to go."

"This is where I need to be." He stood, sliding his cell phone out of his pocket. He looked down at it as his thumb began to move. "I need to call this in."

"*Robert!*" Patterson barked. Carlyle looked over, the younger man's face flush with embarrassment. "Sir, you need to go. It's a half hour to La Jolla if you're lucky. *I* will call it in." Carlyle remained still, his thumb still hovering over the screen. "Sir, you were never here. I confronted him about signing the car out under my name—about his ties to the Byrnes. He attacked me. When

I was about to get the upper hand, he shoved me away long enough to kill himself. Now go."

Carlyle looked at his phone as he took a deep breath, sighing loudly as he processed the words that had tumbled out of the junior detective's mouth. He glanced down at Seegars, visualizing the gun now on the floor, still clutched in his hand, once more entering his mouth.

He turned to Patterson, the younger man seeming to tremble as he waited for a response. He forced a smirk in acknowledgement. "Okay," he conceded as he dropped the phone back into his pocket. "Okay."

"And one more thing, sir?"

"What?"

"I need you to punch me in the face."

■ ■ ■

Tommy had wriggled onto his back, but Enzo was still on top of him, his knees continuing to dig into his sides. Fists rained down in a steady succession, Enzo measuring each strike before finding his way between Tommy's flailing hands. A punch broke Tommy's nose, and when his consciousness flickered back to life, Enzo's hands were gripping his neck, his thumbs pressed into his throat. "Just die, you dumb fuck."

Tommy clawed at Enzo's wrists, fighting for breaths that refused to come.

"That's right, asshole. This is it for you."

Tommy continued to gasp for air that would not come as Enzo forced more of his weight down upon him. He soon felt his own grip weaken as the pressure increased, his eyes sluggishly rolling back as his eyelids closed over them.

They were together in the emergency room again. He was seated on the edge of the hospital bed as she stood beside him, her scrubs still wrinkled as if pulled from the bottom of a pile of laundry, her nametag hanging from a half torn front chest pocket.

She looked once more at his forehead. "This might hurt a little."

"I'm not afraid of a little pain."

Sabrina reflexively scoffed. "All the tough guys cry," she said. "Always. Especially the ones with babysitters outside the room like you got."

"Oh yeah?"

She could see the comment wounding, and allowed herself a flirtatious grin to soften the blow. "Well… we'll see how you do."

"You still haven't said yes to going out with me."

She patted him on the knee with her free hand several times, allowing it to linger as it came down one final time. "Well… we'll see how you do," she repeated as she reached for the needle.

The pressure around his neck gone, he felt his chest spasm as the air poured in. He reflexively gulped, his eyes jolting open to find Enzo sitting upright atop him, his face contorted in pain, his shoulders arching backward as his right arm flung outward and his left hand clutched his side.

Enzo rose to his feet, quickly spinning around before lunging toward the figure now before him. Tommy, now free, rolled onto his stomach, his arms pushing his upper torso off the carpet, his weight on his elbows as he began coughing uncontrollably while continuing to gasp for air.

He glanced back as Enzo hauled Alex up by his shirt—then stiffened. The knife Enzo once held was now deeply buried in his shoulder blade. He watched as Enzo violently flung Alex toward the front door, his head striking it with a sickening thud before he crumpled to the floor. Tommy then looked toward the bedroom as he began to crawl away.

Enzo looked down, watching for movement in Alex but the younger man remained still, a small pool of blood now forming on the tile where his head made impact. His legs suddenly giving out, he dropped to his knees, then onto his hands as he let out a scream: "God fucking damn it!"

He coughed, wincing as a trickle of blood escaped his mouth and trailed to his chin before dropping to the carpet below. He chuckled at how he now found himself, watching the slow, steady stream of droplets fall between his hands.

He grunted as he focused once more on his task, the grin still on his face as his head turned toward Tommy. "We're not done, you and me," Enzo announced as he slowly shifted his body around to face him.

Tommy was now slouched against the wall, his left arm draped over his waist, his hand pressed hard against the still open wound. In his right, his elbow supported by his left hand, was Arthur's Glock, the gun on his right knee as if too heavy to lift.

Enzo glanced at the weapon as he began to crawl toward him, his breath now rapid and shallow as he dragged one hand forward, then the other, his legs trembling as he raised and lowered his knees to pull himself closer. "You're not getting away from me, you fucker," he muttered as more blood escaped his mouth.

Tommy remained frozen, the sensation of his brother's hands around his neck still lingering as he watched Enzo inch closer, the maniacal smirk marking the violence he hoped to dispense etched onto his face. He had seen the expression countless times before, but once more the image of the old man tied to the chair revisited him, Enzo excitedly grinning, his hands strangling the bat as he swung with all his might.

"I've got you now," Enzo announced as Tommy glanced down, Enzo's right hand wrapped around his left ankle. "Come on, you coward. What the fuck are you afraid of?"

Enzo released his grip and pushed himself up. Still on his knees, his shoulders now slumped as he struggled to keep his head up, he abruptly reached back with both hands to the knife still in his shoulder. Two quick tugs later—the second drawing a groan as he bit down on his lower lip—the bloodied knife, bits of flesh and fabric caught in its serrated edge, was in his quivering right hand.

"I think I'm going to fucking gut you, you son of a bitch."

It was always going to come to this, Tommy understood as he remained snug to the wall, looking into his brother's eyes and seeing only undying rage and hate within. Enzo would never relent, would never buckle to the reality before him. He would not stop until stopped.

His own hand shaking, the weapon was slowly raised. Tommy watched as his brother seemed to scowl, the color draining from his face as he turned his focus to the end of the silencer.

Enzo's eyes moved slowly over the gun and their eyes met one final time. "I guess you're a Byrne—"

The gunshot to the chest silenced him forever.

■ ■ ■

Isabella twitched in her chair. She smiled and caressed the rim of her wine glass, her plan now concluded.

Taking a sip, she thought once more to this afternoon, when she had felt nothing upon what she believed was Tommy's death. But this time— Jimmy's—had brought a sensation unmistakable in its intensity. How odd, she thought, that the one she despised most would elicit such a feeling. Hopefully he had suffered for all the pain he had brought this family over the past week. If she knew her Enzo, he certainly had.

She stood to go back downstairs to refill her drink. It would help her sleep after the anxiety of today's events. Tomorrow would usher in a new era as the two sides of the family aligned, and she would need all her strength to deal with Liam Byrne and his three ill-raised offspring.

90

Carlyle entered the apartment and stopped short.

Tommy was on the couch, legs spread, his arms outstretched on the cushions behind him. Beside him, to his right, was a gun with a silencer attached, resting on a green and white kitchen towel, the handle pointed toward Carlyle.

He closed the door. "You alone?"

"Yes," Tommy answered. "They're safe."

"*They*?" Carlyle asked. He paused. "Ah—"

"My brother is safe," Tommy corrected.

Carlyle stepped deeper into the room. "So—you really aren't dead. And it turns out we did have a rat in the kitchen."

Tommy grinned. "Was I wrong on either?"

"Not on the latter, but you look at least half-dead to me," Carlyle said, taking in Tommy's swollen throat, bruised eyes, bandaged nose, and bloodstained dress shirt. "You going to make it? You need an ambulance?"

"I've had better days, but no," Tommy said.

"Who patched you up?"

"A friend of a friend."

"Is that right?"

Tommy nodded. "I still have one or two."

Carlyle looked down at Arthur, whose corpse was lying on his back in the middle of the room. "And who is this?"

"My cousin Arthur."

"Where is the other one?"

"You won't have to worry about him again."

Carlyle scowled. "That wasn't our deal."

"I know, but you get your trophy," Tommy said as he motioned to Arthur, "and my family gets to avoid some unseemly headlines back home. It's been taken care of."

Carlyle reluctantly nodded. A week ago, he would have despised himself for the moral compromises he was now making. Yet here he stood— a man forced by circumstance to accept reality as it was, not as he wished it to be. "Fair enough," he eventually said. "So… what do you suppose happened here?"

"That I will leave to you," Tommy answered as he used the towel to pick up the gun by its silencer and held it out.

Carlyle walked over and took the weapon. He then moved to stand over Arthur, offset the gun a few inches to the right of the first wound and fired— the body motionlessly absorbing the impact. "I disarmed him somehow then shot him with his own weapon," he theorized.

"Works for me."

Carlyle walked over to the dining room table. He put the gun down and turned back to Tommy. "And what becomes of you now that family honor in Chicago is maintained?"

"What do you mean?"

"Well, technically you're dead," Carlyle reminded him.

"I would hope your people are a little better at their jobs than that."

"The coroner owes me a favor. Although after this—" He motioned to the body on the floor. "—after this I might be out of them. I think you can stay dead if you wanted to, though."

Tommy stood from the couch with a wince. He stepped over the body and stopped about five feet from Carlyle, sliding his hands into his pockets. "I wish it were that easy."

"It is, trust me. If you ever wanted out, now is the time."

"I have to go back," Tommy said.

"Are you insane? This is your opportunity to put all that behind you."

"My uncle and cousins are planning to move in and take over."

"So? Let them have it."

"I can't allow that to happen. They'll clear out everyone and start fresh."

"Then let them."

"Look," Tommy began, "I don't expect you to understand what it is we do, much less the people I work with, but they will take everyone out—including families, if necessary. He would never let my wife walk away given everything he thinks she might know. And if I don't go back, everything I've worked for… all the changes away from this garbage… that all goes to hell."

Carlyle glanced down, the past several days once more passing over him. "I get it."

Tommy held out his right hand and offered it to Carlyle. "Thank you, Detective," he said as the two shook. "I appreciate everything you've done. I am in your debt."

"Can I count on that?"

"More than you'll ever know."

Carlyle paused. "Good luck, Mr. Byrne."

Tommy chuckled. "Thanks. This war's only just begun."

EPILOGUE

Joe had been parked down the street for nearly an hour when the call finally came to proceed.

He and Sam had spoken only hours before. Sam had been vague, but he assured him that if all went according to plan his son would be safe. The catch—and with this life he understood there would always be one—was that this fight would continue, starting tonight.

He didn't care, however. He had never wanted this life for Alex, but over time had come to terms with him at his side. He hated himself for having allowed it, and now he faced the very real possibility that he would never see him again. His son was safe, but far from the coming turmoil. Perhaps it was for the best if he never saw Chicago again.

Joe climbed out of the car and walked toward the front door. A single light illuminated the uncovered front stoop, but otherwise the house was dark. The street itself was quiet, the lateness of the evening having long chased everyone indoors. With his back to the street, the collar of his wool coat turned up against wind and his cap pulled low, he would be unidentifiable should anyone stumble across what was about to happen.

He pulled open the screen door and knocked loudly on the white door with his gloved left hand. He waited patiently for a few minutes before he heard the wood creaking at the top of the landing inside, the hallway light coming to life as the sound of footsteps descended from above.

Moretti looked warily at him after first glancing through the panes of the sidelight. Then he opened the door; there was no point in delaying the inevitable. He looked into Joe's eyes, but no words were said. None were necessary as each knew their roles. Moretti finally nodded slightly to acknowledge his acquiescence. They had lost.

Joe was just about to adjust his wrist to let the weapon drop into his hand when a woman's voice from the top of the landing gave him pause. "Who is it?" she called out as he took a step back away from the door. She would say nothing even if he had been identified, but that was not a risk he wanted to take.

"It's no one, dear," Moretti said as he glanced back at her. "Go back to sleep." He turned back to his guest. "I'll be up in a minute," he said as she vanished from the landing.

Joe nodded. "She'll be taken care of," he offered, as the gun fell into his hand.

"Thank you," Moretti meekly offered.

Joe brought the gun up and pulled the trigger twice.

■ ■ ■

Sam quietly entered the foyer of the darkened house. He crept toward the entrance to the room at the back of the corridor, his eyes focused on the dying light in the fireplace. He stood in the doorway along the right side of the entrance, remaining in the shadow of the darkened room as he prayed his black clothes and cap masked his presence.

The great room was empty save for Michael, whose eyes were closed as he slouched in a leather chair by the fireplace, an empty cocktail glass on his right leg, a relaxed hand holding it in place. A half-empty opened decanter of whiskey was on the floor by the right front leg of the large chair.

On his left leg, mostly hidden beneath his arm, rested a P290 Sig Sauer. Sam had missed it at first glance, but now he cast aside hesitation.

He watched for a moment as Michael's chest slowly rose and dipped, listening for any other movement in the house, but none came. He stepped out from the shadows and into the room, quickly positioning himself at an angle slightly in front of Michael. Now just a few feet away, he could hear the gentle snoring as he removed the gun from the back of his pants. As Sam stepped toward the front of the chair Michael opened his eyes.

"Don't," Sam warned, leveling his gun as Michael started to sit up. "Don't move an inch." Michael nodded, and Sam offered up his left hand. "I'll take that, if you don't mind."

Michael took the gun by its barrel and turned the weapon to offer up the grip, which Sam took before flinging it across the room behind him. It hit the rug with a dull thud, Michael watching it bounce away before looking back up. "I guess you got me."

"A goddamn Trojan horse all along."

Michael smirked. "She practically begged us to take it from her."

"Let me guess," Sam said. "You let Enzo take care of Tommy and Jimmy, and then you all take care of Enzo."

"Cut the head off the snake, and the captains always fall in line," Michael remarked. "Even the Irish ones. They know it's in their self-interest to do so. Not that they would've had to bother faking their loyalty for very long."

"And you got the Valcos to agree to that?"

"Not exactly. They fucked over my father, and now we're going to fuck them right back."

"I'll make sure to let them know you all sold them out when we head West."

Michael snorted. "You're not going to live long enough to do anything of the sort."

Sam grinned as he adjusted his finger on the trigger. "You first."

■ ■ ■

Isabella shivered slightly as she sat down on the bed.

She had once loved this house, but as she looked over the guest room, Ciaran still down the hall in the bed they had once shared, she had come to despise it. Too much had taken place here. Perhaps it was time, once all of this was past, to look at somewhere simpler, a place without all the reminders of those points in her life that had brought her pain.

There would be no memories of Ciaran, or of Tommy and Jimmy—only what came next. Under Michael and Enzo, the family would be restored to its proper shape—its proper purpose. It would be better, she assured herself as she kicked off her slippers and slipped beneath the covers. They would survive this, and in time everything would return to order, once the distractions were finally gone.

She heard the creak on the stairs but thought little of it. It would be Michael, she knew, turning in early in preparation for the transition to begin come morning. Outside of his father's day-to-day guidance he would be malleable enough, and Enzo would help keep his cousin in line. The young man was ambitious and had his father's temperament, but Chicago was not Las Vegas, and he would bend to her will soon enough.

There was a light knock on the door. What did that stupid boy want now, she asked herself. She almost called out for him to go away but thought better of it. No, she wanted him to see her anger at the intrusion. His lessons on how to behave would start now.

She climbed back out of bed and slid her feet back into the slippers. She retrieved her thick cotton robe from the chair by the bed and slipped it on, folding one side over the other before fastening it in place with the belt.

Determined to put the young man in his place, she flung open the door—her scowl vanishing as her eyes widened in surprise.

Sam nodded once, his arm steadily rising. "Your son Tommy sends his regards."

ABOUT THE AUTHOR

Greg Emmerth grew up in Spartanburg, South Carolina, and began his creative career in film, writing and directing five projects, including *The Perfect Plan* (2006), *Queerspiracy!* (2007), *The Heart of the Matter* (2008), *3 for Anna* (2009), and *Dirty Sex* (2009). He made his transition to fiction with his debut novel, *Nobody Else*, published in 2013. He currently resides in Atlanta, Georgia.

www.ingramcontent.com/pod-product-compliance
Lightning Source LLC
Chambersburg PA
CBHW072106270326
41931CB00010B/1472